ARISTOTLE

SUNY series in

ANCIENT GREEK PHILOSOPHY

———————————————

Anthony Preus, editor

OTFRIED HÖFFE

ARISTOTLE

Translated by Christine Salazar

STATE UNIVERSITY OF NEW YORK PRESS

Originally published in German by
Verlag C. H. Beck, Munich

Published by
STATE UNIVERSITY OF NEW YORK PRESS
ALBANY

For information, address
State University of New York Press
90 State Street, Suite 700, Albany, NY 12207

Production, Laurie Searl
Marketing, Anne M. Valentine

Library of Congress Cataloging-in-Publication Data

Höffe, Otfried.
    Aristotle / Otfried Höffe.
      p. cm. -- (SUNY series in ancient Greek philosophy)
    Includes bibliographical references and indexes.
    ISBN 0-7914-5633-1 (alk. paper) -- ISBN 0-7914-5634-X (pbk. : alk. paper)
    1. Aristotle. I. Title. II. Series

B485 . H56 2003
185--dc21   2002075875

                10   9   8   7   6   5   4   3   2   1

IT BEGAN WITH ARISTOTLE . . .

For Evelyn

CONTENTS

List of Illustrations   xi
List of Abbreviations and Method of Citation   xiii
Preface   xv

PART I "THE PHILOSOPHER"?

1   The Man and His Work   3
       1.1 The Man
       1.2 The Work

2   Researcher, Scholar, and Philosopher   15

PART II KNOWLEDGE AND SCIENCE

3   The Phenomenology of Knowledge   23
       3.1 Propaedeutic?
       3.2 An Epistemic Hierarchy
       3.3 Freedom and Self-realization

4   Forms of Rationality   31
       4.1 Syllogistics
       4.2 Dialectic (*Topics*)
       4.3 Rhetoric
       4.4 Poetics: Tragedy

5   Proofs and Principles   49
       5.1 A Critique of Demonstrative Reason
       5.2 Axioms and Other Principles
       5.3 Induction and Mind

6   Four Methodical Maxims   61
       6.1 Establishing the Phenomena

6.2 Doctrines
6.3 Difficulties
6.4 Linguistic Analysis

PART III PHYSICS AND METAPHYSICS

7   Natural Philosophy   69
    7.1 Aristotelian Natural Science
    7.2 Motion
    7.3 The Four Causes
    7.4 Continuum, the Infinite, Place, and Time

8   Biology and Psychology   85
    8.1 Aristotle the Zoologist
    8.2 Teleonomy: Organisms, Procreation, and Heredity
    8.3 The Soul

9   First Philosophy, or Metaphysics   95

10   Cosmology and Theology   103
    10.1 Meta-physics
    10.2 The Cosmological Concept of God
    10.3 An Ethical Concept of God?

11   Ontology and Language   111
    11.1 Categories
    11.2 Substance
    11.3 Aristotle's Critique of Plato's Ideas
    11.4 On Language

PART IV ETHICS AND POLITICS

12   Practical Philosophy   129
    12.1 The Autonomy of Ethics
    12.2 The Goal Is Action
    12.3 Outline Knowledge

13   Theory of Action   135
    13.1 The Basic Concept of Desire
    13.2 Decision and Power of Judgment
    13.3 Weakness of the Will
    13.4 Does Aristotle Know the Concept of Will?

14   The Good Life   147
    14.1 The Principle of Happiness
    14.2 The Virtues of Character
    14.3 Justice, Natural Law, and Equity
    14.4 Theoretical or Political Existence?

15 Political Anthropology   163
     15.1 The Relevance of the *Politics*
     15.2 "Political by Nature"
     15.3 Friendship and Other Prerequisites

16 Political Justice   175
     16.1 Elementary Inequalities
     16.2 Rule of the Free over the Free
     16.3 Democracy or Polity?

PART V   The RECEPTION

17 Antiquity and the Middle Ages   189
     17.1 Antiquity
     17.2 Christianity, Islam, and Judaism
     17.3 The Great Aristotelian Renaissance

18 The Modern Age and the Present   199
     18.1 Detachment and Renewed Interest
     18.2 Aristotle Research and Neo-Aristotelianisms

Chronology   205
Bibliography   209
Index of Personal Names   225
General Index   231

ILLUSTRATIONS

1. Plato. Roman copy (from the reign of Tiberius) of a portrait statue made in the middle of the fourth century B.C.E. (Munich, Glyptothek).   4

2. Detail (Alexander) of a battle between Alexander the Great and Darius. Pompei, House of the Faun; probably based on an original by Philoxenus of Eritrea.   7

3. Socrates. Copy of a Hellenistic bust (Rome, Villa Albani).   8

4. Aristotle. Roman copy based on a fourth-century B.C.E. statue (Vienna, Kunsthistorisches Museum).   9

5. Detail (Plato and Aristotle) from Raphael, *The School of Athens* (Rome, Vatican, Stanza della Segnatura).   120

6. Aristotle (Portal Royal of Chartres Cathedral, twelfth century).   194

7. Aristotle at his lectern; MS of the writings on natural sciences, Rome 1457 (Vienna, Österreichische Nationalbibliothek, Cod. phil. gr. 64).   197

ABBREVIATIONS AND
METHOD OF CITATION

Ath.	*Athênaiôn Politeia: The State of the Athenians*
APo.	*Analytica Posteriora (Analytika hystera): Posterior Analytics*
APr	*Analytica Priora (Analytika protera): Prior Analytics*
Cael.	*de Caelo (Peri ouranou): On the Heaven*
Cat.	*Categoriae (Katêgoriai): Categories*
de An.	*de Anima (Peri psychês): On the Soul*
EE	*Ethica Eudemia (Ethika Eudêmeia): Eudemian Ethics*
EN	*Ethica Nicomachea (Ethika Nikomacheia): Nicomachean Ethics*
GA	*de Generatione Animalium (Peri zôôn geneseôs): On the Generation of Animals*
GC	*de Generatione et Corruptione (Peri geneseôs kai phthoras): On Coming to Be and Passing Away*
HA	*Historia Animalium (Peri tôn zôôn historiai): On the History of Animals*
Int.	*de Interpretatione (Peri hermêneias): Hermeneutics*
MA	*de Motu Animalium (Peri zôôn kinêseôs): On the Movement of Animals*
Metaph.	*Metaphysica (Ta meta ta physika): Metaphysics*
Mete.	*Meteorologica (Meteôrologika): Meteorology*
MM	*Magna Moralia (Ethikôn Megalôn): Magna Moralia*
PA	*de Partibus Animalium (Peri zôôn moriôn): On the Parts of Animals*
Ph.	*Physica (Physikê akroasis): Physics*
Po.	*Poetica (Peri poietikês): Poetics*
Pol.	*Politica (Politika): Politics*
Prot.	*Protrepticus (Protreptikos): Protrepticus*
Rh.	*Rhetorica (Rhêtorikê technê): Rhetoric*
SE	*Sophistici Elenchi (Peri sophistikôn elenchôn): Sophistical Refutations (= Topics IX)*
Top.	*Topica (Topika): Topics*

Where they are available, the text is translated from the *Oxford Classical Texts* editions. Passages are cited as follows: *Metaph.* I 1, 981a15 = *Metaphysics* book I, chapter 1, page 981a (of the respective Bekker edition), line 15.

PREFACE

This book introduces a philosopher who is in a class by himself, even within the small circle of great thinkers. In late antiquity he was called "divine Aristotle" (by Proclus). For the Middle Ages, from al-Farabi to Thomas Aquinas by way of Albertus Magnus, he was quite simply "the Philosopher." Even Leibniz said that Aristotle's utterances about the basic concepts of natural philosophy were "for the most part entirely true."

Rather than within a few decades, a serious attack on Aristotle's authority did not occur until two millennia later, in the seventeenth and eighteenth centuries, but when it did happen, it came on a wide front. The attack began in physics (cue: Galileo); it continued in fundamental (Descartes) and political (Hobbes) philosophy, was reinforced by transcendental philosophy (Kant), embraced ethics and aesthetics and, at the end of the nineteenth century, finally reached logic. However, even then Aristotle was not simply *passé*. It is well known that Hegel treated him with great respect; similarly Brentano and Heidegger, as well as Lukasiewicz and the analytical philosophers. Even among biologists, none less than Darwin himself held him in great regard. While until recently criticism of Aristotelian positions—from essentialism through teleology to the principle of happiness—has prevailed, these days there are pro-Aristotelians in the fields of the philosophical theory of action, in ethics, topics and rhetoric, political philosophy, social theory, and even ontology.

Given that, despite all this, knowledge of Aristotle cannot be expected even from students of philosophy, this volume is an attempt to provide a comprehensive introduction to Aristotle with the intent of making him more popular. There is also the added interest of a philosophical dialogue that bridges the centuries, for it would be sterile to bar practical questions while merely repeating his tenets. With Aristotle in particular, one is always faced with the objects of his philosophizing. Thus, we are interested in what the philosopher says, how he conducts his argumentation, and what remains of the intuitions, the concepts and arguments, or at least his style of philosophizing. Also, a confrontation with Aristotle is helpful for gaining a clearer view both of antiquity and of our own times. Occasionally this may open up a viable alternative to current thought.

No one should be deterred by the boundless wealth of commentaries on an author such as Aristotle: a considerable number of texts allow for unprepared reading.

Frequently his thoughts are expressed with such freshness that one only needs a bit of curiosity and patience to understand them. Some texts can even be read "in one go" like a novel, but one should not "devour" Aristotle chapter by chapter, like a murder mystery. Beginners should start with the first book of *Metaphysics* (esp. chs. I 1–2) and the *Nicomachean Ethics* (esp. chs. I 1–6), and then turn to the initial chapter of the *Zoology* (*HA* I 1), the first chapters of the work on categories and perhaps also the opening of the *Physics*. It is—almost—self-evident that there are more difficult texts as well (e.g., *de An.* III 5, *Metaph.* VII–IX, *Int.* 12-14, *EN* VII 1–11), that others can only be decoded if one has certain preliminary knowledge (e.g., *Metaph.* XIII–XIV), and that here and there one encounters obscure, and even contradictory, passages.

The result of a series of lectures, this book owes much to the various suggestions given by my students, in particular Dr. Christoph Horn, Dr. Christof Rapp, and Rolf Geiger.

PART I

"THE PHILOSOPHER"?

THE MAN AND HIS WORK

Pantes anthrôpoi tou eidenai oregontai physei: "all humans strive for knowledge by nature." The opening sentence of one of the most famous books in Western civilization, Aristotle's *Metaphysics,* explicitly speaks about man and knowledge and implicitly about its author as well. As far as the anthropological claim—a natural craving for knowledge—applies, Aristotle is not only an exceptional thinker, but also a great human being.

1.1 THE MAN

It is surprising that we have only a very general idea of Aristotle's personality and biography. The scarce evidence consists of the *Testament,* various letters and poems, as well as honorary decrees of Stagira, Delphi, and Athens. Ancient biographies, on the other hand, can only be trusted to a limited extent. Compiled generations after his lifetime, some have pro-Aristotelian, others anti-Aristotelian bias. The best-known text—in Diogenes Laertius's *Lives and Opinions of Famous Philosophers* (220 C.E. ch. VI)—combines fact and, not always benevolent, fiction (cf. Düring 1957). Thus, he says about Aristotle's physical appearance: "He spoke with a lisp and he also had weak legs and small eyes, but he dressed elegantly and was conspicuous by his use of rings and his hair-style."

It cannot be ascertained whether Aristotle really was a bit of a dandy, but the following is more or less certain: his lifetime coincided with the period in which a form of society common to many Greeks, the free city-state, lost its freedom. Aristotle experienced the Athenian and Theban defeat against Philip II at Chaeronea (338 B.C.E.). He was also a contemporary of Philip's son, Alexander the Great. However, a long time had passed since the Periclean age (443–429), the years when Athens was both politically and culturally in a position of hegemony, when artists such as Ictinus or Phidias created the buildings on the Acropolis, when Sophocles wrote his tragedies, for example *Antigone* and *Oedipus the King,* and philosophers such as Anaxagoras and Protagoras were active in Athens.

Aristotle was born in 384 B.C.E. in Stagira (Starro), a small city-state in northeastern Greece. Since, unlike Plato, he was not a scion of the Athenian high aristocracy and not even an Athenian citizen, his status in Athens was that of a *metoikos* (alien resident), a foreigner with a "permit of residence," but without any political rights. Nevertheless, he was not a nobody. Born to a renowned family—his father Nicomachus was royal physician at the Macedonian court—Aristotle was given an excellent education, which was supervised by his warden after his father's early death. In 367 B.C.E., possibly because of tensions at the royal court, the seventeen-year-old Aristotle took himself to Athens, the center of Greek culture, in order to study with Plato. Plato's school, the Academy, was much more than just a public "gymnasium"; it was the intellectual Mecca for the scientists and philosophers of the time, an international meeting point and a model of the unity of teaching and research, in a way in which it has hardly ever been achieved again.

During a period of twenty years, his "first sojourn in Athens" (367–347), Aristotle familiarized himself with the questions we know from Plato's dialogues,

PLATO. Roman copy (from the reign of Tiberius) of a portrait statue
made in the middle of the fourth century B.C.E. (Munich, Glyptothek)

including the late ones. At the same time he studied with members of the Academy such as Speusippus, Xenocrates, and Eudoxus of Cnidus. However, he did not remain a "disciple" for long: through confrontation with Plato and his colleagues he soon developed his own position. We do not know of any road-to-Damascus experience, any sudden enlightenment that turned the follower of Plato into his critic. Nor do we hear of a philosophical turning point by means of which one could contrast a late Aristotle, or Aristotle II, with an early Aristotle, or Aristotle I. In these aspects, Aristotle's intellectual biography appears remarkably straightforward and downright matter-of-fact.

During his first stay in Athens, the philosopher began to give lectures in a lecture hall provided with a blackboard, various scientific instruments, and two wall paintings, as well as astronomical tables (*Int.* 13, 22a22; *EN* II 7, 1107a33; *EE* II 3, 1220b37; *APr.* I 27, 43a35; cf. Jackson 1920). It was during this period that he produced copious collections of data, especially the first drafts on natural philosophy ("physics"), fundamental philosophy ("metaphysics"), ethics, politics, and rhetoric. It is a matter of controversy whether the writings on logic and scientific theory later combined in the *Organon,* as well as the *Poetics,* were also written during that time.

Plato, the founder and head of the Academy, was forty-five years Aristotle's senior, roughly the same age difference as that between Socrates and Plato. We have no reliable information about the relationship between "student" and "teacher," but presumably Aristotle's feelings toward Plato were similar to the latter's toward Homer. Thus, his criticism of Plato in the *Ethics* (I 4, 1096a11–17) opens almost like Plato's criticism of Homer and the poets in the *Republic* (X, 595b; cf. *Phaidon* 91b f., concerning Socrates): "Of course such an examination is contrary to us, given that those who introduced those ideas were [our] friends. However, . . . for the preservation of truth, we would seem to be obliged not to spare our own sentiments, since we are philosophers . . ." This is the basis of the later dictum *amicus Plato, magis amica veritas,* which means, loosely translated: "I love Plato, but I love truth even more." Socrates is treated with a similar combination of respect and criticism (e.g., *Metaph.* XIII 4, 1078b17–31; *Pol.* II 6, 1265b10–13). We may consider ourselves lucky that Plato was Socrates' pupil and Aristotle was Plato's, that is, that twice in a row an outstanding philosopher studied with another outstanding philosopher, developing his own views against the background of the other's well-considered views.

Aristotle did not interfere in matters of the *polis,* not least because he was a *metoikos,* but he is the founder of politics as an autonomous science. Nevertheless, he cannot avoid political practice entirely: he acted as a mediator between Macedon and various Greek cities, a task for which the "citizens of Athens" thanked him in an inscription (see Düring 1957, 215). However, sceptical about the—finally unsuccessful—political vocation of the philosopher proclaimed by Plato, he did not consider such missions the "natural"extension of political philosophy.

Most of the time, Aristotle concentrated on his studies, his own research, and independent teaching. If one is to believe the evidence on the subject, he was a speaker endowed with incisive wit and gave clear and captivating lectures. A diligent reader, but also a collector and analytic, he is the prototype of the learned professor—not, however, in his impractical guise, but one who is open toward the world, even versed in its ways. His urbanity extended to intellectual matters: Aristotle familiarized himself not only with the views of his own "school," that is, Plato's and the Academy's, but also with the works of the Sophists, the Pre-Socratics, and the medical writers, as well as with Greek lyric, epic, and drama, and not least with the constitutions known at the time.

After Plato's death in 347, Plato's nephew and heir Speusippus (410–339) was made head of the Academy. It was not vexation, though, that made the now thirty-eight-year-old philosopher leave Athens, but political danger, given that Aristotle was considered a friend of the Macedonians, who were threatening the freedom of Greece. Since the political situation required further displacements, his life did not run as quietly as one would expect given the size of his œuvre. Aristotle's ability to keep to his lifework, that is, research, even under adverse circumstances, is astonishing.

Together with other members of the Academy, he spent the beginning of the following twelve "years of travel" (347–335/4) with a former fellow-student, Hermias of Atarneus. Generously provided with all the necessities by this ruler of the city of Assus in Asia Minor, Aristotle was free to devote himself to philosophy and the sciences. It was presumably in Assus that he met his later collaborator and friend, Theophrastus of Eresus (c. 370–288). The philosopher married Pythias, Hermias's sister (or niece), with whom he had a daughter of the same name, followed by a son, Nicomachus. It was probably in the years spent away from Athens that Aristotle collected the wealth of zoological material that, together with the research related to it, would make his reputation as an outstanding zoologist.

After Hermias's death in 345, he moved on to Mytilene on Lesbos. Two years later, upon the request of King Philip, he took charge of the education of the thirteen-year-old Alexander. It is an extraordinary situation that one of the greatest philosophers should take on the responsibility for one who was to become one of the greatest rulers. Nevertheless, Aristotle does not mention his unusual student anywhere in his works, although he is said to have written a text with the title *Alexander, or On the Colonies,* and, more importantly, to have opened an access to Greek culture for his student. For example, he had a copy made of Homer's *Iliad,* which Alexander, an admirer of its protagonist, Achilles, took with him on his campaigns. Aristotle also seems to be partly responsible for the fact that Alexander took Greek scientists along in order to pursue cultural and scientific interests as well as military aims. It would seem, however, that a letter to Alexander, preserved only in Arabic, is spurious (Stein 1968): it is one of the oldest princes' codes, containing advice to Alexander on his behavior toward his subjects, the foundation of Greek cities, and the question whether the Persian nobility should be relocated by force. It culminates in the vision of a world state, a *kosmo-polis* (see ch. 15. 3).

DETAIL (ALEXANDER) OF A BATTLE BETWEEN
ALEXANDER THE GREAT AND DARIUS. Pompei, House of the Faun;
probably based on an original by Philoxenus of Eritrea

Toward the end of his "years of travel," Aristotle accepted a commission for Delphi to compile a list of victors of the Pythian Games. The fact that he was given this honorable commission demonstrates his scientific renown—and his acceptance of it documents once again his far-reaching intellectual curiosity in adding historiography to his other lines of research. He was awarded a decree of honor for his achievement which was, however, revoked in the anti-Macedonian rebellion of 323.

After Greek resistance against Macedonia had been broken by the destruction of Thebes (335), Aristotle, by then almost fifty, returned to the place of his earlier studies. This was the beginning of the "second sojourn in Athens" (335/4–322). Three or four years earlier Xenocrates—a philosopher far inferior to Aristotle in knowledge, acumen, and intellectual flexibility—had been elected leader of the Academy. It cannot be proved that this election led to the split from the Academy, but it is not implausible. In any case, during the following twelve years Aristotle worked at the Lyceum *(Lykeion)* near Mount Lycabettus, a gymnasium open to everyone. Because of its architecture it is also called *Peripatos,* which originally meant "walk," but later came to mean "roofed gallery" or "hall for strolls and discussions."

It remains uncertain whether the circle that formed around Aristotle there consolidated into a firm unit for teaching and research, into a working team. What certainly did not develop is something like a university with a fixed curriculum, exams, and academic degrees. Not even a formal foundation of the school took place, since, as an alien, Aristotle was not entitled to acquire property. In "nationalist" Athens he always remained a suspect stranger, and just one foreign scientist among many as far as Athenian intellectual life is concerned. Aristotle brought his library, which was of extraordinary size for his times, to the Lyceum, as well as a considerable amount of scientific instruments. In the course of public lectures— the philosopher kept up the unity of teaching and research familiar from the Academy—he revised earlier drafts of his thoughts and elaborated a mature version of his didactic writings. He also evaluated his collections of data. Not least, he organized his research by delegating certain areas of research to friends and colleagues, such as Theophrastus, Eudemus of Rhodes, and Meno.

After Alexander's death in June 323, Aristotle left Athens again. Although his political philosophy was, if anything, contrary to Macedonian interests, he was nevertheless afraid of becoming a victim of anti-Macedonian intrigue. He had also been charged with impiety *(asebeia)*, the same accusation that had brought about Socrates' death. Hinting at the fate of that "best, wisest and most just man among those alive at the time"(Plato, *Phaidon* 118a), he is said to have justified his

SOCRATES. Copy of a Hellenestic bust (Rome, Villa Albani)

departure from the city by saying that he would not allow the Athenians to sin against philosophy for a second time (Aelian, *Varia historia* III 36). Aristotle retreated to his mother's house in Chalcis on Euboea and shortly thereafter, in October 322, died of an unspecified illness at the age of sixty-two.

In the *Testament* (Diogenes Laertius, ch. V 1, 11–16) we encounter a considerate man who cares for the well-being of his family. The Macedonian general Antipater, Alexander's governor in Greece, is appointed as executor, Theophrastus as Aristotle's successor at the Lyceum. Aristotle expresses his wish to be buried next to his wife Pythias, and makes arrangements for relatives and servants.

We have portrait busts of Aristotle made at the time of the Roman Empire but based on a Greek original, presumably one made by Lysippus, court sculptor to Alexander the Great, at his master's command. They show Aristotle, aged about sixty, with a beard, wide mouth, strong lower lip and—as the iconographic expression of his outstanding intelligence and powers of concentration—a conspicuously protruding forehead. In the biographical tradition of antiquity one finds the epithets "the reader"(*anagnôstês*: Vita Marciana 6) and "the spirit of (scholarly) discussion"(*nous tês diatribês*: Philoponus, *De aeternitate mundi* VI 27).

ARISTOTLE. Roman copy based on a fourth-century B.C.E. statue
(Vienna, Kunsthistorisches Museum)

1.2 THE WORK

Diogenes' list of Aristotelian works mentions 146 titles, but this does not include two of the works considered most important by us, the *Metaphysics* and the *Nicomachean Ethics*. If one believes the author's count of 445,270 lines and adds the two treatises not mentioned by him, the result is one of almost incredible productivity (even considering the quantity only), an œuvre the equivalent of forty-five volumes of about three hundred pages each. As Aristotle's works were not protected as carefully as Plato's, it seems that less than one-quarter has survived, still amounting to an impressive ten volumes. (On the ancient lists of Aristotle's works, see Moraux 1951.)

Aristotle's writings fall into three genres. Some, stylistically elaborate, texts address educated laymen. Since the audience were outside (*exô* in Greek) the school, these writings are called exoteric or, as they also addressed a larger circle *(kyklos)*, encyclical writings. Among these are the *Protreptikos,* a hortatory text for philosophy, and also many dialogues, such as *On Philosophy, On Justice,* and *On the Poets.* Apart from these "popular"writings there are "professional"texts, the *pragmateiai* or treatises, also called esoteric writings, because they address students and colleagues "inside"(Greek: *esô*) the school. Surprisingly these only treat some central topics very briefly. This can be explained by the fact that Aristotle has already dealt with these topics in his exoteric writings and presupposes a knowledge of them— these writings were, after all, available in the book trade. The third genre consists of collections of research material—about the tenets of earlier philosophers, research into nature (in particular zoology), about politics, proverbs, Homeric questions, etc. The collection of performance dates of the "tragedy competitions," the so-called *Didaskalia,* is lost, and of the most famous collection, that of 158 Greek constitutions, we have only the *Constitution of Athens.*

When comparing the extant works with Plato's, one must not forget that in Aristotle's case all writings of specific literary value, apart from a few fragments, were already lost in late antiquity. In Plato's case, however, what we know are specifically the works of literature, namely, the dialogues. One could blame this state of transmission entirely on the vicissitudes of history, but it may also be the case that Aristotle's dialogues were not transmitted because they did not hold their ground against this outstanding model. Cicero, who is of the greatest importance for the transmission of Greek culture, appears to be following the Aristotelian dialogues particularly closely. Nevertheless, it cannot be denied that, apart from Aristotle and Cicero, attempts to imitate Plato's art of the dialogue in philosophy— e. g., in Augustine, Abelard, Ockham, Galileo, Hume, or Leibniz—all seem to fall short of Plato's standards.

Matters are different with the writings intended for school use. At an intermediate level between lecture transcripts and structurally as well as stylistically refined works, they prepare the way for another textual genre developed by Aristotle, that is, the treatise, which can be "imitated"without problems and still is the form in use for science and philosophy. As far as we know, Aristotle wrote down his most essential thoughts in this form. This could result in a third, internal, reason for the state of transmission: there was no longer a philosophical need for transmitting the dialogues as well. Nevertheless, the loss of the dialogues is regrettable. Firstly, it would be interesting to know which thoughts Aristotle intended to make accessible to a wider audience. Secondly, one would like to get to know their literary qualities, given that Cicero praises their "golden stream of speech" (*flumen orationis aureum*: *Academica* II 119), by which he means the rhythmically and syntactically refined style of an only slightly elevated colloquial language.

It would seem that of the "treatises" only the *Historia animalium,* the *Zoology,* is conceived for a reading, rather than listening, audience. The *Prior Analytics* and the *Nicomachean Ethics,* too, are carefully developed, without the leaps of thought or mere hints that can be found in other didactic writings. However, the majority of Aristotle's treatises are notebooks or either lecture notes or transcripts of lectures, not intended for publication. Presumably most of them are revised versions of a first draft, often made by Aristotle himself, but partly by Theophrastus and other pupils. Therefore, one can expect various layers of text, but also some reorganizing, excurses, annotations, and references. It appears, though, that Aristotle made final, revised versions of some texts, not only the *Nicomachean Ethics* but also the *Categories,* the *Topics,* and the *Analytics.* It is odd that there are several texts on some of the topics, in particular on ethics, on which we have the *Nicomachean Ethics,* the *Eudemian Ethics,* and the *Great Ethics* (the *Magna Moralia,* whose authenticity is disputed).

With great acumen and no less polemic spirit, learned philologists—called to the fore by the state of transmission of the didactic writings—have suggested a plethora of attempted datings, hypotheses of development, and textual emendations (conjectures). However, their work always involves the risk of losing sight of the actual philosophical content, and in spite of all this erudition the chronology of the works still remains disputed. Only the following is generally accepted: The *Topics,* one of the oldest treatises, was written before both the *Categories* and the *Prior Analytics;* the *Rhetoric* and—perhaps—the *Poetics* are both early works; the writings on biology and metaphysics refer to an early form of the logic and theory of proof (contained in the *Topics*), while the *Analytics* present a relatively mature elaboration of these. The *De generatione animalium* is the latest work on biology; as far as ontology is concerned, the *Categories* precede the *Metaphysics,* and within practical philosophy the *Nicomachean Ethics* must be written after the *Politics.*

Given that Aristotle only has a limited range of models at his disposal, he can be considered one of the creators of a sober scientific prose style. He is also the originator of a multitude of technical terms that, by way of their Latin translation, have become a fixed part of philosophical terminology. It has to be added, though, that the ensuing ossification has nothing to do with him. Many of his technical terms are originally questions: among the categories we find *ti*/"what," *poson*/"how big," *poion*/"of what kind," or *pou*/"where"; among the principles of motion, he mentions "made from what," "what," "whence," and "for the sake of what." In any case, Aristotle does not aim at an artificial language of philosophy, but at the specification, differentiation, and occasionally the development of expressions familiar from everyday language. That way he achieves a diction that is flexible and thoroughly unscholastic.

Usually Aristotle writes in a style that is clear, concise, to the point, and rich in variety—apart from some formulaic expressions. Occasionally, we even find the style praised by Cicero, for example in parts of *Metaphysics* XII, of the *Politics,* and in chapter I 5 of the treatise *On the Parts of Animals* (644b22–645a36). In general, however, the texts are dense and often elliptical, as one would expect from lecture notes, and interwoven with interpolations. They also contain abrupt transitions, and some connections remain obscure. It may be possible to read other philosophers by the section, or even by the chapter, but a precise thinker such as Aristotle needs to be studied line by line, even word by word. One needs to read, analyze, and reread, and to be able to follow his line of thought in such a way as to understand an argument that is only hinted at and to bring to philosophical life some "bone-dry" passages by illustration and by further consideration of their relevance ("What does this mean?"). However, those who confront this challenge will find access to a philosophy almost unequalled when it comes to thematic range, phenomenal wealth, conceptual acuity, and speculative power.

Unfortunately, most of this extraordinary œuvre, with the exception of the popular writings, was lost soon after Aristotle's death. The first meticulous edition of his didactic writings was not made until three centuries later, in Rome. According to ancient tradition, the editor, Andronicus of Rhodes, relied on original manuscripts, which had reached Rome by tortuous paths (see ch. 17. 1). This edition is the basis for all subsequent Aristotelian tradition, and it is essentially identical with our extant *Corpus Aristotelicum.* Through Andronicus's edition Aristotle's didactic writings quickly became widely known and commented upon, in the circle of Andronicus as well as later, in particular from the second century C.E. onward. It must not be forgotten, though, that unlike the example of Plato, there was no continual exegetic tradition for Aristotle; the first extant commentaries date to Imperial Rome.

The history of the textual tradition also has another, serious consequence: the systematic arrangement and the subdivision of the texts into four groups are not the work of the author himself, but that of his editor. Led by the idea of a philosophical system structured in a logical way, Andronicus places (1) the writings on logic and theory of science, considered as propaedeutic, at the beginning. Surprisingly, (2) the *Ethics,* the *Politics,* the *Rhetoric,* and the *Poetics* follow. Only then (3) come the writings on natural philosophy (including psychology). The final section (4) consists of texts on first philosophy, which are called "meta-physics" because of their position after (Greek: *meta*) physics, meaning, natural philosophy. On the other hand, the arrangement corresponds roughly to the ancient standard subdivision of logic—ethics—physics, which was already available to Aristotle, albeit in the inverse order (cf. *Top.* I 14, 105b20f.). The fact that, later, Andronicus's second section, ethics, was placed last, has remained there since, and is often disregarded, reflects the low esteem of practical compared to theoretical philosophy prevalent among some philosophers, although not shared by Aristotle.

Even after this rearrangement Andronicus's idea of a system was kept alive. Not infrequently it is the basis for a rigid Aristotelianism determining interpretation until a few generations ago, despite the epochal editions and investigations of the fifteenth and then the nineteenth centuries. The systemic idea was finally refuted by the interpretation based on historical development that originated in two monographs (1912 and 1955[2]) by the philologist Werner Jaeger. Inspired by nineteenth-century historicism, Jaeger sees in Aristotle's œuvre the result of his intellectual development, in which three phases can be clearly distinguished: years of study *(Lehrjahre),* years of travel *(Wanderjahre),* and a period of mastery *(Meisterschaft).* In the intellectual adolescence of his first sojourn in Athens, the "Academy period"—in Jaeger's construct—the philosopher represented Platonic positions and was an "idealist." In the time he spends away from Athens, the *Wanderjahre,* he progressively turned away from this position, and finally, in the *Meisterzeit* after his return to Athens, he pursued phenomenologically and empirically orientated research stripped of all speculation. In brief: idealist metaphysics is replaced by realism and empiricism.

The same model of interpretation has been used on Plato by K. F. Hermann (*Geschichte und System der Platonischen Philosophie*, Heidelberg 1839). It can even be traced back to the third century C.E. and the philosopher, and commentator of Aristotle, Porphyry. The basic idea is not so new, then. In any case, among philologists nowadays there is "a broad consensus that Jaeger's results are to be considered erroneous in their overall conception as well as in many details" (Flashar 1983, 177). Choosing biology and, within it, the classification of the animal kingdom as an example, one can see, on the one hand, how an increasingly complex "system" saturated in experience develops in the course of time, but, on the other hand, there is no question of empiricism in our modern sense, given the element of teleology. From the onset, the uncritical use of ancient biographical material and fragments, as well as the scheme of a linear, almost mechanical development, are questionable. Furthermore, one has to credit the philosopher with a development that is not determined by his emotional state vis-à-vis his teacher, but relies on reasoned insight. Anyway, the idea of development adds so little to our philosophical understanding that one feels drawn to the opposite position, expressed in a lecture by Heidegger in this pithy sentence: "He was born in such and such a year, he worked and died" ("Grundbegriffe der aristotelischen Philosophie," Gesamtausgabe Bd. 18).

2

RESEARCHER, SCHOLAR, AND PHILOSOPHER

Aristotle deals with practically all the research subjects available in his time, adding domains such as topics, including the *Sophistical Refutations* (= *Top.* IX). According to his own testimony, he was the first to explore this field (*Top.* IX 34, 183b16 ff.), and he took it to very high standards straightaway. Aristotle developed a formal logic, a logic of discourse, and a theory of scientific proof, as well as theories of rhetoric and literature. He explains the various forms of knowledge and constructs a theory of their perfect form, that is, of science and philosophy. "Alongside" there are the themes we consider traditional: epistemology, ontology and natural theology, philosophical psychology ("philosophy of mind"), and not least ethics, inclusive of theory of action and political philosophy, as well as a comparative theory of constitutions and political sociology.

It was still possible for the great early modern thinker Kant to give lectures on the natural sciences and provide remarkable contributions to smaller fields of study, but he was no longer one of the great natural scientists. Nowadays researchers tend to be even more narrowly specialized. Aristotle, however, is able to produce epochal achievements on all three levels, that is, in empirical research, the theory of individual sciences, and philosophical proto- or meta-theory. Diogenes Laertius is justified in writing that, where nature is concerned, Aristotle's inquisitive zeal leaves all others far behind, since he tries to indicate causes for even the most insignificant phenomena (V 1). Furthermore, Aristotle stands out as a scholar, whether it is as a historian of philosophy, a constitutional historian, the historiographer of the Pythian Games, or the representative of a scientific Homeric philology. He even makes important contributions to mathematics, albeit only to its method and the theory of the reality of its objects.

In today's debates some of these topics seem like poor relations: which philosopher would still venture into rhetoric or a theory of modern theatre? In Aristotle we can see that—independent of the question whether there are central and marginal topics—at the best, it is the quality of philosophizing that is of a higher or lower rank.

One area is conspicuously absent. As a physician's son, Aristotle is familiar with the practical skills of a doctor as well as the physiological and anatomical theories of his times (cf. the remarks in the *Ethics;* also *Metaph.* I 1, 981a15–24; *Pol.* III 11, 1281b40ff. and *passim*). He only refers to them from the points of view of the theory of science, natural science, and theory of literature, however, while there is no theory or philosophy of medicine. It would seem that two factors are partly responsible. On the one hand, there is no medical research being done in Aristotle's intellectual surroundings, that is, in Plato's Academy. On the other, Aristotle only opens up new areas of research where there is a fundamental shortage, such as in zoology. As for the theory of medicine, it had long been cultivated within the circles of Hippocratic tradition.

Thus, Aristotle's œuvre represents a true encyclopaedia of knowledge, with the exclusion of medicine and common mathematics. It still presents as a unity what has now become fragmented into specialist subjects, and often mutually alienated, namely natural, social, and literary sciences, as well as history of thought. The philosopher undertakes descriptive as well as normative investigations; he occupies himself with empirical research, the theories of individual sciences, and, not least, the various spheres of genuine philosophy. In brief: Aristotle is "one of the richest and most comprehensive (deepest) scientific genii . . . that have ever lived" (Hegel, *Werke* 19, 132).

One could be led to believe that this encyclopedic research is based on the concept of a homogeneous unified science, but Aristotle rejects even its two prerequisites, the idea of a single intention of research and that of homogeneous objectivity. Although he knows about the methodic elements common to all sciences and their common basic concepts and points of view, these are neither developed in a homogeneous fundamental philosophy nor do they lead to a single principle that circumscribes all knowledge in a closed context. He acknowledges final causality only in the modest form of a theory of basic principles of thought. Otherwise, he champions a plurality of common principles which, along with principles specific to particular disciplines, are, however, dealt with by several disciplines—by metaphysics, logic, and considerations on the theory of science, in some ways also by topics and by parts of natural philosophy and ethics.

By his critique of a unified science Aristotle liberates the various fields of research from any kind of "systemic constraint," creating a wealth of relatively independent single disciplines. Specialist research, which has long become commonplace in European science, did not begin, as some believe, after the supposed failure of Hegel's *Encyclopaedia,* but much earlier. Essentially it began with Aristotle. He distinguished three spheres within the framework of emancipation of single disciplines. Kant believed that "ancient Greek philosophy was subdivided into three sciences: physics, ethics and logic" ("Vorrede"to the *Grundlegung zur Metaphysik der Sitten*). Although Aristotle was aware of this subdivision (ch. 1. 2), which had been current in the Academy since Speusippus, a different distinction was more important to him, namely that into theoretical, practical, and productive knowledge (*Metaph.* VI 1; *Top.* VI 6, 145a15 f.). This classification is distinctly modern insofar as it links the questions of subject-matter and leading cognitive interest (see Table 2.1).

Table 2.1

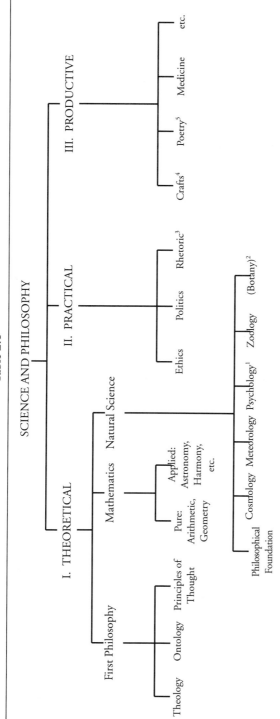

SCIENCE AND PHILOSOPHY

I. THEORETICAL   II. PRACTICAL   III. PRODUCTIVE

First Philosophy   Mathematics   Natural Science

Theology   Ontology   Principles of Thought

Pure: Arithmetic, Geometry

Applied: Astronomy, Harmony, etc.

Philosophical Foundation

Cosmology   Meteorology   Psychology[1]   Zoology   (Botany)[2]

Ethics   Politics   Rhetoric[3]

Crafts[4]   Poetry[5]   Medicine   etc.

1. Secondarily, psychology belongs partly to mathematics, partly to first philosophy.
2. Botany will be practised only by Theophrastus.
3. Rhetoric belongs also to II, but because of its neutral value it belongs chiefly to III.
4. Not practised by Aristotle.
5. This is present only as theory in Aristotle.

Directed toward the eternal, unalterable structures of nature and cognition, the three theoretical sciences strive for knowledge for its own sake: (1) Mathematics consists of pure mathematics, that is, arithmetic and geometry, and applied mathematics, namely astronomy, mechanics, navigation, optics, and harmony. (2) Physics, in the broad sense of natural science and natural philosophy, deals with the entire range of what exists in the world in motion: the stars and the earth, plants, animals, humans, and gods—in brief: the world. Physics begins with the philosophical elements, that is, physics in a narrow sense, and leads from the heavens, cosmology, to the things between heaven and earth, meteorology, and finally to psychology, zoology, and botany. (3) First philosophy consists of philosophical theology, as well as ontology and the theory of basic principles of thought; in a certain sense dialectics (topics), logic (syllogistics), and the theory of science belong in this group as well.

The practical sciences comprise ethics and politics, including economy. Concerned with the changeable human world and the good that can be achieved, they not only pursue knowledge, but also put it to the service of moral practice (see Ch. 12. 2). Finally, the productive or technical faculties are directed toward the production of a work. Artisans belong in this group, given that they manufacture certain things, and so do doctors by intending to achieve health, and poets by intending to achieve a work of art. By contrast, rhetoric is—not exclusively, but to a large extent—an ancillary science to ethics and politics, because its purpose is not merely persuasion, but it can also contribute to *eupraxia,* good actions (*Rh.* I 5, 1360b14). Nowadays, the application-orientated, technical sciences span a far larger and more differentiated field, but their basic structure is the same as it was then: either directly or indirectly, they serve the production of certain works. Neither Aristotle's collections of data nor his historical research have a proper place in this scheme.

All this raises the question how one should best approach a scientific and philosophical œuvre of such universal character. For centuries Aristotle's works were looked to for a system of philosophical tenets that was true as well as all-embracing and constructed by a deductive principle. Although the œuvre is rooted in a well-defined historical situation, it was assumed that its questions were of timeless validity and that its answers could solve practically all the mysteries of philosophy, as well as most problems of the individual sciences. Aristotle's works were read as a system of definitions and distinctions as well as arguments and their syllogistic connections, and thus as a system of doctrines that could be summarized in textbooks, or even philosophical catechisms, for systematic ("scholastic") teaching.

Those who opt for this kind of access pay a high price. By not approaching Aristotle's thoughts from the inside, it is all too easy to emphasize aspects alien to them. If one becomes fixated on an earlier stage of scientific research, however elevated it may be, one shuts out everything that is new, and living philosophizing turns into dead doctrine. The reaction to this is obvious. Self-confident philosophers develop their thought as a critique of, or even in opposition to, Aristotle, so that in the end he is seen as the representative of the *via antiqua,* which is simply outstripped by the *via moderna.*

In neither case is there a need for a dialogue with Aristotle. In the former, there is no need for it because he is supposed to have given us a *philosophia perennis,* a treasure-trove of eternal truths, which we can only read and commentate on again and again, with reverent admiration. In the latter case one can do without a dialogue, because Aristotle is seen as belonging to an era that has long been surpassed—by Galileo in the natural sciences, Hobbes in political philosophy, and by Kant and Frege in theoretical philosophy and logic. Furthermore, Aristotle subscribes to metaphysics, a way of thinking that nowadays needs to be discarded by anyone wanting to be taken seriously as a philosopher.

The following description is based on a different expectation, namely that of an exemplary paradigmatic way of thinking. Those who expect philosophy to provide not only history of thought, but also a knowledge of the world combining experience, acuity of perception, methodical superiority, speculative power, and intellectual openness, will find an outstanding model in Aristotle. Furthermore, quite a few of his concepts were important tools for finding one's bearings in the world for many centuries, and some still are. Among these concepts are the distinction of things that exist independently, namely, substances, and those that exist only with or in independent things, to wit, accidents. To give some examples: the distinction between matter and form, reality (action) and possibility (potentiality), or between theory, practice and *poiêsis* ("technique"). As such distinctions have long become obvious to us, we forget easily that we owe the elaboration of some and the specification of others to Aristotle. Therefore, his philosophy has more than merely exemplary character. Quite a few of the concepts, as well as of the structural and methodological investigations, have kept their relevance until the present.

PART II

KNOWLEDGE AND SCIENCE

Science and philosophy tend to push to the forefront of knowledge to such an extent that anything else—if it may call itself "knowledge" at all—loses status. Aristotle is strongly opposed to this tendency. He grants a fixed place in the world of knowledge to rhetoric and even poetry. Within the sciences he introduces ranks but recognizes more than one criterion, and therefore more than one order of rank. Not least, he advocates more than one method for the sciences. This epistemic flexibility and tolerance result in an unusual horizon that is as broad as it is multilayered. Without lapsing into a randomness without criteria or into an anarchism of scientific theory, Aristotle is open to strict procedures, formal logic, and scientific proof, as well as to linguistic analysis, dialectic, history of thought, rhetoric, and poetry.

3

THE PHENOMENOLOGY OF
KNOWLEDGE

3.1 PROPAEDEUTIC?

In the traditional arrangement, Aristotle's œuvre begins with six treatises called collectively *Organon,* that is, "instrument" or "tool." According to the traditional view, this is an organic whole, a systematic textbook of logic and theory of science, consisting of deductive logic, a doctrine of induction, dialectic logic, and a doctrine of fallacies or paralogisms. According to this view, the textbook does not belong to science or philosophy proper, but—as their imperative prerequisite—it is a kind of pre-philosophy, a logical and methodological propaedeutic.

At a first, fleeting glance the texts of the *Organon* indeed present a systematic unity. The first two parts, the *Categories* and the *Hermeneutic,* in Latin *De interpretatione,* appear to treat the elements of a proposition (capable of truth), concepts or terms and their combination in forming simple sentences or statements (propositions). The next part, the *Prior Analytics,* examines the smallest unit of an argument, that is, the combination of sentences into syllogisms or inferences. Since their combination in order to form a proof is discussed in the *Posterior Analytics,* the first parts of the *Organon* (in the traditional reading) result in a four-part deductive logic proceeding from simple to composite: the logic of concepts *(Cat.)* is followed successively by a logic of propositions *(Int.),* of inferences *(APr.),* and of proof or argumentation *(APo.).* The fifth part, consisting only of the final chapter of the *Posterior Analytics,* deals with the theory of principles of proof which Aristotle calls *epagôgê,* induction. The subsequent *Topics* develops a form of proof that is either alternative or complementary, namely dialectic. Finally, the seventh part is made up by the theory of fallacies contained in the ninth book of the *Topics,* which also appears separately as the *Sophistical Refutations.*

The traditional interpretation that Aristotle compiled a textbook of logic, which he considered a mere tool, was uncommonly influential. In the seventeenth century it was still reinforced by the famous *Logique de Port Royal* (Paris 1662), and in some places it was the basis of the logic course as part of the teaching of philosophy as late as the twentieth century. There is a wealth of arguments, philological as well as philosophical, against this interpretation, beginning with the one that, with the exception of the two *Analytics,* the treatises do not refer to each other in accordance with the system of the *Organon.* Another is that their relative size is disproportionate: the alternative theory of argumentation or proof in the *Topics* is almost as voluminous as the remaining parts of the *Organon* put together. Besides, the concepts mentioned in the title of the first treatise, namely the categories, do not feature in Aristotle's syllogisms. Furthermore, the treatises are never mentioned as a unity. Nor does Aristotle state—as some Peripatetics will do later, in contrast to the Stoics and some Platonists—that logic does not belong to philosophy proper, and is only its tool. Instead, *Topics* (I 14, 105b20f.) mentions logical propositions as a field of their own, along with ethics and physics. Finally, there are thematical arguments as well: the *Hermeneutic* is concerned also with grammar, albeit only for the purpose of understanding logical questions, and the *Categories* deals with questions of ontology and theory of language, that is (if one wants to make these distinctions), not with the tool, but with philosophy itself. Not least, the terms *conceptual logic* and *propositional logic* become inappropriate at this point.

Even if one removes the *Categories* from the *Organon,* concedes a special position to the *Hermeneutic,* and considers the *Sophistical Refutations* an appendix, that is, after a thorough emendation, there are still two reasons left for rejecting the traditional view. One is that the remaining texts, the two *Analytics* and the *Topics,* form two self-contained "autarkical" treatises. They neither presuppose a special logic of concepts or sentences, nor does either text refer to the other. In the *Analytics* and the *Topics* we have two "parallel" types of logic, which are not entirely of a different kind, but which nevertheless differ in their orientation. The other reason is that logical and methodological considerations are dispersed throughout the entire œuvre. The idea of the *Organon* expresses the leitmotif of Andronicus's edition, namely that of Aristotle as a systematic thinker. The idea also belongs to the kind of Aristotelanism that originated in the Middle Ages and continued until our century, but it does not provide an obligation for a study of the original Aristotle.

Among the logical and methodological discussions scattered throughout the œuvre one can distinguish four forms. Firstly, methodical excurses are inserted among the factual considerations (on natural philosophy, ethics, politics, etc.). These are contributions to a special theory of science which "applies" general principles of theories of science to the respective subject (e.g., *EN* I 1, I 2, I 7, and II 2; *de An.* I 1, 402a–403a).

Secondly, we find reflections about a general theory of science, for example in the *Physics* (I 1) and with particular frequency in the *Ethics*. There is a brief but instructive remark at the beginning of the discussion on weakness of will (*EN* VII 1, 1145b2–7); and the sixth book of the *Ethics* introduces not only the knowledge pertinent to moral actions, that is, prudence with its related competences. Given that the *Ethics* considers the *logos* the achievement characteristic of man, it describes in an almost encyclopedic way all its varieties, its five basic forms—art *(technê),* knowledge *(epistêmê),* prudence *(phronêsis),* wisdom *(sophia),* and the spirit *(nous)*—as well as numerous variants. One could also consider as part of this second group the originally independent texts which were later integrated into a larger work. Taken separately, however, they have the value of an autonomous introduction to science and philosophy: (a) The introductory chapter of *On the Parts of Animals* makes a distinction between (general) erudition and science, which is taken up by the first excursus on method in the *Ethics* (I 1). (b) The introductory chapters of the *Metaphysics* (I 1–2) contain a gradation of epistemic possibilities which results in a phenomenology of knowledge. (c) The second book of the *Metaphysics* provides a brief introduction to the study of philosophy and (natural) science. (d) The introductory chapter of book VI of the *Metaphysics* divides the sciences into three sections (see ch. 2).

Thirdly, in the *Rhetoric* and the *Poetics,* Aristotle deals with forms of knowledge outside science. Fourthly, there are the aforementioned texts on logic and theory of science, which are transmitted as autonomous treatises and combined in the *Organon*.

Because of the reasons mentioned above it is better to remove the *Categories,* and the *Hermeneutic* does not examine logical questions exclusively (even though that is its sole purpose), so what remains are mainly the two *Analytics* and the *Topics,* including the *Sophistical Refutations.* Each of these treats a separate field of research—formal logic, theory of proof, theory of discourse, and the theory of fallacies—which Aristotle approaches with the same curiosity and thoroughness he applies to ontology, physics, ethics, and politics. Given that, therefore, these investigations are not only subservient to others, as the word *Organon* implies, but are also carried out for their own sake, they cannot be downgraded to mere propaedeutic. Logic and theory of science are tools as well as objects of philosophy.

In early modern times, the previously almost undisputed esteem for the *Organon* waned. While the *Logique de Port Royal* still referred to Aristotle, others began to search for—to use the title of Bacon's work—a *New Organon* (*Novum organum,* 1620). In opposition to a scholasticism gone sterile, and content with an art of proving, an *ars demonstrandi,* the alternative, an *ars inveniendi,* accompanied the great scientific awakening of the early modern era. From Bacon to Vico, Wolff and Lambert, by way of Descartes and Leibniz, philosophers in general were looking for a new "tool." The malaise expressed by this search is certainly justified in regard to a type of logic that gives most attention to the syllogism, but not against Aristotle himself. One part of his logic, namely, dialectic, is—among other things, of course—an art of research or examination (*exetastikê: Top.* I 2, 101b3). Above all, Aristotle has at his command a much greater arsenal of means of argumentation than just the syllogism. In his treatises he manifests something that is rarely found among philosophers (in particular among contemporary ones), namely an *esprit de finesse* that knows about the plurality of epistemic possibilities and is capable of using them in a masterly way. Besides, the modern age has never discovered a true art of invention either, that is, one that can be taught and learnt. In the following, we shall choose some examples from the wealth of Aristotelian thought; chapter 12 will add some explanations about his ethics.

3.2 AN EPISTEMIC HIERARCHY

The *Metaphysics* (I 1–2; cf. *APo.* II 19) opens with a gradation of epistemic abilities which, with its clear delimitations at both ends, is reminiscent of Hegel's

Phänomenologie des Geistes. The sequence starts from an ultimately first knowledge, namely the perception of single things, and culminates in the highest knowledge possible, that is, philosophy, understood as the cognition of the first principles. Like Hegel, Aristotle, too, succeeds in deploying the wealth of epistemic possibilities without losing himself in mere variety. Compared to Hegel's, however, his claim is more modest: in the end he only focuses on theoretical matters, and here, though not in all of his œuvre, he leaves aside the practical knowledge of prudence as well as rhetoric and poetry. Furthermore, he combines the normative distinction between higher and lower forms of knowledge with an extent of epistemic tolerance as it is rarely encountered and which is, for example, lacking in Hegel.

While—from Plato to Husserl and the Vienna Circle, by way of Hegel—the privileged position of science and (strictly scientific) philosophy devalues other forms of knowledge, Aristotle concedes each stage of knowledge a greater autonomy. In opposition to the prevalent model of epistemic absorption, according to which a lower stage of knowledge is either absorbed ("inclusion") or declared invalid, or even relatively untrue, ("annulment") by the one higher than itself, Aristotle advocates a model of epistemic intensification. For example, the task of perception (*aisthêsis*, cf. *de An.* II 5, III 2 and III 8), that is, the "decisive knowledge of the particular" (*Metaph.* I 1, 981b10 f.), is neither expanded nor diminished in its epistemic rank by the higher stages. Rather, a succession of new epistemic achievements leads to a structural enrichment, and it is only because of the latter that Aristotle speaks of a higher *(mallon eidenai)* and finally a highest knowledge (*hê malista epistêmê: Metaph.* I 1, 982a32 ff.; also at 981a31 f.).

After perception has discerned individual facts, these perceptions are stored in the memory *(mnêmê)*, and provided with cause-effect relationships through experience *(empeiria)*. The first two stages can also be found in animals, but the third is limited to humans. Those who, because of a wealth of experience, know not only *that (hoti)*, but also *why (dihoti)* the relations between cause and effect exist, achieve the distinguishing characteristic of art or skill and science, that is, a knowledge of the general that knows about the concept of a thing as well as its causes. Even though this fourth stage is not quite the highest form of knowledge yet, it nevertheless meets the high standards of what is called *epistasthai haplôs* in the *Posterior Analytics* (I 2, 71b9 ff.). Given that one knows the cause of a thing, one knows that it can behave only in this way and not otherwise; one knows not by chance *(kata symbebêkos)*, but absolutely.

Within this fourth stage there are differences in rank for which Aristotle introduces different criteria, some of them mutually conflicting. According to the criterion "precise" *(akribes*, or *akribeia)*, in the sense of "close to principle" or "with few prerequisites," mathematics is at the top of the hierarchy, and slightly below it one finds empirical natural science, as well as ethics and politics. Again, within mathematics pure mathematics is given precedence over physical mathematics (optics, mechanics, harmony, and astronomy), and within pure mathematics, arithmetic over geometry. Finally, mathematical astronomy is of higher rank than nautical astronomy (*APo.* I 27; II 13, 78b39–79a13). According to a second criterion, that is, the dignity of the subject (*Metaph.* I 2, 982a25–28 and *de An.* I 1, 402a1–4), it is astronomy, that is, cosmology, that has pride of place within natural sciences. Since there is the risk, therefore, of biology—with its wealth of knowledge—being judged inferior, Aristotle introduces another measure, namely the abundance of knowledge, and adds that every natural object has something wonderful about it (*PA.* I 5, 644b32 ff.). Furthermore, in the *Ethics* he advocates a principle of precision as appropriate to the subject, which revaluates the practical disciplines.

There is a further stage above the knowledge about concepts and causes, which consists in the knowledge of first causes and principles (*Metaph.* I 1, 981b28 f.; cf. *APo.* I 9, 76a118–25). Where it is the cognition of the general that is intensified, Aristotle uses the term *wisdom* (*sophia: Metaph.* I 1, 981b28); elsewhere he speaks of first philosophy, leading science, or, where it is understood as an activity, of *theôria*. Given the superlative—"first" causes—this stage cannot be surpassed: in it (theoretical) knowledge has reached immanent perfection.

The gradation of knowledge outlined so far is built up in a teleological (goal-oriented) way, and is quite convincing despite modern skepticism against teleology. For it would mean giving away epistemic possibilities either to look for perceptions only but not for a means to retain them, or to be satisfied with memories without recognizing their interconnections; or again, to collect experiences without taking an interest in the respective generalities (concepts and causes); and finally, to content oneself with simple generalities. Superlative generalities, on the other hand, do not permit any further intensification. A further argument can be adduced in favor of the two highest stages: a person who knows the causes possesses epistemic superiority and is also able to teach the subject (*Metaph.* I 1, 981b5–10).

Aristotle opposes the devaluation of pre-scientfic knowledge by according a merely dominant meaning to the two highest stages. They do not necessarily include preceding knowledge, as with the absorption model decribed above; the lower stages are not contained within the higher ones in the Hegelian sense. As experience shows, those who know about the general do not necessarily know all the particulars contained in it. A scientist can be lacking in knowledge of the particular; for example, a person who has the necessary scientific knowledge as well as diagnostic and therapeutic skills, is not *eo ipso* an experienced doctor (cf. *Metaph.* I 1, 981a18 ff; on the value of *empeiria,* cf. also *EN* VI 8, 1141b18). In a similar way, competence in philosophy does not include any competence in individual sciences. The fact that for knowledge philosophy does not have the same rank as, say, happiness has for practical life, that is, that it is not a perfect knowledge that lacks nothing, contributes to the epistemic emancipation of the individual sciences.

Put simply, the history of philosophy has known an epistemological polarity of "empiricist" disregard for, and "idealist" overestimation of, the general. Aristotle's theory of epistemic gradation steers a promising middle course between the two positions. Although in his theory the higher knowledge is directed toward something general and shows itself to be superior by doing so, the lower stages keep their own value, which puts the higher ones in their place. In the case of the absorption model (inclusion or neutralization), there is nothing lacking in the knowledge of the most general, so that, epistemically, just being a philosopher is sufficient. If one assumes that it is gradation (i.e., mere dominance), however, one postulates what Aristotle himself puts into practice, that is, an interest in the richness of the particular that can only be investigated empirically.

There is a dual argument—regarding the politics as well as the history of science—in Aristotle's favor: if philosophy overestimates its efficiency, the sciences develop the need to emancipate themselves from philosophy, or even to deny it all importance. That way, the epistemic misjudgment soon turns out to be counterproductive. If, on the other hand, the value of the individual sciences is acknowledged, these do not need to disassociate themselves, as they did from philosophy after Hegel, or from theology in the late Middle Ages and the early modern period; instead there is the chance of a productive cooperation. Thus, there are two arguments for the Aristotelian approach, both from the point of view of the politics of science and from that of its history.

One can pass through the gradation of knowledge in two directions: although Aristotle does not do so at the beginning of the *Metaphysics,* in the second excursus on method in the *Ethics* (I 2, 1095a30 ff.), and similarly at the beginning of the *Physics* (I 1)—referring to Plato—he distinguishes between the "inductive" way, going toward the principles *(epi tas archas),* and the "deductive" way, leading down from the principles *(apo tôn archôn;* cf. *APr.* I 2, 71b21 f.; *Top.* VI 4, 141b3 ff.; *Metaph.* VII 3, 1029b3–5). In the latter, that is, the "logical" reflection, one starts from what is "inherently known" *(gnôrimon tê physei),* the general or the causes knowable to the highest degree, and then descends from the top downward to the particulars. In the inductive way, one starts from what is obvious and "known to us" *(gnôrimon hêmin),* especially perception, and then moves upward to the general: "For just as the eyes of bats are disposed toward the daylight, so the spirit in our soul is disposed toward that which is the most evident of all by nature" *(Metaph.* II 1, 993b9–11).

3.3 FREEDOM AND SELF-REALIZATION

Aristotle's phenomenology does not open in a teleological way, but rather with the anthropological thesis quoted above: "By nature all men strive for knowledge." What makes this thesis convincing, despite the skepticism against anthropology prevailing today, is that it postulates not an optimal anthropology, that is, the perfection of human-ness, but a minimal anthropology, that is, an element in the basic makeup of every human being. Besides, Aristotle provides clear evidence: our love *(agapêsis)* for sensual perceptions suggests an inquisitiveness and pleasure in discoveries innate to humans *(Metaph.* I 1, 980a21 f.). It can be found in connection with all senses: there is pleasure in hearing, touching, tasting, smelling, and, most of all, says Aristotle, there is the pleasure of seeing, or visual pleasure. "By nature" means two things here: internal consent—because the craving for knowledge comes from inside humans—as well as the fact that this craving characterizes man as such.

Both are easily confirmed by modern research: the beginnings of the individual by developmental psychology, and the beginnings of the history of the species by ethnology. What is confirmed initially, of course, is the elementary form, that is, the pleasure taken in perception, which humans still share with animals. But there is also an inner assent when it comes to the higher, specifically human, forms of knowledge. Alluding to Plato's *Theaetetus* (155d), Aristotle cites astonishment (*thaumazein: Metaph.* I 2, 982b12–17) by which he does, however, not mean awe in front of the harmony of the universe, but rather wondering about disharmony, that is, skeptical wonder in the face of as yet inexplicable facts. Those who then search for causes and reasons prove by that very action their pleasure in knowledge of a higher degree.

In both cases of simple, innocent desire to know and of its reflected, higher-level variant, one investigates the world *chôris tês chreias* (*Metaph.* I 1, 980a22), or *mê pros chrêsin* (981b19 f; cf. I 2, 982b21). Free of all needs or necessities, one searches for knowledge for itself. Nevertheless, it is always possible to consider usability, and then there are two options within each stage of knowledge, knowledge for its own sake and knowledge for a purpose. Aristotle only speaks of this distinction as far as the fourth level is concerned. Only there he contrasts pure science, *epistêmê,* against *technê,* the term that is the root of "technology" and its equivalents in all European languages. For the actual terms we have to wait for the *Ethics* (VI 3–4), but the *Metaphysics* (I 1, 982a1) already mentions theoretical and productive (manufacturing) sciences. *Epistêmê* fulfils the criterion of the "end in itself," but *technê,* or productive science, does not.

At the elementary stage, Aristotle sees the disinterested desire for knowledge in all men, but only in a few when it comes to science and philosophy. The *Metaphysics* gives a reason that is both economic and social-historical for this limitation, thus anticipating in an astonishing way a more recent scientific trend, namely the combination of the theory of science with the history and sociology of science. While, as an inclination and an interest, disinterested curiosity belongs to the basic human makeup, it only achieves the full reality of science and philosophy at a relatively high level of economic development, at which the necessities and amenities of life have already been taken care of (*Metaph.* I 1, 981b20–25; cf. Plato, *Critias* 110a). However, Aristotle does not point out that, as an additional condition, these criteria are to be interpreted very narrowly, that is, people need to be relatively frugal. Otherwise even rich civilizations, and even rich individuals within them, would be too poor for science and philosophy. A further condition which is not mentioned in antiquity in general is that the scientist's needs have to be provided for by others; in the economic sense, too, disinterested science is an aristocratic undertaking.

The concept of knowledge for its own sake has been difficult to handle for the modern age since Bacon (*Novum Organum,* preface and aphor. I 81) and Descartes (*Discours de la méthode,* Part VI). The more recent theorem of knowledge constitutive interests even attributes an interest to each science: an interest in control to the natural sciences, an interest in understanding and orientation to the humanities and an interest in emancipation and enlightenment to the social sciences. By distinguishing between theoretical, productive ("technical") and practical considerations, Aristotle acknowledges the possibility of knowledge constitutive interests, but he refutes their claim to exclusivity. And the knowledge *chôris tês chreias* is indeed practised in the appropriate treatises—from the *Physics* (as a theory of motion, space, time, and continuity) through the *De anima* (as a theory of the cognitive and noncognitive faculties of humans and animals) to ontology and philosophical theology. In all these cases cognition is on a general level, precluding control, orientation, or emancipation, except for the emancipation from the necessities and amenities of life, which characterizes completely disinterested science.

This esteem of a merely intellectual curiosity could remind the new ethics of science of one form of justification it likes to forget, that is, of a legitimation that is independent of profit and purely internal to science. In Aristotle it is defended with two arguments—or three, if one adds the anthropological status of curiosity. The first argument (which is also political), using the comparison of the fully empowered citizen, surprisingly features in the *Metaphysics* (I 2, 982b26 f.): only a science that is not in someone else's service is free *(eleutheros)*. Today we intend freedom of science as the right to choose topics, methods, and hypotheses, but in Aristotle it has a different meaning. In an epistemic sense a science is free if it rejects all subjugation to a purpose and finds its meaning and goal in precisely that absence of external tasks (since Bacon and also Descartes, however, this kind of science has become discredited).

Aristotle's second argument, voiced in the final chapters of the *Ethics* (X 6–7), uses the latter's principle of happiness, understood as self-realization in an objective, anthropological sense: people who seek science for its own sake realize the capacity peculiar to them, the *logos*. Here the presence of something human has been found that is not present in knowledge for the purpose of orientation or enlightenment. Finally, the value of disinterested research lies in the fact that it is not merely a vehicle for human dignity, but an actual expression of that dignity itself. (In his autobiography *Le premier homme [The First Man]*, Camus shows that this is possible on a fairly elementary level: "In Monsieur Germain's class they realised for the first time that they existed and were the object of the greatest esteem: they were considered worthy of discovering the world.")

4

FORMS OF RATIONALITY

At first glance, syllogistics, Aristotelian dialectic, rhetoric, and poetics appear to be disparate topics. However, despite far-reaching differences, they have one thing in common: they are ways in which human knowledge presents itself, forms of rationality.

4.1 SYLLOGISTICS

Even within an impressive tradition, Aristotle's logic occupies a special rank. In an age when the rest of his œuvre has succumbed to criticism, the logic is still praised unconditionally by Kant (*Kritik der reinen Vernunft,* preface to the second edition) and Hegel (*Logik,* Werke 6, 269). And even after the reorientation of logic by Boole, de Morgan, and Frege, it remains valid for syllogistics, the doctrine of inferences operating with three terms. It also demonstrates considerable originality. With very little work done in the field before him, Aristotle develops logic as an autonomous science that is clear, thorough, practically free of errors, and, for the first time, has the elements of artificial languages. Russell's disdain (1975[8], 212) has long been replaced by the insight that we have a work of "exemplary severity and logical purity" (Patzig 1969[3], 199). The text on the subject, the *Prior Analytics,* leaves aside all psychological, anthropological, and metaphysical aspects. With its concise disposition and masterly concentration on the essential, it constitutes one of the best texts in the extant œuvre.

Presumably Aristotle is building on a method that has been shaped in the disputations at the Academy, and may already have been refined in everyday debates, and is perfected in the sciences, and in particular in geometry. He develops, as its basic element, the cogent or demonstrative deduction *(syllogismos apodeiktikos),* and the proposition, that is, the sentence that confirms or negates something about something, and can therefore be true or false (cf. *Int.* 4), as the former's element (*APr.* I 1, 24a16 f.). There are four modes of simple proposition: according to quality, they can be positive (*kataphatikê:* affirmative) or negative *(apophatikê);* according to quantity, general *(katholou)* or particular *(en merei).*

A deduction *(syllogismos)* is composed of propositions in such a way that "from certain assumptions something different necessarily follows *(ex anankês)"* (*APr.* I 1,

24b18–20, I 4, 25b37–39 and *passim.*). According to its logical core, it is the deduction of a conclusion from its premises, the potential truth of the conclusion depending solely upon that of the premises, that is, it is a purely formal inference.

This inference in the larger sense is already present in the ("pre-syllogistic") *Topics* (I 1, 100a25; cf. *Rh.* I 2, 1356b16–18; *SE* 1, 164b27–165a2). In the *Prior Analytics,* through the addition of further conditions, it becomes a subset of inferences in a narrower sense. The syllogism familiar to us is a qualified inference for which two premises and three concepts are sufficient. Its standard formulation is: "If A is predicated by all B, and B is predicated by all C, then A is predicated by all C." In order to demonstrate that it is not the content that is important but the formal structure alone, Aristotle uses concept variables (A, B, C, . . .) in the case of valid inferences. Only for invalid inferences does he use concrete examples, such as an animal, a human, or a stone (e.g., *APr.* I 4, 26a9). (On syllogisms, see also Corcoran 1974.)

The medieval philosophy of the schoolmen labeled the valid inferences with trisyllabic mnemonic terms. For that purpose the vowels of the Latin words *affirmo* ("I confirm") and *nego* ("I negate") indicate the moods in the following way: a = general affirmative, i = particular affirmative, e = general negative, and o = particular negative propositions. Thus, by far the most important conclusion, the one expressed by the word Barbara, consists of three positive general propositions, and the next by order of importance, Celarent, of two general propositions, one negative *(e)* and one positive *(a),* resulting in a negative general proposition *(e).*

One could be led to expect that these merely logical considerations would bring nothing new, but in fact they achieve formal, if not material, novelty. The connection, initially merely assumed, of two concepts *(horoi),* for example, mortality (= A) and Athenian (= C), is raised from the sphere of mere assumption to the status of certain knowledge by the evidence of a connecting middle term, in this case humanity (= B): all (= a) Athenians are mortal, because mortality applies to all humans and humanity to all Athenians. Written as a formula, this reads (inference Barbara): AaB & BaC → AaC, or:

$$AaB$$
$$\underline{BaC}$$
$$AaC$$

Since late antiquity the (qualified) inference has been expressed in three sentences: "All humans are mortal. Socrates is human. Therefore Socrates is mortal." The form that prevails in Aristotle, on the other hand, highlights the logical structure. It is a single tripartite conditional sentence, consisting of two premises *(protaseis)* and the conclusion *(symperasma).* The copula ("is") is avoided. Aristotle states that something is contained "in something else as a whole" *(en holô einai heteron heterô)*—in which case the form of the inference can be interpreted in terms of set theory—that something "is predicated of by all others" *(kata pantos katêgoreisthai: APr.* I 1, 24b26–30; 25b39). He also uses the terms *subsist / belong to (hyparchein:* e.g., *APr.* I 2, 25a1 f.), and occasionally *is said by (legesthai kata:* e.g., *APr.* II 15, 64a14 f.).

For qualified syllogisms, Aristotle only considers those concepts of a medium generality which, on the one hand, can be predicated of more specific concepts and which, on the other, can be predicated by more general ones. To that purpose he uses neither singular concepts, such as proper names like Callias or Socrates (cf. *APr.* I 27, 43b12 f.), nor categories. Both absences can be explained with the task of securing knowledge within the individual sciences. Categories are absent because they are indifferent toward the peculiarities of all individual sciences, and so are singular concepts because, according to Aristotle, the particular as such cannot be recognized. (On the practical syllogism, see ch. 13. 3.)

Depending on the position of the middle term, three figures *(schêmata)* can be distinguished:

Figure I: A x B & B x C → A x C;
Figure II: B x A & B x C → A x C;
Figure III: A x B & C x B → A x C; or:

I.	II.	III.	(IV.)
AxB	BxA	AxB	BxA
BxC	BxC	CxB	CxB
AxC	AxC	AxC	AxC

Although Aristotle claims completeness for his "system" (*APr.* I 23, 41b1–3), it lacks Figure IV: B x A & C x B → A x C. Lukasiewicz (1958³, 27) considers this an oversight; according to Prantl (1955³, I 367), Figure IV is "practically valueless" from a scientific point of view; Kant calls it "unnatural" (Akad. Ausg. II 53; similarly Ross 1949, 34 f.), while according to Patzig (1969³, § 25), Figure IV cannot be distinguished from Figure I in the framework of Aristotelian method. In the standard formulation of *APr.* I 4 (25b37–39), though, it can be defined. Besides, through the indirect (converse) equivalents, Aristotle recognizes all syllogisms of Figure IV.

The "x" in the formulae stands for the moods. The combination of the three figures with four moods in each of the three partial propositions results in three times $4^3 = 192$ moods, $4 \times 6 = 24$ of which show themselves to be valid syllogisms. Since Aristotle does not count the *a fortiori* valid inferences, that is, those with a particular conclusion, he recognizes fourteen moods only (I = 4, II = 4, III = 6: *APr.* I 4–6), which still makes it a complete count for Figures I–III, though.

Only the (valid) inferences of the first figure are perfect, while the validity of the others needs to be proved by the reduction to perfect inferences (cf. *APr.* I 1). Three types of proof are available for this reduction: conversion (turning around) of the concepts into one of the premises (e.g., "AeB" into "BeA"), *reductio ad impossibile* or *ad absurdum* (proof of contradiction in case of the contrary assumption) and the rarely used *ekthesis* /exposition (e.g., the insertion of a minor term), necessary in modal logic only. Since perfect inferences only occur in Figure I, and it is the only one in which all four moods *(a, e, i, o)* can be deduced, it deserves pride of place; Figure II contains only *a-* and *e-* conclusions, and Figure III only *i* and *o*. Incidentally, if one introduces the conversions of the four moods as well, syllogistics can make do with one single figure.

According to the way in which a concept is related to another, namely, its modality, a proposition can be apodictic (necessary: *ex anankês*), assertoric (actual: *hyparchein*) and problematic (possible: *endechesthai*). Since necessity is mentioned here for the second time, Aristotle distinguishes between two types (*APr.* I 10, 30b32–40). Syllogistic, relative necessity (*toutôn ontôn anankaion*: *APr.* I 10, 30b38 f.), that is, the consequentiality of an if-then relationship, which is also valid for the syllogism in a wider sense, characterizes the syntactic connection of several propositions or clauses: "It is of necessity: *if* AaB and BaC, *then* AaC." Modal, unlimited, or absolute necessity (*haplôs anankaion*: *APr.* I 10, 30b40), on the other hand, concerns the semantic connection of subject and predicate within a single proposition: "A belongs to B of necessity."

Along with assertoric logic, Aristotle also treats (syllogistic) modal logic, or modal syllogistics, again in great detail (*APr.* I 8–27; on the question of contingent propositions regarding the future, see *Int.* 9). He cites no fewer than 111, or rather 148, of its 256 valid syllogisms (cf. Ross 1949, 286 f.). Among other things, he points out that apodictic propositions cannot be inferred from apodictic propositions alone, but only from their combination with assertoric ones. He demonstrates in particular that apodictic propositions do not follow from assertoric ones; this amounts to the axiom of modern empirical science that says that one cannot arrive at laws by means of empirical propositions only. One can, however, and this corresponds to another axiom, deduce new laws from empirical propositions with the help of laws that are already known (cf. Wieland 1992[3]).

By reconstructing Aristotelian modal syllogistics with the help of the more recent means of predicate logic, it becomes possible to represent the high differentiation that is in fact present, but for which Aristotle does not yet dispose of the appropriate descriptive instrumentarium. By doing so, Aristotle's claims of validity can be verified to an astonishing degree (Nortmann 1996).

Aristotle believes that mathematical proof must use the syllogism, or, more strictly speaking, its first figure. Barnes (1994[2], 155) considers this opinion simply wrong. By contrast, Detel (I 177–82) arrives at a more differentiated valuation, using as an example a reconstruction of the theorem of Thales (*APo.* II 11, 94a28–34). According to this, although the creative geometrical achievement only occurs in a mathematical induction, the logical steps necessary for proof can nevertheless be outlined by employing syllogisms.

One tends to read the syllogism from the top, that is, from the premises downward to the conclusion, and therefore deductively, but this use is so rare in Aristotle's œuvre that it almost looks as though he were disregarding his own logic. From a merely logical viewpoint, the syllogism allows two readings: the deductive reading, proceding from top to bottom, and the explicative one, going the opposite way. In this sense Aristotle himself attributes a twofold task to syllogistics: as far as the theory of argumentation is concerned, it is to help recognize the validity of the conclusions, and as for the practice of argumentation, to construct them (*poiein*: *APr.* I 27, 43a22–24), so that one needs to move from circumstances that are already known to the premises that have explicatory faculties (see ch. 5. 1). In its second function, as an explanation or a reason, the syllogism does justice to the problem-orientated style of argumentation effectively practiced by Aristotle. Besides, the ability to perform the essential task, the discovery of the suitable middle term, without much pondering, is a sign of incisiveness (*APo.* I 34, 89b10–20).

4.2 DIALECTIC *(TOPICS)*

The term *dialectic* raises high expectations with philosophers. Thinking of Plato as well as Hegel and Marx, one expects a kind of knowledge that transcends the limited possibilities of individual sciences and makes it possible to grasp the foundations of all reality. Harking back to the original nonspeculative meaning of *dialegesthai*, "to converse," though, Aristotle widens the scope of application of dialectic and, at the same time, downgrades its epistemic rank. His dialectic is concerned with a certain kind of intellectual debate. Concerned neither with truth of the highest order nor "ordinary" philosophy, but being the art of attacking an adversary's thesis or defending one's own, dialectic continues the *agôn* (contest), characteristic of Greek culture, by intellectual means, including obfuscation *(krypsis),* which leaves the opponent in the dark concerning the aim of the proof (*Top.* VIII 1). It is important for philosophy, and yet it is only something like an ancillary science, because it "treats as an exercise what philosophy tries to understand" (*Metaph.* IV 2, 1004b25 f.).

Like scientific proof, dialectic, too, makes use of syllogism: the text on the subject, the *Topics* (I 1, 100a25–27) defines it not differently from the *Prior Analytics.* The difference does not lie in the stringency of formal logic—the *Topics* is not about a softer, less committed logic—but rather, on the one hand, in its not yet qualified, or standardized, form (see ch. 4. 1), on the other, in the epistemic rank of the premises. Scientific proof is based on self-evident propositions, but dialectic inference rests on the so-called *endoxa* (*Top.* I 1, 100a20 ff.). By these Aristotle intends propositions that, unlike the principles of a science, are not by themselves credible. Partly, as in the *Rhetoric,* they consist in the common opinions of the crowd, partly—especially in philosophical debates within the Academy—in qualified and well-founded opinions. The *endoxa,* highlighted by the famous definition at the beginning of the *Topics,* are considered true by all or most people or by all, most, or the best-known experts (*Top.* I 1, 100b18–23; cf. I 10, 104a8 ff.; I 14, 105a34 ff.). Qualified in this way, the *endoxa* are respectable views.

The term is often translated as "probable propositions," but *endoxa* have nothing to do with objective or statistical probability *(probabilitas)*—neither with the a priori probability of the dice nor with empirical probability, such as the relative frequency of an event. Nor do they refer to a subjectively limited certainty *(verisimilitudo),* nor, finally, to the epistemological fact that for some propositions there are only plausible, but no sufficient reasons. The term is meant to be not a diminution, but an emphasis: it refers to propositions that are correct according to everything that the audience—be it the crowd or the experts—knows so far.

Thus, Aristotle pleads neither for a more modest concept of truth nor for a form that is embedded in contexts of life and speech as an alternative to scientific rationality. It is true that, with certain limitations, he develops a "theory of lifeworld rationality" (Bubner, *Dialektik als Topik,* 1990) in the *Rhetoric,* but he does not do so in the *Topics,* not least because he uses the *endoxa* as the premises of an argumentation, and not as its result. Furthermore, dialectic does not result in a consensual theory of truth, since the *endoxa* are seen not as criteria for the truth, but as a prerequisite by which to test the truth of statements. Every debate is dialectical insofar as—from the point of view of the practice of argumentation, but not from that of the logic of validity—it needs to begin with views shared by the debaters. Incidentally, many of the Aristotelian examples are true: some are truisms, others opinions acknowledged by experts, but in any case they are premises that no one wanting to be taken seriously in a debate could stubbornly refuse to accept.

Given that dialectic does not question its premises, the *endoxa,* any further, it cannot in the end achieve more than a demonstration of the internal consistency and coherence of a multitude of theses. If at a later stage than the (early) *Topics,* Aristotle reaches the first principles with a dialectic that, by then, has become sophisticated (*APo.* I 11, 77a26–35 seems to point in that direction; cf. Irwin 1989), then it would mean that he is content with a theory of coherence of truth, or rather a coherentist understanding of science and philosophy (Bolton in Devereux-Pellegrin 1990 and Smith 1993 argue against this). In order to take Aristotle's argumentation in favor of the principle of contradiction (see ch. 5. 2) as coherentist, however, one needs to apply a very broad concept of coherence, which is not restricted to a number (however large) of theses, but includes life in general with its constantly claimed minimum of theoretical and practical reason.

Dialectic is considered useful for three goals: for practice, the exchange of thoughts and philosophy (*Top.* I 2, 101a26–28). What these have in common is the relation with another person (VIII 1, 155b10 f.), since dialectical argumentations usually consist in an alternating of attempts at justification and refutation. There is, of course, also the debate with oneself (VIII 14, 163b3 f.; cf. VIII 1, 155b5 f.), so that we have four kinds altogether. They all follow the same logic of argumentation. In a practice debate exercise performed according to rule (VIII 2, 158a16 f.), someone raises a question, a problem, for example: "Is 'two-legged sensual being walking on its feet' the definition of man or is it not?" (I 4, 101b28–31). Then the defender (respondent, proponent) choses one of the two theses and the attacker (questioner, opponent) attempts to entangle the other in paradoxes or contradictions, so that he has to withdraw his thesis. This institution lives on in the disputations held at medieval universities.

Victory is not the only objective of such agonistic discourse exercises, least of all victory achieved by dishonest means. Since for Aristotle dialectic is at the service of truth, he—like Socrates and Plato—delimits it against the sham wisdom of the Sophists (*Metaph.* IV 2, 1004b26), who turn debating into a trade that, by means of the so-called eristic inference, seeks victory even to the detriment of truth (*Top.* I 1, 100b23 ff. and *SE* 11). Given that a commitment to truth cannot be ensured from within the argumentation, and that, on the contrary, dialectic can be abused as mere technique, a good (moral) inclination *(euphyia)* is also necessary in addition to intellectual dexterity. The "dialectician" must provide the readiness to chose what is true and avoid what is false (*Top.* VIII 14, 163b12–16).

The two other types of dialectical debates are less formalized. In an exchange of views, that is, a chance discussion, one discusses with untrained persons on the basis of their opinion, and in a philosophical or scientific discussion, first a multitude of views is deployed and then their pros and contras are discussed. In these cases dialectic is part of an agonistic intellectual culture modeled on the lawsuit (*Metaph.* III 1, 995b2–4), because the side that carefully weighs the arguments against each other after they have been deployed as completely as possible will be best equipped to deliver the final verdict.

Finally, dialectic is used also by those who nowadays would be discredited as "solitary thinkers" by many. Those who do not have partners for debate practise on their own (*Top.* VIII 14, 163b3 f.). In all four situations it would seem that the critical function of dialectic is in the foreground: propositions are refuted and positions are revoked or overturned. Nevertheless, indirectly dialectic is also affirmative, given that propositions that resist all attempts at criticism are retained as proven.

Those who want to be good at debating always keep the relevant points of view ready, knowing them by heart (*Top.* VIII 14, 163b17–23). By being devoted to exactly that purpose, the *Topics* serves the nowadays neglected field of discourse logic. Its descriptive section is composed of two autonomous parts: the theory of the use of nonscientific, "endoxastic" premises, and the finding or constructing of arguments with the guidance of *topoi* (literally: places). Surprisingly, the *Topics* never defines its basic concept, neither on its own nor in relation to the *endoxa;* according to the *Rhetoric* (I 2, 1358a12–14), it is concerned with general points of view *(koinoi)* which are equally valid for law or justice, nature, politics, and much else. According to the topoi deployed in the *Topics,* they are schemes of argumentation consisting of four elements when in their complete form (which, however, is not always provided). These elements are: a procedural instruction, a general regularity, an indication of the area of application, and an example. The topos provides the appropriate premise for a given conclusion. Where it consists in an *endoxon,* it can be presented to the opponent. If he acknowledges it, one can deduce the conclusions, again with the assistance of the topos, that is, of the procedure mentioned in it.

While book I of the *Topics* expounds the relevant basic concepts—the task, the procedure, the use, and the tools *(prothesis, methodos, chrêsimon, organa)*—and book VIII gives practical advice, the main part of the *Topics,* books II–VII, consist in a catalogue or reference work of the schemes of argumentation that allow the defendant to plan his defense and the opponent his attack. The *Rhetoric* (not only at II 23–25) supplements this collection by topoi for real and apparent enthymemes (see ch. 4. 3) and for refutations. (On the topoi in the *Rhetoric,* cf. Sprute 1982, Part III.)

In order to provide a collection as inclusive as possible, the *Topics* follows the four meta-viewpoints on which the propositions and problems hinge, the so-called predicables. It opens with the topoi of accidents (books II–III) and genus (IV), followed by those of properties (V) and definitions (VI–VII). To pick just a single subsection: regarding the question which of several things is the most desirable, Aristotle brings together elements for a theory of comparative value judgments (book III; cf. *Rh.* I 7) that could still be of interest today for a theory of preference in the economical or social sciences. According to this passage, the following are more desirable: that which is more permanent, that which is more desirable per se, the cause rather than the accident of the good, that which is more desirable generally and not only in particular cases, of two means the one that is closer to the goal, etc.

Since many topoi appear to originate from the repertory of the Academy, the *Topics* provides an insight into the wide-ranging competence expected of a good student at the time. Being the oldest text about logic (as already pointed out by Brandis 1835), it also reveals the latter's "entrenchment in life." Western logic does not originate from the (intra-logical) interest in dissecting the formal structures of thinking in isolation, unrelated to their application. Its origin was an interest, oriented toward its practice in argumentation, in classifying all possible arguments into certain types in such a way that they become applicable purely according to their form, independently of their contents. From this viewpoint one can say that its origin lies in the skilfully conducted dialogue, in scientific discussion (Kapp 1920). Since "naturally" this is not restricted to certain fields, one should be skeptical about suggestions that topics or dialectics are a regional logic with a competence for jurisprudence (Ch. Perelman, Th. Viehweg) or politics and practical philosophy (W. Hennis). In truth it is suitable for any kind of, and not just a particular, science (explicitly at *Rh.* I 1, 1354a1–3).

4.3 RHETORIC

By rhetoric one often understands nothing more than the art of well-formulated speech, occasionally even a mere technique of persuasion, which uses irrelevant arguments or a cynical manipulation of emotions. For Aristotle the speech, in a practical respect, is committed to the leading human goal of happiness (*Rh.* I 5, 1360b4 ff.), and, in a cognitive sense, to that which is plausible in each case (*pithana peri hekaston:* I 1, 1355b11; II 1, 1355b25 f.). However, the former only applies in the thematical sense of dealing with the same subject, not in the normative sense of the orientation toward a virtuous life and a just *polis*. Happiness here is intended in the sense of the "empirical," generally acknowledged goal, not in the "normative" sense of a criterion for goodness or badness (be it that of an individual or that of a *polis*). Instead, Aristotle is aware of the neutral value of rhetoric, in that it can be employed for good as well as for evil. This is contrary to Cicero's (*On the Orator* II 85) and Quintilian's (*The Education of the Orator* XII 2) view that there is some mechanism immanent in rhetoric that can prevent evil persons from using rhetorical means. On the other hand, he is not of the opinion that words *(logoi)* on their own could improve the crowd which, according to his belief, follows its passions (*EN* X 10, 1179b4 ff.). He does, of course, consider a morally good use of rhetoric desirable (I 1, 1355a31), and believes that it has the potential of strengthening virtue when directed at the noble-minded (*EN* X 10, 1197b7–9).

Because of its first duty, rhetoric belongs to ethics and politics, and because of the second, it has a firm place in Aristotle's multilayered theory of knowledge. Rhetoric deals with those spheres in which no necessary propositions are possible, but only mostly valid ones, and about which, since there is no professional competence *(technê),* one needs to consult with others (cf. *Rh.* I 2, 1357a2 ff.). Aristotle assumes that the true and the just are by nature stronger than their opposites, and also easier to prove; in short, more credible. It would, after all, be strange if man were "built" in such a way that, while the body can help itself, the *logos* cannot (I 1, 1355a21 f. and a37 ff.). At the same time, the truth for which rhetoric aims does not concern the necessary circumstances—which are the object of the demonstrative sciences—but only those that could also behave differently and about which only mostly *(hôs epi to poly)* valid propositions can be made. That is exactly the sphere of the matters about which one could deliberate with oneself or with others (I 2, 1357a2 ff.).

Because of its orientation toward the plausible, rhetoric can be considered as belonging to a "theory of life-world rationality" given that three qualifications are introduced. Firstly, there is no antiscientific bias in Aristotle's *Rhetoric.* Secondly, it does not focus on the rational part, the *logos,* alone, but two prerational elements are of equal importance: character *(êthos),* that is, prudence, virtue, and benevolence, by which the orator becomes credible (II 1, 1378a8), and the passions *(pathê:* II 2–11), that is, the disdain, love, hatred, and fear as well as its opposite, confidence, which he must attempt to rouse in his audience. Thirdly, the *Rhetoric* is concerned not with the entire world we live in, but merely with a clearly delimited section thereof, namely public speech in the three varieties of political or advisory oration, ceremonial speech, and court speech, while the important sphere of economical or political negotiation is absent.

Public speech is, however, treated in considerable detail, and Aristotle goes in for what is now called "linguistic pragmatics." In the general section of the *Rhetoric* he examines both the tripartite basic relationship between the orator, the subject of the oration, and the audience (*Rh.* I 3, 1358a37 ff.), and the three means of persuasion (*pisteis:* I 2, 1356a1 ff.) mentioned above: *êthos, pathos,* and *logos.* In the specific section of the same work he deals with the three types of public speech, its position in public life and its aim (I 4–15; I 3, 1358b20 ff.). Furthermore, Aristotle spells out the psychological, ethical, and political conditions by which an orator can awaken the audience's powers of judgment and gain their consent. With topics such as happiness and virtue, material possessions, pleasure, and friendship, chapters I 5–7 (see also I 9) contain the abstract of an ethics; in chapter I 8 we find the summary of a theory of constitutions. Chapters I 10–12 contain the elements of a theory of criminal responsibility (criminal psychology), namely, precise observations on the distinction between unintentional and deliberate acts, as well as advice about different types of motives and the psychology of unjust actions. Chapters II 12–14 develop a richly nuanced psychology of the various stages in life. *En passant,* the knowledge a good orator should have is displayed, so that one gains an insight into the social, legal, and political conditions of the times; the *Rhetoric* constitutes a real treasure trove for anyone wishing to know about the social history of Greece.

The first twelve chapters of book III, which appears to have been a book in its own right originally, contain the elements of stylistics—although Theophrastus would be the first to write a textbook on different styles *(Peri lexeôs)*—and the subsequent chapters treat the structure of an oration (III 13–19). Aristotle demands clarity and pleasantness, but also originality; he deals with errors of style, purity of language *(hellênismos)* and wit *(asteia),* and emphasizes the difference between oral and written representation. He devotes particular attention to the figurative use of words, that is, to metaphor (e.g., *Rh.* III 2, 4, 6, and 10–11; see also *Po.* 21), meaning an abbreviated comparison taken to the point of identification. Aristotle stresses its power for triggering cognition. Thus, for example, by referring to old age as a stubble, that is, a stalk cut off for the harvest, one effects a learning process; by alienation the matter is at the same time made clearer. It is similar with jokes and riddles, where figuring out the point is both enjoyable and instructive (*Rh.* III 11, 1412a26 ff. and b22 ff.). Together with the *Poetics,* the third book of the *Rhetoric* asserts its influence for an exceptionally long period of time, beginning with Cicero, until well after the baroque era, acquiring almost canonical weight in literature and the related sciences (cf. Lausberg 1973[2]). It is, however, true that Cicero's concepts of the good man *(vir bonus)* and the perfect orator *(orator perfectus)* are alien to Aristotle.

The fact that such an ambitious work had for a long time been neglected by research—the major contributions are still those of Spengel 1851, Cope 1877/1970, F. Marx 1900, and Solmsen 1921—and has only been given some attention quite recently (see Kennedy 1991, Furley-Nehamas 1994, and Rorty 1996, preceded by Grimaldi 1980), reflects the preference of recent philosophy for a strictly scientific character, and perhaps also a "Platonic" prejudice against rhetoric. In Greece, however, both strictly scientific and rhetorical argumentation were held in high esteem (on Greek rhetoric, see Kennedy 1963; Cole 1991).

With regard to its thematic range and because of its philosophical intent, Aristotle's *Rhetoric* is far superior to the works of his predecessors, the Sophists Gorgias of Leontini, Lysias and Thrasymachus of Chalcedon, and Isocrates, the author of a formal and stylistic work on rhetoric. Even Cicero's *Ars rhetorica,* which was to become so famous later, cannot compare with it. While, according to Aristotle (*Rh.* I 1, 1355a19 f.), his predecessors prefer the court speech, he also treats the political oration as well as the ceremonial oration. And while his predecessors focus on the virtuoso display of means for arousing *pathos,* Aristotle sets greater store by *logos* and claims to have discovered its element specific to rhetoric, the enthymeme (I 1, 1354a11 ff.). On the other hand, he does not overestimate the value of rhetoric. Only an intellectual such as Cicero, who is prevalently a rhetorician, could believe that it is the sign of perfect philosophy to speak at length and beautifully about the most important questions ("copiose . . . ornateque dicere": *Tusculan Disputations* I 7).

One could speculate on the reasons why Plato's well-known critique of rhetoric turned out so sharp: perhaps neither he nor his role model Socrates were able to deny a certain affinity to the Sophists. As is understandable among competitors, Plato goes out of his way to distinguish himself from his opponent in his dialogue *Gorgias* (462b ff., 480a ff.). Part of this criticism can only come from someone who does not need to worry about his livelihood. On the other hand, the severity of Plato's judgment may also result from the consideration that Socrates' rejection of superficial rhetoric may have been responsible for the (fatal) outcome of his trial. Furthermore, at the time (long before Aristotle's *Rhetoric*) the self-definition against Sophists and rhetoricians was part of the shaping of a proper identity for philosophy, given that it wanted to be anything but a form of dexterity relying on mere routine, directed at aims such as the acquisition of power and the obtention of pleasure. In other dialogues wholesale rejection is replaced by the demand for a better form, that is, for a rhetoric that is based on knowledge and recognizes the truth of things according to (Platonic) dialectic *(Phaedrus* 266b f., 276e f., and *passim).*

Aristotle takes seriously the objections voiced in the *Gorgias*. He also tries to comply with the demands made in the *Phaedrus*—only in part, however, since they amount to the postulate that true orators necessarily have to become philosophers. In keeping with his critical stance toward a homogeneous science, Aristotle rejects this strategy of absorption. Instead, he is looking for an ability specific to rhetoric, which could furthermore be learned by any citizen in accordance with democratization. In contrast with Plato, he does not treat the topics "from top to bottom," but always in relation to the respective situation in which the speech is given. (For the relation to Plato, cf. Hellwig 1973.) Where Aristotle deals with ethics or psychology, he is not performing "basic research," but rather "applied ethics" and "applied psychology."

Within the scheme of the sciences, rhetoric is situated between dialectic and practical philosophy (*Rh*. I 2, 1356a26 f.). Like dialectic, it relies on a store of viewpoints over which, even though they may not be self-evident, one can nevertheless expect agreement. It can also be compared with dialectical dispute insofar as the orator presents counter-arguments against views and arguments he expects from the audience. Here the audience also has the function of a judge, since the decision whether the arguments have been invalidated is theirs entirely (*Rh*. II 18, 1391b11 ff.). The third accordance with dialectic, namely that rhetoric, too, examines a subject common to all sciences (*Rh*. I 1, 1354a1 ff.), only applies within limits, though. Dialectic *qua* scientific discipline deals with the general, rhetoric more with the particular (I 2, 1358a23 ff.), and therefore only rhetoric is concerned with the psychology, inclinations and emotions of the audience. For rhetoric this is also "natural," because it addresses larger audiences, at times even crowds, with whom a dialogue is not possible.

On the other hand, rhetoric has an affinity with ethics and politics, because the orator wants to influence decisions and thus rhetoric constitutes a part of political practice. Furthermore, its aim is not to persuade, but to serve the attainment of happiness, the goal of ethical as well as political practice, but only as a concept of neutral value. It is only in this weak sense, and not because *eo ipso* it serves what is good, that rhetoric can be seen as no longer morally questionable so that Aristotle can give it a positive valuation and overcome the "Sophists-contra-Plato" alternative.

In a rhetoric aiming for credibility it is the orator's arguments (*logoi:* II 18–26; cf. also I) that count, along with his character and his ability to rouse passions. In principle, rhetoric has at its disposal the same two means of argumentation as does demonstrative science, that is, induction and deduction. However, both are adapted to the specific purposes of rhetoric, concision and brevity on the one hand (cf. II 22, 1395b23 ff.; III 18, 1419a20 ff.), and what is only probable (*eikos:* e.g., II 24, 1402a9 and *passim*) on the other. For both reasons the orator uses—in the place of ordinary induction—a pertinent example (*paradeigma:* cf. II 20). It should have the rank of an analogous precedent and appears in three forms: the mythical or historical account, the simile, and the fable. This rhetorical induction is characterized by the merely tacit assumption of a universal proposition, which is either too obvious for being stated or not actually valid for all cases. With its method of inferring valid advice from particular cases, this means of argumentation is particularly suitable for the advisory speech, since "we judge the future, prophesising from what has happened" (I 9, 1368a30 f.).

The second rhetorical tool, most tightly argumented and practically free of emotions, is the enthymeme, that is, the rhetorical syllogism, which should constitute the core of rhetorical argumentation (*sôma tês pisteôs:* I 1, 1354a15). In fact, by supplying reasons and proofs, it is particularly suitable for the law court, since there what has happened is as yet not clarified (a32 f.). In the case of the enthymeme—literally "idea," "thought"—according to the classical description, part of the conclusion can remain unsaid (*en thymô:* "in the heart"). Needless to say, this does not mean that the orator "covers his hand," but rather that he either leaves out one of the premises because he can assume that it is known, or that, for a better effect, he leaves it to the audience to make the conclusion for the particular case at hand; in either case something that is self-evident remains unsaid. However, Aristotle does not provide the *en thymô* interpretation. According to the criteria of rhetoric—conciseness and brevity—the enthymeme can also mean that the deduction is performed "not from a great distance": neither with many intermediary steps nor with far-fetched arguments. Furthermore, the enthymeme treats facts that are not necessarily valid, and therefore make deliberation necessary. (On the question of enthymemes, see Sprute 1982, part II, and Burnyeat in: Furley-Nehamas 1994 and Rapp 1996.)

As a theory of deliberation, rhetoric allows for a contemporary application that goes beyond the obvious application in the spheres of social sciences and of communication and media studies. The theory of discourse of our times sees public debates in the pattern of a discourse internal to philosophy directed at the final foundations of the matter. In real life there are elementary obligations to be fulfilled, such as fundamental and human rights. In public debates it is usually not these obligations that are controversial, but the question how they are to be put into practice and how they are to be weighed against each other in the case of conflicting requirements. These debates take place under non-ideal conditions, since, strictly speaking, neither side is neutral. Given that Aristotle thematizes exactly that kind of situation, namely, the debate between interested participants influenced also by passions, he offers an emendation, or even an alternative, to the theory of discourse. His *Rhetoric* contains the elements of a theory of "civic discourse," that is, of a theory of arguments and counter-arguments among (equal) citizens.

4.4 POETICS: TRAGEDY

The philosopher who is considered the poet among the great thinkers, and who indeed combines his philosophy with artistic demands, sees poetics as a rival whom he rejects. Despite his love for poetry and his admiration for Homer (*Republic* X, 595b-c; see ch. 16. 1), Plato condemned "imitative" poetry not only for moral, but also for political and ontological reasons (*Republic* II–III and X; *Sophist* 235e ff.; *Laws* VI–VIII). He believed that it gave rise to erroneous ideas about the gods and about justice and injustice, and also that, by arousing desires and passions, it clouded reason. According to the Sophist Gorgias (Diels-Kranz 82 B 11 and 23), poetry can even deceive and has the same effect as wizardry and magic.

Here, too, Aristotle distances himself from Plato as well as from the Sophists. In keeping with Greek tradition, he considers the poets the best teachers of the people—he believes that it is even their duty to provoke strong emotional responses. The tolerance regarding theory of science familiar from Aristotle's phenomenology is also visible in his dialectic, rhetoric, and again in the poetics. Like intellectual debate and public speech, poetry, too, is measured by its own criteria and not by a one-dimensional conception of rationality. In consequence, Aristotle has no problems with acknowledging that one can also achieve a certain kind of knowledge through poetics. Without modifying the special rank of philosophy, he agrees with the verse from Aeschylus *tô patei mathos* ("learning from suffering"; *Agamemnon*, V.177). One can learn from the experience of emotional conflicts and even catastrophes, even though it is learning in an affective rather than an intellectual sense (Höffe 2000).

Aristotle's *Poetics*, like his *Rhetoric*, belongs to the most influential works of its kind up to our times. For its status in the Enlightenment it suffices to cite Lessing who, in the *Hamburgische Dramaturgie* (vol. 2), criticizes recent French theatre with reference to Aristotle. Even Brecht, who calls his dramatic art "non-Aristotelian" (*Schriften zum Theater*, vol. 3, 1963), develops it "in essence according to the Aristotelian foundation" (Flashar 1974, 35). Furthermore, Aristotle's interest in poetry is not limited to his *Poetics*. He also wrote a dialogue *On Poets (Peri poiêtôn)*; he made systematic collections of material, such as the *Didaskaliai (Catalogues of the Dramas)*, and in the *Aporêmata Homêrika*, the *Homeric Questions*, he treats questions of Homeric philology. From the point of view of subsequent reception and influence, however, it is only the *Poetics* that is important. (See, e.g., Lucas 1968, Fuhrmann 1992², Halliwell 1986, Rorty 1992.)

According to the literal meaning of the title, Aristotle is aiming to make a contribution to productive art *(poiêtikê)*. Primarily, he is concerned neither with criteria for the evaluation of literary works of art, that is, with literary criticism, nor with a universally valid theory of literature—although there are remarkable elements of both—but rather Aristotle wants to show his contemporaries how literature is "produced" (cf. *Po.* 1, 1447a8 ff.). Here Aristotle is reluctant, perhaps wisely so, given the generality of the goal, to proffer an unequivocal definition. To this purpose he deals with the most important literary genres of his times, having opened with a detailed exposition of the basics (chs. 1–5). Within his poetics by genre, Aristotle treats tragedy in the greatest detail (chs. 6–22); this is followed by the epic (chs. 23–25), while the final chapter is a comparison of the two genres. It would seem that the third genre mentioned in the introduction, comedy, was treated in the lost parts (cf. *Po.* 6, 1450a21 f.). Towards the end (chs. 20–21), the section about tragedy contains some general reflections on linguistic form *(lexis)*, amounting to an elementary grammar concerned with conjunctions, articles, nouns, verbs, declensions, and sentences.

In the final chapter on tragedy, a concept we tend to consider as typically modern—alienation *(xenikon)*—occurs for the first time in the context of literary theory (22, 1458a22; cf., e.g., *Rh.* III 2, 1404b36). Although Aristotle only relates the term to linguistic means (with the injunction of using glosses, metaphors, paraphrases, etc., instead of the usual expressions), and not yet to dramatic technique, the latter is present according to content as well, as one can see, under the heading *para tên doxan* (against expectation: *Po.* 9, 1452a4): unexpected and astonishing events result in beautiful stories *(mythoi)*.

However, the basic aesthetic concept of the *Poetics* is *mimesis,* which sounds more like pre-modern literary theory, in particular when translated as "imitation." What may be feasible in painting—i.e., to paint grapes so lifelike that the birds pick at them—should not be attempted, neither by epic, tragedy, or comedy, nor by music, for which the use of mimesis is also claimed (*Po.* 1, 1447a13–16; cf. *Po.* VIII 5, 1340a39). Aristotelian mimesis, perhaps best translated as "representation," expects the artist neither, as would Horace's *Ars poetica* (V. 268 f.), to strive after classical models, nor to mirror reality like naturalistic theatre of illusion. Directed against overly fantastic inventions, *mimesis* means any kind of imitation or production of something similar to reality—as it was or is (the tragedies of Euripides), as one says or believes it to be, or also as it should be (Sophocles; 25, 1460b10 f. and 33 f.). In all three cases, poetry is not interested in imitating superficial characteristics of reality, but rather in representing consistent actions and characters. Tragedy ought to represent people nobler than they are in real life, while comedy presents them more vulgar (*Po.* 2, 1448a16–18). In contrast with painting and mere narration, a second meaning of mimesis, enactment, plays a part in the dramatic arts. (Both meanings are already present in Plato's *Republic:* dramatic imitation at III 392d–394c and the general representation of the similar at X 597c.)

The root of the kind of mimesis characteristic of poetry lies in ordinary mimesis, that is, the propensity for imitation innate to humans, together with a sense of harmony and rhythm (4, 1448b5 ff. and b20 ff.). Founded on the pleasure derived from learning (b12 f.), poetry committed to mimesis is part of man's predisposition for knowledge. Aristotle even considers poetry to be more philosophical than historiography because, by depicting human possibilities as prototypes, the poet is able to present something universally valid, while historiography remains beholden to the sphere of the particular (9, 1451b1 ff.).

Myth is considered the "soul of tragedy" (6, 1450a38). Largely stripped of its religious power, however, it does not signify much more than the fable, that is, the story or the plot. The poet can draw his subject matter from three sources: not only (1) from real life, but also (in confirmation of the fictionality of poetry) (2) from his conviction of how things ought to be, and (3) from oral or written tradition, in which case transmitted myths must not be tampered with (14, 1453b22 f.). The result should be a plot that is so self-contained and, unlike the epic, so free of distracting episodes that the whole is altered if even a single part is transposed (8, 1451a32–35). Actions should take precedence over character (6, 1450a26), as the fortunes and misfortunes of the protagonists are decided by single actions.

There is hardly anything else in all of Aristotle's writings that has provoked such a flood of literary output since the Renaissance as the concept of tragic pleasure, which is not explained much further (tragôdias hêdonê: 13, 1453a35 f.; cf. 14, 1453b12). It expresses the author's interest, within the framework of his poetics of genre, in an aesthetics of reception and, within the latter, in the second option in the later alternative of "instructive or entertaining theatre" (cf. Horace, Ars poetica, V.333: "aut prodesse volunt aut delectare poetae"—"the poets want either to be useful or to delight"). The immediate effect on the audience is to be neither moral nor intellectual gain, but rather aesthetic pleasure (hêdonê). A purification (katharsis) should occur through pity and fear (di' eleou kai phobou: Po. 6, 1449b27; 14, 1453b12 f.), and it is because of this purification that Aristotle, unlike Plato, considers tragedy as innocuous from the point of view of morals.

The emotions in question are by no means superficial, but they are, so to speak, substantial sentiments reaching to the core of human existence. Tragedy uses examples of outstanding persons who are blessed with both fame and fortune and are for that very reason in particular danger, in order to show what can happen to any ordinary person: disasters caused not by nature or the licence of others, but at least in part by themselves. We may prefer a different interpretation, such as Sophocles' Antigone seen in moralizing black-and-white depictions, as a morally exemplary protagonist heroically opposing an immoral tyrant. However, according to Aristotle, tragedy shows how people who are neither entirely virtuous nor completely evil, neither saints nor criminals, commit an error (hamartia: Po. 13, 1453a8–10) because passion narrows down their aims and intentions. In Sophocles, too, it seems that both protagonists, blinded by self-righteousness, perceive a complex situation in a simplistic way and err for that reason. While it is Creon's duty to punish the traitor Polyneices, Antigone's brother, this does not need to be done by denying him burial. Antigone for her part is justified in insisting on burial for her brother, but she can be blamed of intransigence.

A further element of the "theory" of tragedy that was to be so influential for the history of European drama is that Aristotle elevates to an ideal a certain phase of Greek tragedy, Sophocles and in particular his Oedipus the King. The example of Oedipus, "the best of the mortals" (Oedipus the King, V.46), turning into "the worst man" (V.1433) in the end, demonstrates with unsurpassed acuity the transitoriness of renown and happiness; from one moment to the next the protagonist is hurled from the pinnacle of fame into the deepest abyss of disgrace. On the other hand, Euripides is considered "more tragic than the other poets" (13, 1453a29 f.).

Oedipus's fate of ending in the greatest misery despite his only limited guilt—both the killing of his father and the marriage with his mother are the result of ignorance—locates human existence close to the absurd. Whether it has religious foundations or not, tragedy—understood by Nietzsche as the art form of pessimism (*Die Geburt der Tragödie*, 1872)—shows that there is no reassuring or comforting meaning to it all. Conscious of not really understanding the way of the world, except in the sense of being subject to the (unfathomable) will of God, tragedy develops a language of noncomprehension, consisting of lamentation, prayer, grief, and horror. This is where the therapeutic function sets in, which is, however, not explained in the surviving *Poetics* in the way in which the *Politics* mentions it (VIII 7, 1341b39 f.).

The decisive concept of catharsis has two meanings before Aristotle: in medicine it designates the effect of emetics and purges, in religious life the ritual cleansing of "defiled" persons. Taken as an analogy with the medical term, the catharsis of tragedy signifies that the emotions, such as sympathy with suffering that is only partly deserved, as well as fear of failing in spite of one's best intentions, are to be stimulated—by the construction of the plot, not the stage setting (14, 1453b 3 ff.)—in the way a physical illness first erupts and then subsides, so that the final regaining of an inner equilibrium is experienced as relief; and precisely that is tragic pleasure.

In an attempt to avoid a supposedly humanist and Christian understanding of pity, Schadewaldt (1955, in Luserke 1991, 254) claims that the emotions are to be intensified to such an extent that the suffering "softens the [beholder's] heart and brings tears to his eyes." Aristotle's concepts of fear and pity (*Rh.* II 5 and II 8) on their own do not support this interpretation, but the story *(mythos)* presented does. This is true for both the extremely heightened emotions of the protagonists and the grand but ominous plot, but in particular the extreme force of the misfortune, such as brother killing brother (Eteocles and Polyneices), a son his father (Oedipus), a mother her son (Medea), or a son his mother (Orestes) (14, 1453b20 f.).

According to other, less plausible interpretations, tragedy is supposed to teach the viewers by deterrent examples to rein in their own passions. This moralist-didactic interpretation, prevalent in the Italian Renaissance and French classicism, was rejected by Lessing in favor of the task of transforming the passions into virtuous abilities through catharsis. According to Goethe *(Nachlese zu Aristoteles' Poetik),* catharsis is not a possible effect, but a structural characteristic of tragedy (cf. Bernays 1880, Flashar and von Pohlenz in: Luserke 1991; Halliwell 1986, appendix). One could make the objection to Aristotle's theory of tragedy that the emotions provoked in the audience cannot be determined in advance, but both the author and the director attempt just that. The fact that Aristotle does not enter into the unspectacular but "rational" part of tragedy, which follows his own ethics, does not deserve criticism either. It is true that the *Poetics* consider neither the temperance of minor figures, such as Ismene in *Antigone* and Creon in *Oedipus the King,* nor the end of the *Oresteia,* when Athena by rational persuasion manages to placate the vengeful Furies. However, these elements are not part of what matters to Aristotle, of the unrenounceable core of tragedy. It is more surprising that tragedy does not play any part in the *Ethics*. It does not feature at all in the passages about pleasure, and in the discussion of voluntariness it does so only counterintuitively: the reason for which Euripides' Alcmaeon allows himself to be incited to matricide is "ridiculous" (*EN* III 1, 1110a27–29).

There are good reasons to believe that the two main concepts of Aristotelian poetics, mimesis and catharsis, are still valid even today. Whether on stage or film, they represent exemplary possibilities of life in their large examples. In doing so they are neither satisfied with simple entertainment nor intent on delivering a moral message, but rather they display powerful passions, force us to suffer with them, and grant us relief after sufficient sympathy. Perhaps tragedy can serve as a model for an important task of dynamic societies, namely a "culture of timeliness" in view of new problems (cf. Höffe 1993, ch. 16). Sophocles' *Antigone* shows, by way of contrast, what is important when faced with new tasks. Only those who escape the danger Creon and Antigone succumb to, that is, blindness caused by self-righteousness, can be open to the complexity of the new situation. Where there is such openness, one "only" needs to make careful considerations and direct one's interests accordingly.

PROOFS AND PRINCIPLES

5.1 A CRITIQUE OF DEMONSTRATIVE REASON

While philosophy has its origin with the Ionian natural philosophers, theory of science as an independent discipline didn't begin until two centuries later. With the *Posterior Analytics* it established itself at such a high level of perfection that for centuries its history coincided largely with the history of the interpretation of that text. However, this was not a creation *ex nihilo*. Aristotle grapples with the major, mutually competing, views of the times, such as Plato's theory of recollection *(anamnêsis)* where he does so by using the dihaeretic method (*APr.* I 31 and *APo.* II 5), Antisthenes' skepticism regarding the possibility of science, and Xenocrates' opinion that the only possible form of science is the circular definition. The subject is higly developed and represented by numerous examples, in particular those taken from mathematics, as well as, in chapters II 11 and 13, from biology, medicine, historiography, and ethics. Thus, a far-ranging practice of the sciences is followed by meta-science.

Nowadays meta-science of that kind usually proceeds in an empirical-reconstructive way; it defines the practice, aims, methods, and prerequisites of a science. The alternative, critical, theory searches for the various cognitive interests in order to evaluate them. Aristotle stays one step behind both possibilities: he demands knowledge without further qualification, "simply knowing" (*epistasthai haplôs: APo.* I 2, 71b9), which aims only at fulfilling the previously raised cognitive demands without any diminution. This ideal cannot be dispensed with, neither in the name of other cognitive interests nor out of modesty.

In the *Posterior Analytics,* knowledge that attempts to realize that ideal, that is, science, is given a fundamental justification. Natural intellectual curiosity experiences its immanent fulfilment only where the criteria mentioned by Aristotle are fulfilled, that is, where one knows the *aitiai*, the causes or reasons, of a fact and where these are explanatory or justifiable; where one knows, that is, that the fact has to be as one claims and no other (*APo.* I 2, 71b9–12). It is therefore not surprising that Aristotle's ideal and its criteria are still recognized in epistemic practice, even if they hardly are in the theory of science. To this day we consider it an epistemic deficiency when reasons are either absent or have no explanatory power.

Furthermore, according to Aristotle proof exists not only for the necessary but also for what is mostly valid, not, however, for the accidental (*APo.* I 30; cf. *Ph.* II 4 and *Metaph.* VI 2; see ch. 8. 3).

In the present revival of interest in Aristotle, theory of science is surprisingly absent. Outside of research literature—such as McKirahan 1992 and Detel 1993, and before them Barnes 1975 (1994[2]), preceded by Ross 1949—there is no systematic interest comparable to the "rehabilitation" of Aristotle's ontology and practical philosophy, or the appreciation of his logic. Anscombe and Geach (1973, 6) even state: "His theory of 'scientific proof' is something which needs the 'pardon' he asks for." In general, critique refers to a tripartite standard interpretation: (1) it should be possible to compress the content of an Aristotelian science into a few, not further deducible, basic propositions, that is, into axioms that are grasped by induction *(epagôgê)* and intuition *(nous)*, and are always true and therefore irreversible; (2) because of the axioms a so-called final justification is possible; (3) the sciences are focused on ontological essences and conditions based on the law of causality. One might say that the characteristics are axiomatics, fundamentalism, and essentialism, in short, the "AFE ideal" (see Detel 1993, II 263 ff.).

The ideal appears to exert a certain fascination, since it anticipates early modern rationalism and the *more geometrico* systems of Descartes, Hobbes, and Spinoza. However, from the standpoint of scientific practice it is possible to argue successfully that: strictly axiomatically, there can be only one science whose axioms make no truth-claims and that is mathematics; that necessary truths cannot be obtained by induction; that scientific propositions, fallible as they are, are ever only of provisional value; and that essentialism, being metaphysical, is outdated. In fact, by advocating the AFE ideal, one forces the sciences into a strait-jacket that is alien to them. On the other hand, the obsolete ideal facilitates a dramatical *mise en scène* of oneself; it makes it possible to claim the collapse of any previous theory of science and present one's own contribution as a magnificent new beginning.

At first glance one can find in the *Posterior Analytics* much that confirms the standard interpretation: see for example chapters II 3–7 about axiomatics in the modern sense. However, a closer reading reveals a theory that is conceptually richer, altogether enlightened and certainly subtle. While it does not always hold out against today's views, it stands up without difficulties to modern standards. The very inception is remarkable, being a step back beyond empirical-reconstructive and critical theories.

It is also impressive how Aristotle—explicitly as well as implicitly—opposes naïveties in the theory of sciences, such as a logic of induction that assumes that it can manage without anticipating the general. Indeed, large sections of the text can be read as instructions for avoiding methodological errors. It also serves for overcoming the legend, still alive in the history of science, that the trilemma of causal thinking (the "Münchhausen Trilemma") was recognized as late as the nineteenth century, by Fries, and then rediscovered by the Popperian school of thought in the twentieth century. Furthermore, Aristotle suggests an alternative, worth considering, to fundamentalism which was desirable to early modern rationalism, but is obsolete today. He has known since the *Topics* (II 3, 110a32–37 and VIII 2,

157a34–b33) that general propositions can be fallible. Not least, the *Posterior Analytics* serves as a model of scientific prose: the author argues succinctly, soberly, and, to all appearances, in fairness toward his predecessors.

The text opens with the programmatic thesis that all knowledge, with the exception of perception, is based on previous knowledge (similarly at *Metaph.* I 9, 992b30 ff. and *EN* VI 3, 1139b26–36). According to Barnes (1994[2], Introd.), Aristotle is aiming for a theory of textbook-style representation of all knowledge. However, the fact that he is not dealing with mathematics and other sciences only, but also with dialectic (here: *logoi,* disputations) and rhetoric (*APo.* I 1, 71a3-11) makes this questionable; Aristotle is not interested in an encyclopedia of all sciences exclusively. Nor is he interested merely in the didactic question of how to transmit knowledge. Against the background of the puzzle *(aporia)* in Plato's *Meno* (80d ff; cf. *Phaidon* 72e–77b) that one "learns either nothing or that which one knows already" (*APo.* I 1, 71a29f.), Aristotle is concerned with the necessary elements for research and teaching, that is, with any way of acquiring knowledge.

The necessary preliminary knowledge could be understood as meaning, heuristically as well as biographically, that learning is always adding something to one's knowledge; it never occurs out of nothing, but only supplements or corrects what one already knows. Aristotle, however, raises a question concerning the logic of argumentation and answers it with an ultimately first or absolute preliminary knowledge; the systematic beginning consists of true and unrestricted first propositions, the principles. Because of these, science is constituted by the interplay of two essentially different elements, of syllogistic ("deductive") proof and (inductive) insight into the no longer provable principles.

By proof *(apodeixis,* in Latin: *demonstratio)* one generally understands a "top-down procedure," that is, the kind of deduction or derivation of propositions from other propositions that is familiar as the way from the principles (ch. 4. 2). However, one would look almost in vain for such a procedure, the "geometrical method," in Aristotle's actual philosophy. Even where one finds syllogisms, they do not assemble to form a system, either complete or partial, of knowledge based on principles. Is there a gulf, therefore, between the scientific ideal of the *Posterior Analytics* and Aristotle's actual practice, so that one is forced to consider wrong either the theory of science or his philosophy?

At closer scrutiny this variance dissolves. Like its element, the qualified syllogism, proof itself can be read not only from top to bottom, but also the opposite way: one looks for the causes and reasons of possible statements and follows them all the way up to the principles. This kind of procedure, too, is called "proof," in the sense of the question: "Can you prove that?," used both within and outside science. The reply follows the "bottom-up procedure" first. It seeks the explanatory reasons for a proposition that is already accepted as true, such as "The angle within the semicircle is a right angle" (formally "AaC"), or the fact that there are lunar eclipses. Aristotelian science is primarily interested in explanation or justification and only secondarily, as a check, in deducing. With the basic element of a proof, that is, the syllogism, the reasons have an exactly determined task. Since the proposition to be proved has the form "AaC," it is their task to prove the connection of the concepts A and C by using the middle term: the fact of "having a right angle" (A) applies to "all" (a) "angles in a semicircle" (C), because "one half of a full circle corresponds to rectangularity" (B) (*APo.* II 11, 94a28–36).

Popper believes that justification is entangled in an *aporia,* or rather in the trilemma that all three conceivable possibilities fail: neither infinite regress nor the logical circle provide an explanation, and the cessation of the procedure only leads to dogmatic opinions. Aristotle is familiar with the trilemma, at least with its rudiments, to judge from his treatment of Antisthenes and Xenocrates (cf. *APo.* I 3, 13, and 19–22; on infinite regress, see also *Metaph.* IV 7, 1012a12–15). However, since he agrees with Antisthenes' critique of infinite regress and of cessation of the procedure, he only deals with the third option. Three arguments can be raised (*APo.* I 3) against the latter, that is, the circular definition, which deduces AC from AB and BC, and AB from AC and the inversion of BC, CB (cf. *APr.* II 5). According to one argument (73a6–20), a circular definition is entirely possible, but only for convertible propositions (BC → CB) whose concepts designate the properties *(propria)* of a thing (*APo.* I 3, 73a7) and therefore have the same extension—e.g., for humans "capable of grammar" and "capable of laughter." More important is the other objection, namely that here the condition of a proof presupposing what is earlier and more familiar has been violated (72b25–32). According to the third objection, in the end the circular definition leads to triviality: "If A, then A." Thus, the circle proves everything—and consequently nothing (72b32–73a6).

Aristotle counters the critique of justification with its modification. One could call it a critique of demonstrative reason in the Kantian sense. The major part of the *Posterior Analytics* is an "analytics of demonstrative reason" in the sense that it deploys the right and the tasks of proof together with its conditions. This includes the opinion that the concepts used in proof—subjects as well as their predicates—are arranged in a hierarchy that is clearly delimited both downward, against the specific, and upward, against the general (*APo.* I 22). In this way Aristotle believes that he can avoid regress. For the subject matter of science, its essence or a part thereof, he sees, very convincingly, the downward limit in the particular—for example, in biology in the individual specimen of a natural species—and the upward limit in the highest genus of the definition of a being, thus, for biology, "living being." For the possible predicates, the properties or attributes, he notices a double limit. Downward they can have no greater measure of specificity than the individuals whose properties they are, and upward they are limited because in the end they lead to one of the categories (of which there is a limited number). Aristotle does not seek a final explanation for the ensuing question from what the categories result, but he checks the regress in a pragmatic way (see ch. 11. 1).

Aristotle also resists the arrogations of a proof that makes itself absolute. His "dialectic of demonstrative reason" consists of two parts, the cognition of principles, as a necessary supplement to proof (*APo.* I 18, 31, II 19) on the one hand, and reference to methodological errors on the other. He refers to infinite regress and the circular definition (I 2), the sophistic method of proving (I 5), the confusion of true proofs with explanations based only on symptoms (I 13), the dispensing with perception and induction (I 18) or their overestimation (I 31; on both, see also II 19), as well as the error of believing that one can prove the essence *(ti estin)* by subdivisions of concepts *(dihairesis)* (II 5).

5.2 AXIOMS AND OTHER PRINCIPLES

The preliminary knowledge necessary for proof consists in prerequisites that are neither provable nor in need of proof, the principles *(archai,* literally, "beginnings"; on the multiple meanings of the term, see *Metaph.* V 1). As far as the principles act as a foundation of all knowledge—Kant aptly translates them as *Anfangsgründe* ("initial reasons")—Aristotle's theory of science indeed has "fundamentalist" character. However, it is with good reason that the three types of principles can still be found in science. Principles can be subdivided into: (1) the small number of axioms that, like the law of contradiction, are presupposed by all knowledge and even by every action; (2) hypotheses; and (3) definitions that are necessary for specific spheres of knowledge respectively *(ta idia;* cf. I 30). Aristotle also uses the joint term *theses* for hypotheses and definitions *(APo.* I 2, 72a14–24). By attributing great importance to the principles of the individual sciences, Aristotle turns his back on the project of a unity of science, without, however, rejecting a fundamental philosophy. It is clear that Aristotle advocates the autonomy of the various branches of research because of his insight into the theory of science.

1. HYPOTHESES AND DEFINITIONS

By hypothesis Aristotle understands not a provisional statement, but an assumption regarding the existence of the elementary objects whose substance is included by the definitions. Thus, the hypothesis of arithmetic states that numbers exist, that of geometry that points, lines, and planes exist, and that of biology that living beings exist. Although hypotheses are presupposed in chains of evidence, they are not used as their principles.

It is a different matter when it comes to definitions *(horismoi).* They appear as the premises of proofs, but they are not placed at the top by an arbitrary or conventional stipulation. Provisional definitions render widespread views, while fully valid definitions have the power of explanation and are the result of the appropriate reflections. Because of its importance, Aristotle devotes more than half of the second book to the theory of definitions (II 1–10; on the interpretation of this sometimes difficult text, see Detel 1993 I 324 ff. and II 542 ff.) After a detailed discussion of the difficulties (II 3–7), he deals with four kinds of definition, each representing a different answer to the question "What is it?" *(ti esti: APo.* II 10, 93b29). The first kind—called nominal definition since Mill—only states what a name (e.g., triangle) or an equivalent expression signifies *(ti sêmainei: APo.* II 10, 93b30). Being devoid of any explanation, it is of scientifically provisional character and does not feature in the final enumeration (II 10, 94a11 ff.).

The second kind of definition answers the question "Why is it?" (93b32), which is left open in the nominal definition, by a reason with explanatory powers. It is related to "proof" in the sense of justification or explanation (cf. 94a12 f.)

and differs from it in its external arrangement only. In Aristotle's example, thunder, the proof goes: "Because the fire in the clouds goes out, it thunders," while the explanatory and, at the same time, fully valid definition reads: "Thunder is the noise that originates at the extinction of the fire in the clouds." With the exception of mathematics, it would seem that the affinity with proof, claimed by Aristotle, is still valid. The definitions that form the systematic, but not heuristic, beginning of a science are not simply laid down, but they are based on cognition. The third kind of definition is in fact only a subspecies of the second: it corresponds to the conlusion of a proof: "Thunder is a noise in the clouds" (*APo*. II 10, 94a7f.).

While the second and third kind define objects of minor importance, the fourth is concerned with the basic subject matter of a science. It is achieved by a specific collection of properties, illustrated by the example of a natural number (II 13, 96a24–b1). Attempts at defining the latter were never made by Greek mathematicians, but they were by some philosophers, beginning with the Pythagoreans. According to Aristotle's "cluster theory," one looks for a cluster of properties each of which reaches beyond the object to be defined, but which, taken together, only apply to the one particular element—for example, for the number three, "number," "odd," and "first in a certain way."

Metaph. VIII 2 (1043a14 ff.) contains an additional theory of definitions, which belongs to ontology rather than theory of science. Going back to the ontological pair of concepts, matter and form, one could define a potential house by matter, in this case stones, bricks, and timber, while the form is necessary for an actual house. In an artifact the form consists in the object's function: a house is a building (literally "container") that provides shelter for things and living beings. (For the theory of definition, see also *Metaph*. VII 5, 10–12 and VIII 6, as well as *Top*. VI–VII.)

The definitions are part of necessary preliminary knowledge in two ways. In the case of the basic objects, one needs to know in advance what they signify and that they exist. With the properties that one adjudges to or denies an object, on the other hand, meaning is sufficient. (Aristotle's example of the triangle is misleading, because one tends to understand it as an object, while it is to be understood as a property of points and lines.) A proof can only be carried out by someone who fulfils the trifold prerequisite (cf. *APo*. I 10) of knowing, in the case of geometry, (1) the definition of the basic subjects (point, line, plane, etc.), (2) their existence, and (3) the definition of possible properties (straight, curved, triangle, etc.), and who, according to a fourth, general prerequisite, is also familiar with the general principles of thought.

2. AXIOMS

This term for the principles spanning all disciplines has its origin in the art of disputation. It designates propositions whose assumption can be expected right at the beginning of a disputation. Its root, *axioun,* means "to consider worthy," and axioms are propositions that are beyond any reasonable doubt and therefore credible in a strict sense. These conditions may be valid in relation to a certain topic; in that case there is an accordingly limited a priori. In the *Posterior Analytics* (I 10, 76b14) and the *Metaphysics* (IV 3–4 and 7; cf. III 3, 997a5–15; XI 4, 1061b17–33), the term no longer has this relativity and designates only the presuppositions that can be made in any debate and even in any action. Axioms of this kind are also the most certain principles—one cannot be wrong about them—and are furthermore the easiest to recognize, in brief: they are of the order of an absolute a priori.

Since all things are quantifiable under certain aspects, general mathematical propositions—for example, the one stating that even numbers subtracted from even numbers result in even numbers—are valid, according to Aristotle, not only for mathematics but for all knowledge. Nevertheless, he does not call that proposition an axiom (*APo.* I 10, 76a41 and b21; I 11, 77a30), as it has general validity not in an absolute sense, but only in relation to quantification (cf. *Cat.* 6, 6a26 ff.; *Metaph.* V 15, 1021a12).

The essentially first axiom, the law of contradiction, says that it is impossible for something (e.g., the designation "human") to apply and not to apply to one and the same thing in the same relation simultaneously (in a logical rather than a temporal sense). According to the second axiom, the law of the excluded middle, there is no middle term in mutually contradictory statements, but rather something has to be either claimed or denied about something. Nowadays, both cases would be referred to as logical theorems, perhaps with the addition that they are immediately evident. It appears as though the principle about the excluded middle had been rendered obsolete by three-valued logic (Lukasiewicz, more recently U. Blau, etc.): with its third truth value—"indeterminate," along with "true" and "false"—it formalizes problems that arise, for example, with contingent statements about the future. However, Aristotle only applies it to those pairs of propositions in which indeterminacy is impossible. In *Int.* 6–9 he expounds when this is the case.

Although axioms cannot be proved, their validity is not merely asserted. Aristotle stages a demonstrative game in form of a dialogical refutation (*elenchos: Metaph.* IV 4; cf. Cassin-Narcy 1989, Rapp 1993). The opponent of the law of contradiction is requested to perform a minimal epistemic task and is then informed that in doing so he already presupposes the law of contradiction. The required task can, for example, consist in a certain claim, such as claiming that the law of contradiction is not valid. Aristotle justifiedly sees this as a *petitio principii*, since who claims a fact is already assuming the validity of the law of contradiction (1006a18–21). A thorough refutation sets in earlier, when the opponent is only talking (a12 f.) and *eo ipso* designates something that is to be valid for both participants in the discussion (a21). In the moment in which the designation is unequivocal—*this*, rather than that delimitable section of reality—the opponent is in fact already drawing on the denied axiom. Therefore, the law of contradiction is enlisted even in the smallest epistemic task or in minimal linguistic communication. Today we would perhaps say that, as the condition for any possibility of cognition or linguistic communication, the law of contradiction has transcendental character, albeit only in the sense of a negative criterion.

It is in Aristotle's subtle as well as penetrating argumentation that the law of contradiction achieves its most fundamental importance. According to Kant, it is merely the basic postulate for all analytical judgments (*Kritik der reinen Vernunft,* B 189 ff.). Since, for Aristotle, all correct designation depends on it, the only way out for the opponent is to say nothing at all. If he does so, however, he cannot call himself an opponent; closed to any kind of *logos,* he ceases to be human, as Aristotle says in a vivid image, and resembles a plant (*Metaph.* IV 4, 1006a14 f. and 1008b10–12). However, this possibility is contrary to his experience. If the opponent believes that he should go somewhere, he will do so rather than keep still; that is, he embarks on something determinate. He does not throw himself into a well first thing in the morning, or into an abyss, just because they happen to be on his way (*Metaph.* IV 4, 1008b14–17). Thus, we draw on the principle in pre-theoretical everyday life as well, and this also occurs in the veritable minimum of self-determination and circumspection that begins even in the subhuman sphere. Since by theoretical reason in a loose sense we understand the ability for self-determination, the law of contradiction shows itself to be the condition for the possibility of all theoretical as well as practical reason. This argumentation can be taken as coherentist provided one applies a loose concept of coherence (see ch. 4. 2).

Since D. Hilbert, logic and mathematics have been making use of the so-called axiomatic method, which will be adopted by other formal sciences. Here two axioms, referring to delimitable individual sciences, have two characteristics: they are consistent and independent of each other, but otherwise they can be defined freely. Axioms are exchangeable; they each determine a different system of theorems and, like the axiom on parallels in Euclidean geometry, they are conventional or decisionist in character. By contrast, Aristotelian axioms are valid for any science and even for any action. Being the very first theorems (and therefore without alternative) whose validity is generally admitted on the basis of one's experience of cognition and action, they are examined not by scientists belonging to individual branches of science (*Metaph.* IV 3, 1005a29 ff.) but by philosophers (1005a21).

Let us take stock with a view to the "AFE" interpretation: axioms such as the law of contradiction, on which actions also depend, are not only logical theorems, but theorems—or rather, meta-theorems—of theoretical as well as practical reason. These are not axioms in the sense of the AFE model; one can deduce neither knowledge nor the principles of actions from Aristotelian axioms. By proving themselves to be true in practice, they have performative character. Their certainty consists not in unrenounceable, propositional knowledge, but in the fact that any speech or action can occur only in accordance with the axioms. Knowledge of the greatest certainty in this sense occupies the position of final justification without being exposed to the current critique of the latter. With his theory of axioms—at least in the case of the law of contradiction—Aristotle attains to a modest and at the same time well-founded fundamentalism. He achieves a final proposition without declaring it the foundation of a theoretical or practical system. The essentialism of his axioms is no less convincing, given that it indicates a requisite, if minimal, core of essence for cognition and actions: whatever one may designate, do, or not do, as long as something distinct happens, one acknowledges the law of contradiction.

The elementary definitions demand a more wide-ranging essentialism. Scientists want to express something that is essential for the respective matter in the fully valid definitions (real definitions), if not in the explication of linguistic expressions (nominal definitions). For example, a concept of animal life intends to say how the life in question differs from other entities and what it is as such. Even when Aristotle attempts, in the zoology, to determine the specificity of individual species with an accuracy sufficient for their definition, his essentialism is not questionable. After all, laws as they are characteristic of modern natural sciences such as physics are not needed there.

In brief: in spite of some critique of details, Aristotle's fundamentalism is not to be rejected on grounds of theory of argumentation or science, and his essentialism is not replete with dubious metaphysical premises.

5.3 INDUCTION AND MIND

The final chapter of the *Posterior Analytics* explains how to recognize the no longer provable presuppositions (*APo.* II 19; see also I 18). Aristotle rejects Plato's thought of an innate knowledge of the principles with the argument that no one knows about these things from birth (cf. *Metaph.* I 9, 993a1 ff.). However, going back to the introductory thesis—i.e., no learning without previous knowledge—he also rejects the opposite view that knowledge of the principles is not innate. Instead, he develops a position that, at the same time, recognizes the refuted positions as elements and modifies them. Knowledge of the principles is innate only potentially *(dynamei).* For it to become real, however, three elements need to collude: *aisthêsis* (perception), *epagôgê* (induction), and *nous,* a term variously translated as "intellect," "mind," or "insight," and occasionally as "reason." For the *Ethics* (I 7, 1098b3 f.; cf. I 2, 1095b4), a practical form of *epagôgê,* namely, *ethismos* (habit), is needed.

Aristotle does not pursue the question how the three elements work together. The relation between *epagôgê* and *nous* is not even made an issue; the two elements are only treated separately (on *epagôgê,* see *APr.* II 24; *APo.* I 18; II 19, 100a1–b5; *Top.* I 12; VIII 14, 164a12–15; *Metaph.* X 3–4; *EN* VI 3, 1139b27 ff.; on *nous,* see *APo.* II 19, 100b5–17; *de An.* III 4–8; and *EN* VI 6 and 12). Furthermore, it is conspicuous that the *Posterior Analytics* mentions three types of principles at the beginning, but the explication of the axioms is left to the *Metaphysics* (III 2, 997a4ff. and IV 3–4). Also, the argumentation of *APo.* II 19 is easier to reconstruct if it relates not to the axioms, but only to the two other principles—the general concepts specific of a particular science and the corresponding assumptions of existence.

The fact that the relevant cognition of principles begins with perception suggests the empiristic explanation that the general concepts are derived from perception by mere abstraction. However, perception could also be just the factor by which the cognition of the principles becomes reality. (On perception, cf. *APo.* I 18 and I 31; *de An.* II 5–III 2, as well as III 6 and 8; *Metaph.* IV 5–6 and *Peri aisthêseôs/ On Perception;* cf. Modrak 1987, Welsch 1987, and Detel 1993, I

233 ff.) According to the non-empiristic reading, while perception concerns the individual, for instance, Socrates, it is not directed at its particularity, but at the general, namely, man. Perception remains unrenounceable for cognition, but the general is only potentially accessible to it. It only reaches reality with the assistance of the mind, that is, through a more active effort. However, this does not happen "at one go," but in a cognitive process called induction, which leads from perception, via memory and experience, to the cognition of the principles.

Aristotle did not develop a detailed theory of induction. At the beginning of the *Metaphysics* he speaks only of perception but not of induction, and in the programmatic chapters of the *Posterior Analytics* (I 1–6), conversely, of induction but not of perception. Since Popper, induction has been considered an epistemically inferior solution to the question how to obtain empirical general statements from observations. Aristotle is not so foolish as to employ induction for the statements to which Popper's misgivings apply most obviously, that is, for negative, singular statements of existence (e.g., "There is no unicorn"); he mentions only the positive general statements which could be the actual problem case for Popper as well. In contrast with the latter's, however, only a small number of Aristotle's examples belong to a natural science that lays down laws or makes claims similar to these. Induction does not feature in the collection of zoological data, the *Zoology*, but it does so in the discussion of general principles of natural philosophy (e.g., *Ph.* I 2, 185a14; V 1, 224b30; V 5, 229b3; *Cael.* I 7, 276a14 f.) as well as in very general philosophical theorems (e.g., *APo.* II 7, 92a37 f.; *Top.* I 8, 103b3; *Metaph.* X 3, 1054b33; X 4, 1055b17), and not least in the domain of rhetoric, albeit in a few cases only (*Rh.* II 20, 1394a11–14).

According to the *Topics* (I 12), induction consists in an ascent *(ephodos)* from the particular to the general, for which a few examples will be sufficient: "If the best helmsman is the one who knows his job, and if the same is true of the charioteer, then in general the one who knows his respective job is the best." If one were to call this "imperfect induction," one would miss the essential point, namely, that a few expressive cases might be sufficient. Aristotle introduces something like an "exemplary induction," but he does not consider to what purpose and under what conditions it works and when it does not—such as in the supposed connection between longevity and the absence of bile (*APr.* II 23, 68b15 ff.). In the example in the *Topics,* the universal proposition appears to have a characteristic that does not apply to the connection between longevity and the absence of bile: it is analytic. "To know one's job" (= A) means "to be very good at that job" (= B). Nevertheless, there is a gain in knowledge, since the induction leads from what is already known, the particular, to what is yet unknown, the general—in this case the fact that A and B are identical in meaning. As for the rest, Aristotle does not attribute great scientific importance to the generalization of individual cases into a general fact. The logical writings only mention it occasionally and only as a second-rate kind of proof (*APr.* II 23, 68b35–37). The reason is that it does not provide a (general) justification but only explicates a (general) fact.

In being content with just a few cases, induction is cognate with the example *(paradeigma;* cf. *Rh.* II 20, 1393a26 f. and 1394a9 ff.; *APr.* II 24; and *APo.* I 1,

71a10f.). The pertinent example, the elliptic induction, abbreviated for rhetorical purposes, has its place even in scientific debate. The opponent is to be forced to acknowledge the general principle by the quoting of individual cases, since he would show himself to be a "spoil-sport" if he refused to acknowledge it despite the absence of proof to the contrary. Aware of the fact that an (exemplary) induction "is more persuasive, clearer, better known to perception and familiar to the masses, while the syllogism (on the other hand) is more convincing and more effective for debate" (*Top.* I 12, 105a16–19), an experienced debater is more likely to use inferences in a professional debate, and induction in an everyday discussion.

At the beginning of the *Posterior Analytics,* Aristotle practices a different kind, more familiar to modern theory of science, namely, the general or enumerative induction. The reason is that, in the proofs for the necessity of preliminary knowledge, he aspires to completeness (*APo.* I 1, 71a3–11). Aristotle generally shows a preference for general propositions as an "opening move": like the *Posterior Analytics,* the *Physics,* the treatise *On the Parts of Animals,* the *Metaphysics,* the *Ethics,* and the *Politics* all open with a proposition of general validity, based on an induction. In the continuation of the discussion, too, it plays an important part, both as an enumerative and an exemplary induction.

The cognition of principles involves an induction only insofar as one arrives at the general step by step from the perception of the particular. In this case it is neither a comprehensive scrutiny of all particular cases that matters nor is it possible to infer the general from just a few observations. From this point of view there is neither an exemplary nor an enumerative induction, but rather a third possibility, which one could provisionally call a creative insight or an intuitive induction. Aristotle likens it to an army that regroups in its flight, when first one of the fleeing soldiers stops, and then little by little the others rally to him until the initial order is regained (*APo.* II 19, 100a11–13). The image is not meant to illustrate how rest originates from motion, but how, from the mere plurality, the multiplicity of soldiers, its principle, the order of the army, is realized. Just as the fleeing soldiers represent only a potential order from which the original formation results by persistance, one can turn into reality, by the persistance of perceptions, what had always been contained in them potentially.

The intellectual competence instrumental for this is the third determining element after perception and induction, the mind *(nous).* While the cognition of principles begins with perception, it does not originate from it. It is essentially noetic cognition, resting on the capacity to grasp the general in the particular, not step by step, but in an unmediated way. The induction proceeds step by step, so that in the strict sense there is no intuitive induction, but an induction preparing for intuition (cf. Liske 1994). Perception represents the particular; the mind achieves the punctual becoming-aware of the general; induction—partly by trying out possibilities, partly as reconstruction of an insight—takes in a discursive way the path from the particular to the general in which the mind succeeds intuitively, "at a stroke."

6

FOUR METHODICAL MAXIMS

As mentioned above, Aristotle's methodological views can be found not only in the *Organon,* but also in excurses or remarks scattered throughout his treatises. A passage in the *Ethics* (VII 1, 1145b2–7) is concise, but it is also meant to apply to other topics. In general, three things matter here: (1) establishing the phenomena *(tithenai ta phainomena),* (2) working through *(diaporêsai)* the difficulties, and (3) proving *(deiknynai)* the credible opinions *(endoxa),* at least the most and the most important. "For when the difficulties are solved and the credible opinions remain, one has given sufficient proof." (Similarly *Ph.* IV 4, 211a7–11 and *EE* VII 1 f., 1235a4–1235b18.) According to the *De anima* (I 1, 402a10–22), there is no unified method that is the same without differentiation for all science, but the aforementioned passage only appears to contradict this, since the three elements do not have the meaning of precise procedures but of methodical maxims. Furthermore, they do not exhaust Aristotle's instrumentarium: what is conspicuously lacking is linguistic analysis, which should be discussed in addition, in a certain sense as the fourth maxim.

6.1 ESTABLISHING THE PHENOMENA

We all know the situation of someone being convinced that a certain course of action is right and yet not following it. We call this weakness of will or lack of self-control *(akrasia).* Aristotle considers Socrates' opinion that this cannot happen an obvious contradiction of the phenomena *(EN* VII 3, 1145b22–28). In order to save it, he develops a theory that takes Socrates' misgivings seriously without denying the possibility of lack of self-control. He proceeds in a similar way with Parmenides', Melissus's, and Xenophanes' view that nothing else can exist beside the one Being *(Metaph.* I 5, 986b18 ff.). He counters their attempt to establish a theory against a clear phenomenal basis with a charge of insufficient consistency. Conceptually, he says, Parmenides knows only the one, but according to perception he admits various things, so that he finds himself forced to obey the phenomena, in this case everyday experience. Incidentally, he finds greater clarity in Parmenides' "obedience" than in the "uncouth views" of Melissus and Xenophanes.

Elsewhere, too, Aristotle refers to everyday experience, for example, in the teleology he cites the experience that an acorn always produces oaks, and the procreation

of humans always produces humans. Phenomena also need to be established in astronomy, because many observations are unreliable (*APr.* I 30, 46a20; cf. *APo.* I 13,
78b39 and 79a2–6; *Cael.* III 7, 306a5–17), as well as in zoology, since a description
of the animal kingdom must begin from the stock of phenomena before embarking
on any classification (*PA* I 1, 639b5–10 and 640a13–15). Occasionally Aristotle follows the first maxim without spelling it out, for example, in his critique of the view
that there is no science (*APo.* I 3). In general, he warns against bending the phenomena to make them fit a pre-established theory instead of looking for a theory
that fits them (*Cael.* II 13, 293a23–30).

As Owen (1961) says, what Aristotle calls phenomena are not always of the
same kind. Astronomy, zoology, and other empirical sciences need to ascertain the
foundation of experience, the that *(hoti),* before they can explore the why *(dihoti),*
that is, the causes and reasons. In their case the phenomena correspond to empirical data. In philosophy—in the theory of science, natural philosophy, ethics, and
ontology—on the other hand, the phenomena are interpretations, that is, opinions, so that the first methodical maxim merges into the second. However, the first
maxim hints at something that is not expressed by the second: the apprehension
that a way of thinking that strays too far from conventional views could lead to ab-
surdity *(atopos:* e.g., *Ph.* I 2, 185a11). Faced with interpretations, "establishing the
phenomena" means to give an intuitively plausible, if vague, opinion a justification
and conceptual acuity. By means of the theory established in the end, however, the
phenomena not only become intelligible, but they are also interpreted more precisely and not infrequently in a different, or even radically different, way.

6.2 DOCTRINES

Aristotle assumes that his audience thinks less about texts than about the world—
that is, about the world of disputation, perception, poetry, and public speech, and
in particular the natural and social world. This is the reason why, unlike most
philosophers in our times, he generally starts immediately from the thing itself
rather than from the history of the discussion so far. On the other hand, Aristotle
is not the first person to think about the world, nor does he want to give the impression of being the first one to do so thoroughly. On the contrary, he allots a remarkable amount of space to earlier teachings *(doxai).* There is practically no
treatise, nor a topic within the treatises, in the context of which he does not mention his predecessors. This is never done merely in order to report the state of discussion. Unlike Theophrastus, who merely collects the tenets of the natural
philosophers *(physikoi),* according to problems, in his treatise *Physikôn doxai,* Aristotle prefers to conform to the maxim expressed in his book on aporia: one should
only deal with one's predecessors insofar as their views differ either from each other
or from one's own (*Metaph.* III 1, 995a24–27).

In dealing with his predecessors' teachings, Aristotle is helped by the fact that
much of this material has already been treated in debates at the Academy and has
become part of the school's body of knowledge; some of it has even become established as formulae. Furthermore, he compiles extracts of written reports by subject

(*Top.* I 14, 105b12–15). Not least, he has the capacity of representing the position of others with precision; for instance, he is remarkably concise at *Metaph.* XII 1 (1069a34–36), where he lists the positions of Plato, Xenocrates, and Speusippus in the space of three lines. Occasionally he introduces earlier opinions with an almost pedantic accuracy. In discussing the question how many and what kind of natural principles there are (*Metaph.* I 3–10; similarly, *Ph.* I 2–9), he deals separately with the contributions of Thales, Anaximenes, and Diogenes of Apollonia; he leaves Hippo aside, whilst considering worth mentioning Heraclitus, Empedocles, and Anaxagoras. He considers Hesiod, Parmenides, Leucippus, and Democritus, the Pythagoreans and Socrates, and discusses Plato in particular detail, including his unwritten teachings *(agrapha dogmata).*

Since the Greek for "opinion" is *doxa,* we speak of the "doxastic method." Aristotle recognizes what are probably the two most important requirements in the ethics of science, that "we must, on the one hand, investigate things ourselves and, on the other, be instructed by other researchers and, if necessary, borrow views of theirs that differ from ours" (*Metaph.* XII 8, 1073b13–17; cf. *Cael.* III 7, 306a11 ff.). By explaining the opinions of his predecessors, acknowledging their achievements without envy, by attempting to give a certain amount of justification to every opinion contradicting his own (*EE* VII 2, 1235b16 f.), claiming originality on principle only where it is justified, and by overcoming deficiencies and other defects and contributing his own thoughts, Aristotle fulfils a condition that, according to Kant, is part of the scientific character (*Kritik der reinen Vernunft,* Vorrede 2nd edn.): he is helping philosophy along toward visible progress (cf. *SE* 34, 183b17 ff. and 184b3–8).

Sometimes it may look as though Aristotle were only sifting through recognized opinions in order to separate the chaff of falsehood from the wheat of truth. This impression is, however, contradicted by the aforementioned requirement of investigating things for oneself, especially since certain things have often remained unnoticed (*Metaph.* III 1, 995a27 f.). Even where a topic has already been discussed extensively, Aristotle develops his position from creative processes of judgment, often by way of a definite negation. According to the introductory book of the *Metaphysics* (I 3–9), it is the so-called theory of the four causes that avoids both the "more modest" theory of principles of many of Aristotle's predecessors and Anaxagoras's assumption of an unlimited number of principles. The author proceeds in a similar way at *Cael.* I 10, 279b4 ff. and III 1, 308a4 ff.; *de An.* I 2–5; GC I 1–2; *Metaph.* XIII; *EN* VII 3; and *Pol.* II.

Texts that give the impression that there had been no serious philosophy before them make the author appear to be an outstanding genius or an intellectual lawgiver setting up a direction and a measure for future generations. Aristotle, however, can do without such stage setting for his own person: with a few, well justified, exceptions—syllogistics, topics, and most of the zoology—he does not claim any original discoveries. Rather, he is content with his greater wealth of thought and clarity in defining. It is in practical philosophy in particular that scientific opinions are supplemented with common views (*legomena;* e.g., *EN* I 2, 1095a18 ff.; I 8, 1098b27 f.), or interwoven with them (e.g., *EN* I 9,

1098b22–29). Occasionally the opinions of the experts contradict those of the many (*EN* I 3, 1095b19 ff.) and thus selection becomes necessary. The criteria Aristotle enumerates for it still appear plausible today: wide distribution, a certain amount of justification, venerable age, and the support of recognized authorities (e.g., *EN* I 8, 1098b16–18; 9, 1098b27 f.).

The way in which Aristotle relates to his predecessors expresses more than merely the claim that scientific or philosophical progress is possible only after a thorough study of the literature. While he understands himself as the continuation, even the culmination, of a long row of scientists and philosophers, he nevertheless refutes the idea of linear progress by, for example, adducing earlier thinkers as witnesses against Plato. He also acknowledges that the beginning is the greater part of the whole (*SE* 34, 183b22 f.), and thus concedes his predecessors the greater achievement. Finally, he also refers to non-scientists, such as Solon the lawgiver, Greek literature, historiography (e.g., Herodotus: *Po.* 9, 1451b2), or aphorisms (*Metaph.* I 2, 983a3). In all this he demonstrates his accurate sense for the history of thought. Certainly the pathos of modern thinkers claiming to define philosophy anew is alien to Aristotle.

However much Aristotle may refer to doctrinal or current opinion, he does not consider it a criterion of truth. He does adjudicate to common opinion a *probability* of truth, given that all humans carry inside them something that is related to truth (*EE* I 6, 1216b30 f.) and that they cannot miss truth in their entirety (*Metaph.* II 1, 993a30 ff.), but nevertheless, even at their best, recognized opinions are true but not clear. Some opinions are too narrow, some too far-flung, while others are superficial or confused, so that it is the philosopher's task to help them achieve clarity (*to saphôs; EE* I 6, 1216b33 f.). In the explanation of the *sophos,* for example, Aristotle first collects the current opinions *(hypolêpseis)* and subsequently names the characteristics resulting from them that are also justifiable (*Metaph.* I 2, 982a8–21). He proceeds in a similar way in other passages.

Since W. Hamilton it has become popular to interpret Aristotle's references to recognized opinions as commonsense philosophy, and H. Sidgwick, G. E. Moore, and J. Rawls read Aristotle's ethics as an expression of the commonsense morals of the Greeks. In practice, however, Aristotle makes higher truth claims. He no more shares the preference of some of the Pre-Socratics for formulating their doctrines as paradoxes, that is, as opinions contrary to those of the crowd, than he does Plato's paedagogical fervor, as in the call for the reversal of the soul, particularly obvious in the simile of the cave. This does not, however, stop him from rejecting out of hand the opinion of the many when the occasion calls for it. In his plea for the theoretical life, the commonsense interpretation of happiness as something visible, such as pleasure, wealth, or honor (*EN* I 2, 1095a22 f.) is opposed by uncommon sense. The conclusion of the treatise about the unlimited, too, is the opposite of what is normally understood by it (*Ph.* III 6, 206b33). In various other passages Aristotle only cites the experts *(sophoi).* Nor does he shy away from forming concepts that are alien to everyday understanding, such as that of the "unmoved mover" (see ch. 10.2), the "most goal-like goal" (see ch. 14. 1) and the distinction between "passive" and "active" intellect (see ch. 8. 3). Not least, the content of his ontology cumulates in an idea that is doubtlessly alien to common sense, that of the of the intellect thinking itself (see ch. 10. 2). In brief: Aristotle's relationship to common sense and current opinion is too varied—alternatingly hermeneutical, critical, or affirmative—to allow for considering him a commonsense philosopher. Possibly one could speak of a qualified commonsense thinker open to criticism (see ch. 12. 2).

6.3 DIFFICULTIES

Given that Aristotle's treatises themselves do not fulfil the ideal of knowledge expressed in the *Analytics,* one could generally contest their systematic claim, and speak of merely aporetic thought. While this anti-systematic interpretation does not do justice to Aristotle's philosophy on the whole, it does hit upon something essential. Literally, *aporia* means "impassable way," and aporias are difficulties or problems rooted in the thing itself which often appear as questions and are then presented as antithetical possibilities, as alternatives, according to the rules of Aristotelian dialectics. Incidentally, the great significance of aporias (cf. *Top.* I 2, 101a34–36) also contradicts the aforementioned commonsense interpretation.

The theory of definition in the *Posterior Analytics* is a good example: Aristotle's own theory (II 8–10) is preceded by a detailed exposition of the difficulties (II 3–7). He proceeds in an analogous way for the theory of the cognition of principles: before outlining it, he names and comments three aporias (*APo.* II 19, 99b20–32). The analysis of time, too, is accompanied by a detailed exposition of its aporias (*Ph.* IV 10; VI 1–8), as is the treatment of weakness of will (*EN* VII 3). An entire book of the *Metaphysics,* the book of problems or aporias—III (B)— is dedicated to the difficulties faced by fundamental philosophy (cf. *Metaph.* XI 1–2). In other passages, the aporias are interspersed with Aristotle's critique of his predecessors (e.g., *de An.* I 2–5), and sometimes they serve indirectly as a confirmation of his own doctrine (e.g., *Metaph.* XII 10, 1075a25 ff.).

It is not as though Aristotle attempted to resolve the aporias as quickly as possible, but rather he allows them to become clearly visible first. Previously familiar views—be they common ideas or well-known doctrinal opinions—are at first represented as questionable and then subjected to a working-through of their questionableness, which is the literal meaning of the frequently used term *di-aporêsai* (e.g., *Ph.* IV 10, 217b30; *Metaph.* I 9, 991a9; III 1, 995a28; *APo.* II 19, 99b23). In this way it is possible to witness the emergence of Aristotle's scientific and philosophical insights. For this, the introductory chapter of the books of aporias (*Metaph.* III 1, 995a27–32) refers to a definite negation: the detailed knowledge (i.e., as complete as possible a knowledge) of the a-porias, that is, the "paths that cannot be taken," results in eu-poria, the "path that is good and easy to walk." The aporetic interpretation can base itself on the first part of the argumentation: indeed, there is a need for philosophy where there are obstacles in the form of "tricky problems." With the second part, however, it reaches its limit: philosophy ought not just to represent the obstacles, but also remove them, thus becoming more than a mere journey, or an endless search. Therefore, the philosopher needs two kinds of things: along with acuity and an awareness of problems, he also needs a highly developed "constructive" ability.

As a rule, the obstacles result from views or theories that are either too simple or too contradictory. The discussion of the aporias then leads to a theory that is both more complex and free of contradictions. In this context, Aristotle practices a basal rational optimism, the opposite of "dogmatic" fallibilism: if one knows the obstacles, one can remove them; if one sees through the difficulties, one is able to solve them. In the *Ethics* (VII 4, 1146b7 f.) he says trenchantly that the solution of the difficulty is the discovery (of truth). In fact, it is possible to make a truth claim where the relevant aporias have been removed, but this claim is not absolute: as soon as new obstacles appear, they need to be worked through again.

6.4 LINGUISTIC ANALYSIS

Linguistic analysis constitutes one of the most important procedures in working through the aporias, and in Aristotle's philosophy in general. According to the *Topics* (I 13, 105a21–25), one side of it, conceptual distinction, belongs to the four "tools" *(organa)* that are a help in finding syllogisms. Again, the *Metaphysics* offers a clear illustration. Book V, the first transmitted encyclopedia of concepts, still worth reading today, presents no fewer than thirty basic concepts in their multiple meanings *(pollachôs legetai;* cf. also *dichôs legetai,* the double meaning: e.g., *APo.* I 2, 71b33; *Ph.* I 8, 191b2; *GC* I 7, 324a26 ff.; *Metaph.* V 23, 1023a27; *EN* VII 13, 1152b27). A string of further concepts is added in the treatises, such as "unlimited" *(Ph.* III 4-4), "life" *(de An.* II 1, 413a22), or "actions" *(EN* 12, 1136b29 f.). Related to conceptual differentiation is the parsing of what is initially said in an undifferentiated way *(Metaph.* VII 17, 1041b1 ff.). By this and other procedures Aristotle preempts modern philosophy: the recognition that truth has to be distinguished from appearance *(SE* 1, 164a20 ff.) is reminiscent of Kant's transcendental dialectics; the idea that philosophy can be a therapy against the bewitchment of the intellect provoked, for example, by equivocation, the confusion of things with their signs *(SE* 1, 165a6 ff.), or other pitfalls of language, reminds one of the philosophy of linguistic analysis of our century. With Aristotle, however, the philosophical investigation of linguistic foundations remains one of several methods, and the claim to exclusivity made by modern linguistic analysis—aiming to commit philosophy to the description of linguistic structures only—is alien to him.

The entire procedure is carried along by confidence in the knowability of the world and, at the same time, skepticism vis-à-vis first appearances. Only this combination explains the great power of persuasion that Aristotle usually has. The epistemic optimism makes it worthwhile to undertake the exertions of research, and the skepticism toward the supposedly apparent makes it necessary. There is, however, no skepticism concerning the possibility of truth as such in view. Perhaps any philosopher has the right to be skeptical about skepticism in principle if, like Aristotle, he succeeds in obtaining a wealth of new knowledge from his familiarity with the state of discussion by means of acuity and constructive thinking.

PART III

PHYSICS AND METAPHYSICS

7

NATURAL PHILOSOPHY

The early modern age dealt severely with Aristotle as a natural scientist. Beginning with Bacon, who denied him with what he credits Anaxagoras, Democritus, Parmenides, and Empedocles, namely, any "trace of the knowledge of nature" (*Novum Organum* I, aphor. 63), the many-voiced criticism came close to the reproach that Aristotle had obstructed scientific progress for almost two millennia. However, this reproach does not even do justice to the Aristotelianism of the time. While it is true that, in some areas, Aristotelianism hampered the natural sciences by a certain dogmatic ossification, in other areas they emerged from a school influenced by Aristotle, namely that of Padua (see ch. 18. 1). Most of the critique against Aristotle himself appears anachronistic, such as that regarding geocentricity, since it was assumed by all great mathematicians and astronomers of his time. As for the rest, a modern theory such as that of epigenesis can claim Aristotelian roots (see ch. 8. 2). At any rate, by studying Aristotle one gets to know a significant inquiry into nature that is not so radically different from that of modernity.

7.1 ARISTOTELIAN NATURAL SCIENCE

It is often said that the experiment in the modern sense is unknown to Aristotle. In fact, he relies far more on direct observation, be it of nature itself or of the reflexes relevant in language; he also makes do without devices such as binoculars or microscopes. Nevertheless, he knows the rudiments of the experiment. Thus, he undertakes dissections of animals; for example, he describes the dissection of moles' eyes in the *Zoology* (cf. ch. 8. 1). He also observes the development of embryos in hen's eggs from the same clutch (*HA* VI 3, 561a6–562a20) and uses this observation to defend his own theory against a competing one. Furthermore, as we shall see, the "experimental method" is not all that important for his kind of biological research.

As far as physics is concerned, it is said that Aristotle is far removed from Galileo's thesis that the book of nature is written in the language of mathematics. In reality he sees both the differences and the overlap between mathematics and physics (*Ph*. II 2, 193b23–25), and in the *Physics* he investigates themes concerning mathematics and physics equally, such as the infinite and the continuum (see ch. 7. 4). In the process he explains the conceptual preliminaries for the mathematical intellectual devices that early modern physics will use to deal with problems of continuity and infinitesimal calculus. Furthermore, he assigns to applied mathematics those natural sciences in which mathematicization will have its triumphs, namely, mechanics, optics, and astronomy. And in biology, or rather zoology, the field in which his contribution to empirical natural sciences is greatest, mathematical assertions are far less important than the description of shapes (morphology) and functions (physiology), even in modernity.

Partly, the exaggerated critique is due to a confusion between Aristotle and Aristotelianism. The critique of universal teleology is part of this, that is, of the assumption that the entire universe is governed by purpose. The view, still preponderant among "philosophically erudite" biologists, that according to Aristotle the world is a context that is meaningful in itself, directed toward values, goals, and purposes, as well as ontologically varied, a *natura naturans* streaming innocently from within itself, does not have its origin in Aristotle. Another part of the critique is based on the fact that Aristotle is, so to speak, read from the wrong perspective, that is, from the angle of physics rather than biology, and from that of "ordinary physics" rather than the fundamental research that explains topics like the infinite or the continuum. In one aspect, at any rate, Aristotle works no differently from his modern colleagues. Unlike some Platonists with their excessive speculation, he allots a fixed place to the search for experience (cf. *Cael.* III 7, 306a5–17) and demands a clearly delimited explanation proper to each natural event. In contrast with the "wild experimenting" without theory which, according to Bacon, generates "even more shapeless and incomprehensible definitions" than Aristotle's attitude (*Novum Organum* I, aphor. 64), he is led by theoretical interests.

On the other hand, there are clear distinctions. While early modern natural science subjects itself to human goals, all that matters to Aristotle is knowledge (*tou eidenai charin hê pragmateia: Ph.* II 3, 194b17 f.). This purely theoretical interest has the expedient consequence that there is no need for a separate ethics of science, neither one directed against eventual abuse, nor an ethics of risk; Aristotle can afford to be content with an ethics immanent in science. Being essentially a free activity, Aristotle's natural science carries its moral justification within itself. Even in sheer quantity the relevant writings have great significance, given that they amount to more than half of Aristotle's transmitted work. The other writings are biological and psychological treatises (see ch. 8) and only four other texts.

The treatise *On the Heaven* treats astronomy as a cosmology. Basing himself on the works of Eudoxus and Callippus, Aristotle represents his geocentric conception of the world: according to this, the relatively small Earth—"a mere nothing, so to speak, compared to the surrounding universe" (*Mete.* I 3, 340a6–8)—is situated, spheric and immobile, in the middle of the world (*Cael.* II 14). Contrary to the tradition from Anaximander to Plato, the world, consisting of concentric spheres containing the moon, the sun, the planets, and finally the fixed stars, is considered as un-generated and imperishable. Aristotle's universe is spatially limited, but temporally unlimited.

The "things in suspension," *ta meteôra*, that is, the physical processes happening between heaven and earth, are investigated in particular detail (cf. Strohm

1984[3]). Aristotle's meteorology, based partly on his own observations, partly on those of his predecessors, is far more than mere weather lore. The philosopher provides the relevant work for antiquity in a field that is already confusingly varied, especially in hydrology and mineralogy. Theophrastus builds on it, and so does the Stoic Poseidonius (135–51 B.C.E.). Transmitted by the Syrians and Arabs, its influence extended well beyond antiquity.

Aristotle concerns himself most of all with the philosophical foundations of nature and the investigation of nature. The *Physics*—according to Heidegger (1958, 240), the "fundamental book of Western philosophy, never sufficiently thought through"—provides, in the literal sense of the title, a general teaching about nature, or natural philosophy. In certain points it is to be supplemented by the treatise *On Coming-to-be and Passing-away* (for an introduction, see Craemer-Ruegenberg 1980; for a more in-depth treatment, see the commentary by Wagner 1989[5]; Wieland 1992[3]; Judson 1991 and Gill-Lennox 1994). Not limited to a restricted class of natural objects or processes, it is neither experimental nor theoretical physics, but rather proto-physics. Nor does it tend toward speculative physics with the goal of creating a systematic connection between all natural phenomena. Engaged not with Nature writ large, but with the *physei on,* the being by nature, it asks what natural things are and how they can be explored scientifically. This brings to the fore a characteristic of philosophy, that is, the investigation not of the unknown, but, as Hegel puts it, of "what one normally considers as known" (Werke 18, 39). Aristotle establishes the relevant deliberations as an autonomous science, conceptually distinct from both mathematics and first philosophy. By not building on the preliminaries of metaphysics anywhere, with the exception of the very first principles of thought, the axioms, he demonstrates the autonomy of physics in the strongest possible terms (as Buridan, one of the pioneers of modern physics, would demand it).

Aristotle did not compile the *Physics* as we have it. Books I and II, about principles and causes respectively, may have been independent books originally. They can, however, also be read as two separate introductions of equal status to books III–V, which in turn present themselves as a relatively closed treatise about natural processes. Book III deals with motion and infinity, book IV with space, the void and time, book V again with motion, and book VI with continuity. Books VII and VIII each stands on its own, and they appear not to have been connected with the other books of the *Physics*. The crowning conclusion of natural philosophy, and at the same time the link with first philosophy, book VIII again treats motion. Some important elements of book XII of the *Metaphysics,* such as the thesis of the eternity of the world (cf. also *Cael.* I 3–II 1) and the concept of a first unmoved mover *(to prôton kinoun akinêton)* first appear here. Surprisingly, an explicit theological component, namely, the equating of the unmoved mover with God (see ch. 10), is lacking here.

7.2 MOTION

Early modern natural philosophy expresses its subject matter as "matter in motion," thereby remaining within Aristotelian tradition, according to which natural objects are constantly subject to some kind of motion. The object undergoing these changes is called matter or stuff *(hylê)*, and what happens to it is *kinêsis*—motion, change, process—or *metabolê*—change, reversal. (When the two words are used as technical terms, the former is subordinate to the latter.) Motion not only is at the center of Aristotelian natural philosophy, it also plays an important part in the *Ethics* (see ch. 13. 1 on the fundamental concept of striving) and in the *Politics* (V–VI about the decline and stability of constitutions). While motion itself is not the subject matter, it is the factor that calls philosophy into action in the subject matter, that is, in the substances *(ousiai)*: it is motion that is worth querying.

What is investigated in early modern times is primarily motion from one place to another, and thus motion that can also be generated deliberately. Its dynamics differs greatly from the Aristotelian kind. For example, Aristotle's "contact causality" contradicts the law of inertia: when an object is thrown, it is the medium, air, that keeps the body in motion *(Ph.* VIII 10, 266b25–267a12; cf. *Cael.* III 2, 301b22–30). However, in order to pass an objective judgment, one must not disregard the fact that in most of the incriminated theorems irrelevant secondary thoughts mingle with fundamental theses. Since many of the elements are treated only in a marginal way, the Aristotelian dynamics criticized in early modern times is "less a piece of Aristotelian teaching than a catalogue of errors and vices opposing Aristotle's natural philosophy drawn up by the thinkers subscribing to the 'mechanist world view'" (Craemer-Ruegenberg 1980, 107).

Considerably more wide-ranging than the early modern concept of motion, Aristotle's comprises four classes of motion (e.g., *Ph.* III 1, 201a9–15), corresponding to the four categories in inverted order: What (substance), How (quality), How big (quantity), and Where (place) *(Metaph.* XII 2, 1069b9–14). Natural processes consist in (1) changes of place (of humans, animals, planets, etc.) *(kinêsis kata topon/phora)*, (2) quantitative changes, of something becoming smaller or larger *(auxêsis kai phthisis)*, (3) qualitative changes, such as something becoming hot or cold, or someone falling ill or getting well *(alloiôsis)*, and finally (4) changes in substance, coming to be and passing away, for example, the generation of a human being *(genesis kai phthora)*.

Empirical natural science of the kind with which we are familiar seeks laws that regulate certain natural processes, but Aristotle takes one step farther back by asking for the factors that are equally relevant to any kind of change. He obtains them through confronting existing views *(Ph.* I 2–6). If, like Parmenides, one assumes only a single principle and, at the same time, the absence of change, the variety and changeability of nature cannot be explained. Presupposing, on the other hand, an infinite number of principles, as Democritus does, does not make real nature any more explicable, because an unlimited multiplicity, being unknowable, explains nothing. With regard to this passage *(Ph.* I 4, 187b10–13), Ockham, in his commentary on the *Physics,* the *Expositio in libros Physicorum Aristotelis,* was to put forward his principle of economy, the so-called Ockham's razor, according to which philosophy and science should make do with as few principles as possible. Aristotle, however, considers the assumption of an unlimited number of principles not unnecessary but erroneous, since it makes cognition impossible (see ch. 7. 4).

The way out of his predecessors' difficulties, hinted at above, lies in an intermediary position defined by several, but a limited number of, principles. Between the absolute nothing, which Aristotle, like Parmenides, rejects, and its opposite, absolute being, he places an in-between solution, relative nothing and equally relative being. Since these can be understood both as lack and as possibility, they result in two pairs of opposites: privation-nonprivation and potentiality-actuality, or potentiality-action. Together with their respective underlying concepts, they constitute the two characteristic groups of three of the natural principles, that is, the triadic models of explanation.

According to the first model (*Ph.* I 6–7 and *Metaph.* XII 1–2), there must be (1) something *whence* the motion occurs, that is, a starting-point, (2) something *where* it moves *to,* that is, a final point, and in addition (3) something upon which it occurs, that is, something underlying or a substratum *(hypokeimenon)* which undergoes the change. It seems odd at first that the point of departure is conceived not as neutral but as negative, as a lack *(sterêsis;* literally: deprivation, privation), and complementarily the final point as positive, as a shape or form *(eidos, morphê).* This way of expression is shown to be plausible, though, both by Parmenides' problem and by some examples. Thus, in order to explain the process of becoming learned or healthy, one begins from the final point, namely, learnedness or health, presenting it as being the form (to be reached); the starting point, on the other hand, is presented as absence, to wit, as ignorance or illness. In a similar way, the seed of a tree is a fully grown tree, even though it is still in a state of "lack." Even for transitions from cold to hot or from wet to dry, this way of expression is justified in a rational sense. Viewed from the result that needs to be explained, the starting point lacks something; in retrospect it is a state of not-yet.

In order to determine the substance (What) of the change *(ti esti kinêsis: Ph.* III 1, 200b14), Aristotle introduces a pair of concepts that was to influence Western thought far more than the contrast between privation and form: that between *dynamis,* that is, possibility, capacity, or potentiality, and *energeia*—realization, actuality, or action. The latter concept is related to that of *entelecheia,* the achieved realization in the sense of "having-reached-the-goal *(telos)"* (*Ph.* III 1–3; *Metaph.* IX 3, 8, XI 9). The second pair of concepts gives "being" a dual sense. The unhewn stone "is" already a statue, the seed "is" already a tree, and the apprentice sculptor "is" already a sculptor—even though this is only the case in retrospect and in the mode of possibility, while the finished statue, the fully grown tree and the trained sculptor "are" in the mode of actuality. Since one retains one's capacity even when resting from one's activity, the *de Anima* distinguishes between a total of three levels, given the two levels of reality (II 1, 410a10 ff.) and potentiality (II 5, 417a10 ff.). One possesses a certain knowledge either (1) in the sense of a child having only the possibility, or (2) in the sense of an adult who has acquired a capacity, but, being asleep, does not actualize it, or finally (3) in the sense of actualization. Thus, by means of the second pair of concepts, Aristotle defines motion as an actuality *(entelecheia)* of that which is potentially *(dynamei)* (*Ph.* II 2, 201a10 f; on the interpretation, cf. Kosman 1969).

The concepts of possibility and actuality are related to those of matter/stuff (*hylê:* against an interpretation that is too narrowly "material," cf. Happ 1971) and form/shape *(eidos, morphê)*. Incidentally, both pairs of concepts appear again in the ontology (see ch. 11. 2), albeit from a different point of view. The *Physics* introduces the concepts in order to understand the motion of things, while the ontology (*Metaph.* VII–IX) does so to understand their constitution. A further difference is that the *Physics* merely examines objects composed of matter and form, while first philosophy also concerns itself with autonomous form, without matter (*Ph.* II 2, 194b14 f.).

Just as a brick is, on the one hand, the matter from which the house is built, on the other it is the form into which the clay is baked; so one and the same thing can be matter from one point of view, and form from another. Unlike the different parts of a statue, matter and form are not two objects that can exist independently of each other, but rather they designate the two roles or functions whose interaction explains the generation of an object. Thus, a statue is generated from marble as well as from the mental design *(logos)* of the sculptor (see also *Metaph.* VII 3, 1029a3–5); an animal consists of tissue (bones, flesh, and blood) "put together" according to a certain construction plan. Matter and form are concepts of reflection for two aspects of one and the same object, which in reality only ever appears in the connection of matter and form, as exemplified in Aristotle's example of the snub nose (*Ph.* II 2, 194a6 and *passim*). Matter and form play a dual role: marble is both the matter from which the statue originates and that of which it consists. In the former case it is the predecessor of the statue, in the latter that which is permanently present in it. Analogously, "form" refers to both the mental design, from which the statue originates, and the shape realized in the statue.

Whether he is speaking about privation-form, potentiality-actuality, or matter-form, in his explanations of change, Aristotle, as in his critique of Democritus, always rejects infinite regress (*eis apeiron: Metaph.* XII 3, 1070a2–4; cf. VII 8, 1033b4 ff. and *Ph.* III 4, 204a2–6). Two aspects are important in this connection. On the one hand, when a piece of iron ore is made into a sphere, the result is not roundness, but only an iron sphere. On the other hand, a well-defined explanation suffices: in the example, the matter of iron ore is presupposed as given. Nevertheless, one can pose oneself the further question where the ore comes from. Aristotle gives the same answer formally as present-day natural scientists: he calls the elements of which the ore is composed the fundamental components of matter altogether. (On the supposed *horror infiniti,* see ch. 7. 4.)

Surprisingly, the *Physics* is not just about natural objects, but also about things made by human hands, the products of the craftsman's art *(technê),* or artifacts. Aristotle has two reasons for this. The first consists in a structural analogy: both the leading concept, motion, and the two pairs of contrasts, whence—where to and potentiality—actuality, suit nature and art equally well. One must not take Aristotle's words that art imitates nature (*hê technê mimeitai tên physin: Ph.* II 2, 194a21 f.) in the sense that only things existing in nature can be copied. Nor does Aristotle plead for a (premodern) art, which does not yet pose as an "arrogant mistress of nature" (Zekl 1987, 247), but rather he points out the fact that one first finds the precise structure in nature.

The second reason for dealing with *technê* as well lies in the fact that the contrast provides nature with a more distinct profile. Like all fundamental concepts of philosophy, *physis,* nature, has more than one meaning. According to the dictionary of concepts (*Metaph.* V 4), the first and original meaning of "nature" is the substance of things which move according to an immanent principle; natural things carry the principle of motion and rest in themselves (*Ph.* II 1, 192b13 f.; cf. *Cael.* III 2, 301b17 ff; *GA* II 1, 735a3 f.; *Metaph.* XII 3, 1070a7 f.). Furthermore, "nature" is the stuff or matter *(hylê)* from which forms in the sense of the first concept of nature originate, also the process of generation and growth of such natural forms, and not least the origin of these motions. What does not feature in this list, however, is Nature with a capital *N,* a quasi-person circumspectly and wisely arranging the world. "Nature" for Aristotle is merely a collective word, the embodiment of all things and processes, inclusive of the regularities, in which there is a source of movement. Manufactured things, on the other hand, result from movement imposed from without; they lack an immanent *(emphyton)* drive for change (*Ph.* II 1, 192b18 ff.). It is true that the germ carries within itself the program for becoming first a young shoot, then a small tree and finally a fully grown tree. Similarly, in an animal growth, motion, and procreation occur from within itself. A house, on the other hand, does not build itself out of bricks and beams, but it only does so with the assistance of the architect and the workmen.

Looking at today's intelligent machines, one could get the idea that the gap between them and living organisms is shrinking. However, no computer, however intelligent, has the ability that even an alga possesses, namely that of nourishing itself and procreating. Citing the Sophist Antiphon, Aristotle illustrates the difference between natural objects and artifacts by a thought experiment: bury a wooden bedstead and imagine that in decaying it would put forth a shoot. This would not become, as children expect when burying a plum stone, a "bed tree," or a new bed, but merely wood (Ph. II 1, 193a12–14).

It would be possible to understand the innate source of movement of natural objects in an absolute sense, and Plato knows such pure self-motion, albeit in relation to the soul (*Phaedrus* 245c-d) and finally the world soul, that is, nature in general. Aristotle, however, is not concerned with this, but with individual natural objects (see Bonitz's *Index Aristotelicus,* 835–39). Looking at them, he realizes that they are dependent upon the environment (*periechon: Ph.* VII 3, 246b6; VIII 2, 253a16 f.) as a concomitant cause; as a *pars pro toto* example he mentions the sun (*Ph.* II 2, 194b13). Natural things are not absolute and complete self-movers, but only relative and partial ones; even plants and animals are moved self-movers.

Surprisingly, Aristotle speaks of self-motion not only in the case of organisms, but also in that of nonorganic natural processes, where it sounds like sheer superstition. Falling is not programmed into a stone in the same sense as growth is into an organism. On the other hand, properties immanent in the stone have some joint responsibility for its falling (it is heavier than the atmosphere), so that one can speak of self-motion to a certain extent: when stones are neither held up nor resting on something, they fall downward on their own.

Aristotle devotes a separate treatise to the fourth kind, the simple and complete change directed at the substance *(ousia): On Coming-to-be and Passing-away (Peri geneseôs kai phthoras;* cf. *Ph.* I 7 and *Metaph.* VII 7), which contains a theory of first elements. In contrast with tradition, this does not begin with the four known basic substances, fire, water, air, and earth. The reason is that, since they can be transformed into each other, they cannot be the true *basic* substances. For the truly elementary stuff, Aristotle coins the concept of a first, shapeless matter *(prôtê hylê).* Together with the four elementary qualities, hot, cold, dry, and wet, it belongs to the final and unchangeable conditions for generation and passing away.

Aristotle's view that the four basic substances originate from combinations of the four elementary qualities—earth from cold and dry, water from cold and wet, air from hot and wet, and fire from hot and dry—can be assigned, without qualms, to the realm of antiquarianism. What remains relevant, however, is the question whether "there is" matter that undergoes all changes, a first matter absolute. Johnson (1958), Robinson (1974), and C. J. F. Williams (1982, 211 ff.) answer the question in the affirmative, while Gill (1989, 243 ff.) negates it. The debate hinges on the exact understanding of the phrase "there is." Given that the essential property of first matter is merely the lack of any property, being formless and pure potentiality, it cannot exist as a being. Aristotle himself says that matter of that kind cannot be recognized as such *(Metaph.* VI 10, 1036a8 f.). By saying so he does, however, not exclude the concept of an absolute *sterêsis,* or of a "deprived" substratum (cf. *Metaph.* VII 3), on which the four basic substances can form. In this sense, first matter is merely a concept of reflection. It is not an element occurring in the perceptible world, but a moment that necessarily has to be presupposed in order to explain the generation of the elements as well as the transition from one element to another.

7.3 THE FOUR CAUSES

According to Aristotle, science *(epistêmê)* differs from mere experience *(empeiria)* by its methodical question for the Why. The appropriate replies, the *aitiai*—a word originally meaning accusation or charge—represent all the factors "guilty" of the occurrence of the given. In Latin the word is translated as *causa,* in English as "cause," or sometimes more appropriately as "reason." In early modern times causality is understood primarily as that of a particular kind, namely the relation between the effect and the cause of an event. An event, E_1, is the cause of event E_2, if E_2 happens not only "after" but also "under the influence of" E_1. Aristotle, too, is familiar with this type. However, in opposition to the Ionian natural philosophers as well to Plato and the Academy, he advocates a more comprehensive understanding, a pluralism which he contrasts, with some pride, with the "more archaic" forms of the explanation of nature.

Aristotle opens his theory of causes with the observation of an elementary equivocation: *legetai aitia pollachôs (Ph.* II 3, 195a29). In the subsequent linguistic analysis he distinguishes between four classes of causes *(ta aitia legetai tetrachôs:*

Metaph. I 3, 983a26 f.), which answer an equal number of why-questions. The causes designate the necessary and, taken together, sufficient, conditions for every (natural or technical) change. Like the categories, the causes cannot be be reduced to a single highest species; while there are many sub-classes, there is no common unifying category.

In the relevant passage (*Ph.* II 3), Aristotle adduces a different example for each cause. It may be that by doing so he wants to give an idea of the wide area of application. Let us begin with his first, classic example, the bronze statue. In order to explain its creation, one first needs to know the Out-of-what *(to ex hou gignetai)*, that is, the matter *(hylê)*, which is bronze. The Scholastics would call this the *causa materialis,* the material cause. Secondly, one needs to know the form, pattern, or essential concept *(eidos, paradeigma, logos ho tou ti ên einai),* the *causa formalis,* or formal cause, in Scholasticism. In the present example it is the project in the sculptor's mind, according to which he arranges the material. Aristotle mentions the ratio of "two to one," by which he means the form of the octave interval. Thirdly, one needs to know the principle (origin) of the change *(hothen hê archê tês metabolês/kinêseôs)* called *causa efficiens,* or efficient cause. In the example it is the artist Polycleitus, who sculpts the statue. Aristotle also mentions the giver of advice which, assuming that one follows it, explains the corresponding action, and also the father who generates a being of his kind. The fourth cause is the Because-of-what *(to tou heneka)* or purpose *(telos),* the *causa finalis* or final cause. In the case of the statue, the purpose consists in its function, such as cult worship or decoration; for the giver of advice in the completion of the action, in the case of generation in the child; and in Aristotle's own example the purpose of taking walks is health.

The four causes designate different directions of scientific research, which it also makes sense to distinguish even though, contrary to Aristotle's assumption (e.g., *Ph.* II 7, 198a22), not all four questions always arise. Incidentally, causes two to four can become one (198a24 f.; cf. II 3, 195a4–8): the essential form of the lion is at the same time the purpose toward which the development of a lion moves—from the sperm to the fully grown animal. This process is set in motion through reproduction by an animal of the same animal species; lions only generate lions, not hares or deer.

In early modern times, the finality or teleology supposedly at work throughout nature (e.g., *PA* I 1, 641b10–642a1; cf. Balme 1972, 93–98) became the target of sharp criticism. However, this critique disregards the fact that the question for purpose or goal is simply found among the usual questions for causes. Furthermore, for Aristotle hidden but purposefully active powers have, at the best, metaphorical meaning. He also takes care to distance himself from the all-embracing teleology of Plato's *Timaeus,* and also from the kind of "pious interpretation of nature" that bases the purposefulness of nature on a god. In some passages, however, he mentions god and nature in one breath, for example, when he says at *Cael.* I 4, 271a33 that the god and nature do nothing in vain.

It would appear that where Aristotle speaks of "purpose," early modern natural science frequently assumes mere chance. It is worth noting that Aristotle, too, contemplates the possibility of chance and even distinguishes between two kinds of it (*Ph.* II 4–6; cf. *Metaph.* XII 3, 1070a4 ff.); he only introduces the concept of purpose after discussing those. An example of one of the two kinds of chance, *tychê,* lucky or unlucky coincidence, is that of someone going to the marketplace in order to listen to an oration and encountering a debtor who on this occasion repays his debts (*Ph.* II 4, 196a3–5; II 5, 196b33 ff.). Or a man digs his field and finds a pot full of gold coins (*EN* III 5, 1112a27). Since Aristotle considers this type of chance possible only in beings capable of action, in the case of natural processes only the other type is possible: *automaton,* that is, "by itself." For example, a horse runs away for no special reason and thereby escapes some mishap (*Ph.* II 6, 197b15 f.). Beside this "good coincidence," there is, of course, a "bad coincidence" as well, such as a falling stone injuring somebody (II 6, 197b30–32).

Aristotle relates both kinds of chance to a purpose that is, however, reached or missed in an irregular, unpredicted, and unplanned way. Consequently, he considers as given an either-or form of teleology, or rather deficient modes, assigning *automaton* to *physis* and *tychê* to *technê.* In the case of *tychê,* the fact that it refers indirectly to a nondeficient, true teleology is not contested, since, as Aristotle says with good reason, one could conceivably go to the marketplace with the intention of meeting one's debtor. What is controversial is the question whether one can speak of actual, true purpose in the case of natural processes. Even those who are skeptical toward Aristotle's affirmative answer can acknowledge two things: on the one hand, the answer is not speculative, but it refers to expedience as it can be encountered regularly in nature. Thus, for example, the incisors enable humans to cut food, while the molars enable them to grind it (*Ph.* II 8, 198b23 ff.). On the other hand, Aristotle explicitly refutes the anthropomorphic view that nature has the capability of desiring goals and chosing the means leading to them (*Ph.* II 8, 199a20 f.). Functionality in any realm other than the human occurs without any awareness of purpose; it is retrospective and involuntary.

Aristotle does not ask himself the question following from this, namely how teleological natural connections are directed, that is, what, other than goal-oriented intelligence, makes expedience possible. Consequently, while the thought of an evolution determined by chance is alien to him, it is nevertheless not contrary to his teleology. It is only applied to four areas outside the question of evolution: to 1) the construction of organisms and the function of tissues and organs, 2) the reproduction of species, 3) inorganic processes, and 4) cosmology. In each of these areas the basically analogous concept acquires a different nuance, and thus the question of its range cannot be answered globally. The first and second areas belong to the sphere in which Aristotle's idea of purpose is particularly well rooted, namely, biology (see ch. 8. 2), where in principle teleological thought still remains meaningful. In the third area, however, only treated in passing by Aristotle, it is unconvincing. The fourth area will be discussed later (see ch. 10. 2).

7.4 CONTINUUM, THE INFINITE, PLACE, AND TIME

Four treatises, which nowadays are studied by a small number of experts only (but see Wieland 1992[3], paragraphs 17–18)—partly because of their difficulty, partly because their problems do not attract the usual reader of Aristotle—belong to the best part of Aristotle's œuvre and even of ancient natural philosophy. Within the *Physics* they are distinguished by the greatest accuracy and consistency. I am speaking of the treatises about the unlimited or infinite (*Ph.* III 4–8; cf. *Cael.* I 5–7), space (*Ph.* IV 1–5), time (*Ph.* IV 10–14), and continuity, or the continuum (*Ph.* VI; cf. *de An.* III 6, 430b6–20). All four subjects could be discussed from the standpoint of mathematics, but Aristotle treats them as common and general aspects of the experience of nature (*Ph.* III 1, 200b22 f.). The fact of motion forms the backdrop to them. Of course, this is not merely a certain angle to be taken, but also involves a certain concept of mathematical objects.

While the earlier part of the *Physics* investigates the natural object, as far as motion is possible in it (Ph. I–III 3), here the natural object is left aside and the inner preconditions for motion are queried. In doing so, time and place are the basic prerequisites for the experience of nature, while the unlimited and the continuous are necessary in order to understand the two preconditions. According to Aristotle, time is unlimited, as is the sequence of natural numbers, and the natural processes in their continuous sequence are unlimited in a different sense. Again Aristotle uses his predecessors as points of reference. In opposition mainly to Zeno's famous paradoxes, but also to the atomists, especially Democritus (cf. Furley 1967), as well as the Pythagoreans and Plato, he searches for a theory that can comprehend without contradiction what we know already (cf., e.g., *Ph.* VI 2, 233a13 ff.).

1. With the exception of changes in substance, the natural processes known at the time have a beginning and an end, but between these two extremes they are infinitely divisible; they occur in a *continuum (syneches).* This infinite divisibility enabled Zeno to set up four paradoxes of increasing strength: 1) that a runner cannot move; 2) if this is nevertheless possible: that the fast runner Achilles never even catches up with a tortoise; (3) should he be able to do so: that a flying arrow stops in the air, that is, that no one moves even for a moment; 4) if this is nevertheless the case: that in a chariot race the chariot going at half the speed covers the distance in the same time as that going at twice the speed, that is, that half the time is the same as double the time. To explain the second paradox only: when Achilles reaches the spot where the tortoise had been, the latter has already moved on so that its lead decreases but never disappears entirely (*Ph.* VI 9, 239b5 ff., as well as VI 2, 233a21 ff. and VIII 8, 263a5 ff.; cf. Salmon 1970, Ferber 1981).

Aristotle does not push the paradoxes aside but, on the contrary, he leads us fully into the "labyrinth of the continuum"—as Fromondus (1631) and Leibniz (in: *Philosophische Schriften,* ed. C. I. Gerhardt, II 268) were to call it. It is only after a detailed and emphatic illustration of the difficulties that he shows the way out of the labyrinth. The theory of continuity developed in the end is an example of didactic writing of unusual subtlety and consistency. While the founders of modern natural science never use it for a reconsideration of Aristotle's position as a natural scientist, they never question it either. On the contrary, this didactic passage is part of the foundations that are not thematized and are relativised much later, in this case by quantum theory. Whether it devalues Aristotle's thesis that the minimal particles claimed by atomists such as Democritus (e.g., Diels-Kranz 68 A 57) and later by Epicurus (*letter to Herodot*, 40f.) do not exist is a different question.

Aristotle resolves Zeno's paradoxes through the clarification of a concept. By defining the boundaries between two related phenomena, that which touches *(haptomenon)* and sequence *(ephexês),* he determines the continuous as something with unified external limits (*Ph.* VI 1, 231a22). A continuum is infinitely divisible and yet, contrary to Zeno's assumption, it does not consist of true parts. If motion consisted of the smallest particles, it would be possible by fits and starts only, as we know it from the early days of cinema and for subatomic nature in quantum theory; the flying arrow would be at rest at any point of its trajectory (cf. VI 1, 232a13 f.). If there is to be continuous motion, the respective lines (of motion) consist not of (an infinite number of) points but of lines only (cf. VI 3, 234a8) and the temporal distance consists not of an infinite number of present points ("nows") but again of temporal distances only (IV 11, 220a20 f.). Being unlimited but divisible into like things only, the continuum is at any rate irreducible.

Aristotle concedes to Zeno that the unlimited is involved in motion, but he points out that Zeno disregards the dual meaning of the former (VI 4, 233a24 ff.), that is, its infinite extension or addability and its infinite divisibility (*prosthesei kai dihairesei:* III 6, 206a15 f.). In the Achilles paradox Zeno understands the unlimited as an infinite quantity of distances, in the example of the flying arrow as an infinite number of points; in either case he sees it as infinite extension that is valid for time and the number series but not here, for continuous, that is, infinitely divisible, motion.

2. In the treatise on the infinite or unlimited *(apeiron)* Aristotle not only introduces its even greater equivocation (II 4, 204a2–7), he also refutes false conceptions. In contrast with the Pythagorean or Platonic substantivation of the unlimited as an autonomous substance, Aristotle considers infinity the accident of an accident, that is, the definiteness of a quantity: "infinite" is the property of an extension or a number (III 4, 203a4–16 and III 5).

In order to develop a more precise concept of infinity, he uses the still relevant distinction between the actually *(kat' energeian)* infinite and the potentially *(dynamei)* infinite (II 6, 206a14 ff.). He then goes on to claim that the infinite is only thinkable in the mode of possibility, comparable with matter *(hôs hê hylê),* because the infinite as such is neither recognizable nor determined *(agnôston; ahoriston:* III 6, 207a25 and a 31; cf. I 4, 187b7–13). It is, he writes, thinkable in the mode of reality as well, but only in the way in which one says that the day and the Olympic Games (the basis of chronology for the Greeks) exist (III 6, 206a 21 ff.). The comparison allows for two readings and it would seem that Aristotle means the first. According to this, an individual exemplar of days or Olympic Games is never present as a whole in the way that a tree, a human, or another substance would be; only a certain part is present at any given time. Given that days and the Games are continua, this part can be subdivided into infinitesimally small fractions and therefore into an infinite number of them. According to the second reading, only a definite exemplar is present at any given time, but there are always others—days or Olympic Games—to follow. Thus, as with the first reading, there is potential infinity.

In order to understand the potentiality of the infinite, one should not think of the ontological concept of *dynamis,* that is, potential being, according to which, for instance, a block of marble is a potential statue (III 6, 206a18 ff.). What is relevant here is the kinetic concept of *dynamis* (*Metaph.* IX 6, 1048a25), that is, the ability to do or suffer something (*Metaph.* IX 1, 1046a16 ff.). According to Aristotle, the division of a continuum is a function of thought (*noein: de An.* III 6, 430b7; Wieland 1992³, 300 ff., rightly speaks of an "operative character") which remains *dynamei* insofar as it never reaches an end, given that each element is followed by a new one (*Ph.* VI 6, 206a27 f.). Contrary to general opinion, it is not the case that the infinite has nothing outside itself—that would be the perfect and the whole *(teleion kai holon)*—but there is always something else outside it (III 6, 206b33 ff.).

One often attributes to the Greeks, and in particular to Aristotelian philosophy, a general tendency to shy away from the infinite, a *horror infiniti,* contrasting this attitude with the modern "Faustian" penchant for the infinite. This view needs revising where the infinite divisibility of the continuum as well as the infinity of the number sequence and of time are concerned. It is true that Aristotle advocates a world that is limited in space and the mass of its matter (*Ph.* III 5, 205a31–35). In particular, he rejects infinite regress for sequences of argumentations and conditions (e.g., for causes at *Metaph.* II 2), because he considers it impossible for something to depend upon an infinite number of arguments or conditions. However, for sequences of motion he admits the infinite.

3. The treatise about place *(topos)* deals not with an abstract locality but with the relatively concrete object by which one answers the question "where?" Not least for this reason the Kantian definition—space as an independent a priori, as pure intuitive form—does not occur. Aristotle starts from a problem which Augustine (*Confessiones* XI 14, 17) would take up in reference to time: no one doubts the existence of place, but nevertheless no one knows exactly what it is. In order to work out the adequate definition, Aristotle first deploys the phenomena that need explaining: (1) the fact that all bodies are somewhere, that is, that they have a certain place; (2) the possibility of change of place: when someone sits down, the person takes up the place that had been occupied by a different body, namely by air; (3) the three dimensions of up-down, front-back, and left-right. He reaches the definition by an astute process of exclusion, true to the maxim familiar from the *Ethics* that the good path *(euporia)* remains when all the puzzles (aporias) have been removed (see ch. 6. 3): while place has all the essential properties of bodies, that is, extension in its three dimensions, it cannot be a body because if it were, change of place would be impossible. However, it is not a cause in the sense of the four-cause theory despite certain points the two have in common. Place, like sheer matter, lacks any kind of qualitative and substantial determination, and like form, place, too, has a limiting effect.

Zeno's assumption that place has to be somewhere for the very reason that it exists leads to the aporia that the place in which place exists also needs to be in a place, etc. Given that infinite regress is out of the question, only two options remain to Aristotle. According to the first, space is the interstice or empty space between boundaries that can be filled by any kind of body. As the consequence of this option—there are places without bodies, i.e., empty space—leads to untenable consequences, there remains only the option that becomes the final definition. According to this, place is the inner boundary of the next body at rest enclosing another body (*Ph.* IV 4, 212a2 ff.). This definition is well suited to bodies, thus the place of water is, for instance, the glass, the tub, or the riverbed, and above it is the contiguous air. The entirety of bodies, namely, the universe, however, is no longer in a place.

It would be worthwhile pursuing the question whether Aristotle considers place as a whole including smaller places as its parts. If this is the case, he preempts part of the Kantian insight that space has intuitive rather than conceptual character. Needless to say, the essential difference remains that for Aristotle space belongs to physical objectivity, while for Kant it belongs to transcendental subjectivity.

4. The discussion of time *(chronos)*, the unchanging measure of change, opens with two difficult questions (*Ph.* IV 10, 217b29–218a30). The first is: does time belong to what is or to what is not? After all, part of it has already passed, while another is still about to happen; something that contains such an amount of nonbeing can hardly "be" on its own account. The second question is: is what separates the past and the future, that is, the now, always the same or always different? According to Aristotle's reply, time is neither autonomous nor, as Plato assumes in the *Timaeus* (37d), something created (*Ph.* VIII 1, 251b17 ff. and *Cael.* I 10, 280a28 ff. refute this). Rather, it exists as an epiphenomenon of natural processes, or more precisely, as an experience made by the mind faced with natural, meaning, changing, things.

Natural processes always occur in time without, however, being identical with it. While place is related to the static, that is, bodies, time is related to the dynamic, that is, change. Not only is time countable, or rather measurable, it also has a recognizable direction: there is an earlier and a later. Consequently, Aristotle defines time as the "number of motion according to the earlier and the later" (*Ph.* IV 11, 219b1 f.), adding "since it is the number of a continuum, it is continuous" (220a25 f.). Because of its continuous character, the understanding of time cannot be based on the now, although the now is what is best known (219b29). By adding now-points, one no more achieves a distance in time than one reaches a distance in space by adding points of space (*Ph.* VI 10, 241a2–6; on Aristotle's theory of time, cf. Sorabji 1983.)

It is astonishing that Aristotle already poses himself the question whether time is "added in thought" within the soul (*prosennoôn: de An.* III 6, 430b1; on psychological time, cf. *Peri mnêmês* 449b), but he rejects this option of time as an element of subjectivity, as Kant would phrase it. While he considers the soul as a necessary prerequisite of time, this is intended only in the sense that time has operative character: it is connected with counting. Time is not mere duration but a mass of units of time; their measure is not based on the now but on temporal distances between two now-points, such as hours, days, months, and years. Counting, on the other hand, is dependent upon a counting instance, namely, the mind (*Ph.* IV 14, 223a22–29). Thus, according to Aristotle, time neither exists through the soul nor is it preformed in the latter, but time does not exist without the activity of counting performed by the soul.

The fact that Aristotle does not preempt Kant's thought of an independent a priori—time as pure intuitive form—may have something to do with his theory of mathematical objects. He sees them as abstractions of the experience of nature; mathematical objects are contemplated separately from natural objects, but in reality they do not exist separately. (On Aristotle's theory of mathematics: *Metaph.* XIII–XIV; see Heath 1949, Annas 1976, Graeser 1987, and Detel 1993, 189–232.) Aristotle's concept of numbers takes its bearings from a counting of things that refers to the respective adequate unit of measurement, that is, to their genus or species. Thus, when it is horses that are being counted, the measure is "horse," when it is humans, it is "human," and when it is human, horse, and god, the measure is "living being" (*Metaph.* XIII 1, 1088a8–11). One can say therefore that when there is an equal number of sheep and dogs, the number ten is the same, but the ten-ness is not (*Ph.* IV 14, 224a2–4). In brief: since Aristotle does not consider mathematics a construct of intuition preexisting in nature, he achieves only a physical theory for both time and space.

Time is measured by clocks. In conformity with tradition, Aristotle recognizes a first and last clock, namely, the pure circular motion of the first heaven (*Ph.* IV 14, 223b18–10). Needless to say, it has its rank of an absolute clock—and there is also absolute time according to it—not for physical reasons, that is, general reasons of natural philosophy, but for more specific cosmological ones.

8

BIOLOGY AND PSYCHOLOGY

8.1 ARISTOTLE THE ZOOLOGIST

Although discussion has become more wide-ranging recently (see, for example, the magazine *Biology and Philosophy,* 1986 ff.), biology is not among the main interests of present-day philosophers; for Aristotle, however, it represents an important sector of empirical as well as theoretical natural science. Leaving botany to Theophrastus, he devoted the most extensive part of his writings to zoology (including biological anthropology or human biology). However, in turning toward zoology, he had to overcome an epistemic barrier: the Greeks, including Aristotle, believed that the realm of the stars ranked more highly than that of humans and animals. This attitude, which threatened to lead to the neglect of non-cosmological research into nature, is opposed by Aristotle's famous plea in favor of a comprehensive natural science that values equally the various spheres (*PA.* I 5, 644b22–645a36). Whilst not upturning the usual ranking or putting cosmology last, he acknowledges zoology as equal using the three following arguments.

According to the second of those, the superiority of cosmology is counterbalanced by familiarity: plants and animals are closer to humans than are the divine stars (645a2–4). According to the third argument, even the lowest animals have something admirable about them because of their functionality (645a4–26). However, the most important appears to be the first argument which is based on greater scientific profit (644b22–645a2). While the greater dignity of cosmological objects and the more intense joy involved in knowing them is not accompanied by a large quantity of material for observation (cf, *Cael.* II 12, 292a14 ff.), there is an abundance of the latter to be found in the investigation of plants and animals as long as one makes the necessary effort. According to Plato, observation only provides pleasure for the senses but does not achieve any true knowledge (*Timaeus* 28a). According to Aristotle, however, in biology not only pure theory is possible but so is an *episkepsis,* that is, an examination that interferes with its object and investigates its parts (blood, flesh, bones, etc.) more closely through dissection. Thus, for example, he twice describes the dissection of the hidden eyes of the blind mole (*aspalae: HA* I 9, 491b28; IV 8, 533a3). The remarkably precise description of the octopus, including its particular form of reproduction, namely, hectocotyl-ization, would appear to be based on dissection (IV 1, 524a3–20).

True to his plea for epistemic equality, Aristotle is the founder of zoology not only as a scientific discipline: he distinguished several specialist spheres (general foundations, anatomy, physiology, behavioral studies, etc.) and composed mono-graphs of high scientific standing on each of them. While, according to one his-torian of science, "the origin of modern biological thought consists partly in its emancipation from Platonic philosophy," he can say that "no one living before Darwin has made a contribution to our understanding of the living world as great as that made by Aristotle. . . . Almost every branch of the history of biology needs to begin with Aristotle." (E. Mayr, *Die Entwicklung der biologischen Gedanken-welt*, 1984, 73).

Part of the texts has been lost, among them the seven books of the *Anatomi-cal Descriptions (Anatomai)*, but the most important texts have been preserved: *On the Parts of Animals (PA)* and the *Zoology (History of Animals; HA)*, as well as *On the Generation of Animals (GA)*, *On the Progression of Animals (Peri poreias zôôn)* and *On the Motion of Animals (MA)*. Furthermore, there are the texts on biologi-cal psychology, the so-called *Smaller Writings on Natural Science (Parva naturalia)*, which are of high quality despite their brevity. Among those are *On Sense Percep-tion and its Objects, On Memory and Remembrance, On Sleeping and Waking*, and *On Dreams*. One could say that the treatise on memory is among the best ever written on the subject (see Meyer 1855 and more recently Balme 1972, Düring 1961, Gotthelf 1985, Gotthelf-Lennox 1987, and Kullmann 1979[2]).

Aristotle's zoology is distinguished by such a wealth of observational data and such highly differentiated terminology that with good reason it was the foundation (together with the logic) of the philosopher's actual fame for centuries. It was Dar-win who once wrote enthusiastically that Aristotle is "one of the greatest observers, if not the greatest, who ever lived" (letter to Crawley, 12 February 1879). The sur-viving material is of such extent that it is hard to imagine that it was all produced by one person; one is inclined to believe the anecdote in Pliny (first century C.E.), according to which Alexander the Great put several thousand people at the philosopher's disposal (*Natural History* VIII 16.44). Nevertheless, the anecdote is totally implausible and it would seem that for his material Aristotle draws partly on his own observations, partly on literature, such as Hippocratic medical works, and in particular on inquiries among fishermen, shepherds, hunters, bee-keepers, and other experts.

Aristotle is often accused of producing a natural science that ventures general statements without investigating all the facts at first. To begin with, the "theory" of induction outlined in the *Posterior Analytics* (see ch. 5. 3) contradicts this claim. Even though Aristotle occasionally relies on a "telling single case," for a scientific induction he nevertheless demands knowledge of all the species belonging to a genus (*APr.* II 23, 68b27–29). His critique of Democritus follows the same crite-ria (*GA* V 8, 788b9 ff.). It is particularly in the zoology that he adheres to his maxim: he collects facts before risking explanations. Repeatedly he points out the existence of observations because of which a theory can be formed, or elsewhere the lack of observations making caution necessary when forming a theory (cf. *APo.* II 14 f. and *PA* 674b7 ff.).

Let us take the example of Aristotle's most voluminous work, the *Zoology:* divided into two thematic fields, anatomy (I–IV 7) and physiology (IV 8–11) on the one hand, and behavioral studies or ethology (V–VI and VIII; there are, however, doubts regarding the authenticity of VII and IX–X) on the other, it presents its subject matter to the extent to which it was known at the time. We read about domestic animals (sheep, goats, dogs, camels, etc.), wild animals (bears, lions, hyenas, and other mammals), countless insects, worms, and parasites, birds, amphibians, and, in particular detail, about marine creatures. The ethological books do not discuss questions of animal psychology but rather they deal with reproduction, birth, and nourishment, as well as the way animals adapt to the climate and the change of season, and with disease. They provide detailed information about, for example, the beginning and duration of fertility, the way and time of copulation and the duration of pregnancy, as well as about a great variety of types of nutrition, including the fattening of pigs, and not least about the migration of birds or fish and hibernation. However, according to the principle of theory of science that states that one needs to "start from what is familiar" (see ch. 3. 2), the text begins with humans (*HA* I 6, 491a19 ff.; similarly at *PA* II 10, 656a9 f.).

Needless to say, there are some errors among the large number of statements, thus for example the mating of insects is described incorrectly (*GA* I 16, 21a3 ff.). Aristotle also considers possible (equivocal) generation without parents, or spontaneous procreation (*HA* V 19, 551a1–7); however, one needs to keep in mind that it would not have been possible before Pasteur to prove that even microorganisms do not consist of inanimated matter. Furthermore, he claims that palpitations are possible in humans only because they are the only beings to live in expectation of the future (*PA* III 6, 669a19 ff.). One must not reproach Aristotle seriously for not remaining free of error in empirical experience or theory, but rather one must admire the many accurate observations—even more so if one considers that they are achieved without present-day technical devices.

As an empiric, Aristotle wants to represent nature in its sheer immeasurable variety, while as a theoretician he seeks, as far as possible, to give a systematic connection to this variety. Therefore, the systematic collecting is followed by evaluation, that is, the sifting and examination of the material, which is not always homogeneous. In doing so, Aristotle continues the dialectic of the Academy, whilst replacing, in a remarkably undogmatic manner, its schematic dichotomy with several suggestions for a structure based on experience. (On the critique of dichotomy, see *PA* I 2–3; on the criteria for biological classification, see *Top.* VI 6; *APo.* I 31, II 5, II 13; *Metaph.* VII 12; also *Pol.* IV 4, 1290b25–37; in particular *HA* I 1–6, *PA* I 2–4, and *GA* II 1.) The most important suggestion begins with two main genera, namely sanguineous and bloodless animals, corresponding to the distinction between vertebrates and invertebrates. The sanguineous animals are subdivided into viviparous and oviparous, the bloodless into mollusks (cuttlefish and octopodes-cephalopods), malacostracans (shrimps, lobsters, and crabs), crustaceans (including shells), and insects (*HA* II–IV). As was noted by Meyer (1855,

344 ff.) already, Aristotle is not aiming at a strict systematics of genera and species in the modern sense. What he wants to achieve by distinguishing recognizable characteristics is not essentially a classification of the animal world but a definition of its last (natural) species (*eschata eidê*, cf. *PA* I 2, 642b5 ff.). Given that definitions are found by way of divisions (*APr.* I 31; *APo.* II 5 and 13), a "system" of zoological definitions at the same time, as a side effect, produces the basic skeleton of a zoological classification (cf. *HA* I 1, 486a5–25).

In different contexts Aristotle distinguishes the animals, according to their habitat, into aquatic, terrestrial, and occasionally flying animals; also, according to their way of life, into herd and solitary animals, furthermore into diurnal and nocturnal or tame and wild animals (e.g., *HA* I 1, 487a15 ff.). The various forms of reproduction also appear as criteria for classification, as well as the degree of development of the new-born offspring (*GA* II 1).

Finally, Aristotle brings all of nature into a hierarchical order, the ladder of nature (*scala naturae*). The order of ranking—from the imperfect to the perfect—begins with inanimate things and, by way of plants and animals, leads up to man. There is a continuous gradation between the inorganic and the organic and then between plants and animals (*PA* IV 5, 681a12–15; cf. *HA* VIII 1, 588b4–6), and at times it is dubious whether something belongs to the higher or the lower step (*HA* VIII 1, 588b12 f.). In *PA* (IV 5, 681a9–b12) Aristotle lists intermediary forms between plants and animals such as the testaceans (*ostrakodermata;* cf. *GA* II 23, 731b8 f.). As far as the body is concerned—and only in that respect—he recognizes an intermediary form between quadruped mammals and humans: the ape (*HA* II 8–9, 502a16–b26). Above humans is the world of perfect processes, of the eternal circles and fixed stars, and the pinnacle of the hierarchy is the Unmoved Mover (see ch. 10).

Although we have become skeptical about ontological hierarchies, Aristotle's ladder (with the exclusion of the world above humans) seems altogether plausible to us. Its measure is the differentiation of organs and the amount of functional capacities. (The measure is reminiscent of the ontological pair of concepts, matter and form, insofar as, as a rule, matter designates something that is slightly less structured and form something that is slightly more structured.) Thus, plants have no kind of sense perception, while lower animals have only traces of tactile sense, higher animals have a sense of smell and taste; the even higher ones possess all five senses as well as memory and (rudimentary) learning and, according to the *Ethics* (VI 7, 1141a24–28), even of intelligence in the sense of foresight. Finally, only humans have the capacity of reflection and of consciously recalling something to memory (*HA* I 1, 488b24–26). As far as living habits are concerned, the lower animals know only self-preservation and reproduction, higher animals pleasure in procreation and care for their young. In lower animals the latter ends with birth (mere brood care), in higher ones it includes rearing and in the highest animals—not different from humans—the care continues until the young are ready to be independent (*HA* VIII 1, 588b24–589a2; *GA* III 2, 753a7–14). Even higher than mere care is life in social groups (*HA* VIII 1), but only humans are capable of this good life (*eu zên; PA* II 10, 656a5 ff.), which is the condition for the continuation of biology in ethics and politics.

8.2 TELEONOMY: ORGANISMS, PROCREATION, AND HEREDITY

More recent natural science distinguishes between teleological processes that are merely following a built-in program and those that are controlled consciously. In the former there is only an inner purpose—teleonomy—but in the latter there is a purposefulness directed by conscience, that is, true teleology. In biology Aristotle claims only teleonomy as it is still recognized today. He neither believes that all purposefulness can in the end be explained in a non-teleological manner (for him teleology is more than just a *façon de parler*), nor does he assume mysterious teleological factors, because for him teleology is an observable natural phenomenon.

He sees a first kind of teleology in the function of tissues and organs. According to *PA* II 2, the bones exist for the sake of the flesh, that is, they protect and support it. The blood vessels are needed for the blood; the liver serves the digestion ("cooking") of food; the legs exist for progression, while the purpose of nails, claws, hooves, and horns is the preservation of life. This teleology of organisms in its turn serves certain purposes on a second level, namely the basic functions of life. These are arranged in a hierarchical structure and correspond to the aforementioned hierarchy of plant-animal-human.

Aristotle recognizes a second kind of biological teleology in the reproduction of a living being of the same species and with some of its parents' characteristics (cf. Lesky 1951 and Kullmann 1979[2]; on the history of embryology, see Needham 1955[2]). The words "a human procreates a human" are used repeatedly (*Metaph.* VII 7, 1032a25; XII 3, 1070a8; a27 f.; XIV 5, 1092a16 and *passim*). The topic of reproduction, differentiation of the sexes, and the theory of heredity is dealt with in the treatise *On the Generation of Animals*. An investigation based on an extraordinary wealth of data, it presents its topic both from a general point of view and separately for the various classes of animals as well as for plants. According to Aristotle, besides sexual procreation there is also, as mentioned above, spontaneous generation and, in some animals such as certain kinds of eels, parthenogenesis (*HA* IV 11; nowadays these animals are considered hermaphrodites).

In order to explain heredity, Anaxagoras as well as the atomists Leucippus and Democritus advocate a view that appears in writings of the *Hippocratic Corpus* and is later taken up by Darwin: the "theory of pangenesis" (*The Variation of Animals*, 1868, II, 357 ff.). According to this theory, genetic material derives from all (Greek: *pan*) parts of the body. The aforementioned Pre-Socratics combine it with the view that a little human (Latin: *homunculus*) is already formed in advance (or pre-formed, wherefore it is also called "theory of preformation") within the genetic material. Aristotle opposes this opinion with a position that would later become known as "theory of epigenesis," supported especially by the anatomist Caspar Friedrich Wolff (*Theoria generationis*, 1759, §§ 232 and 235), and would replace the predominant theory of epigenesis.

Aristotle procedes in his usual way. First he presents the counter-theory together with its arguments (*GA* I 17), then he invalidates the arguments (I 18), and only subsequently he develops his own theory (I 19 ff.). To name only some of his objections: 1) even characteristics not yet present at procreation, such as a beard or greying hair, are inherited; 2) so are characteristics without material elements, such as the gait; 3) in plants the husks are also transmitted although no part of them enters into the seed.

The way in which Aristotle achieves his counter-theory is not speculative but markedly modern, that is to say, experimental, using the example of the chicken. Every day he opens a hen's egg, observes the progress of its development (*HA* IV 3) and then makes a generalization. According to the latter, the organs of a living being develop successively, the characteristics of the genus developing before those of the species (*GA* II 3, 736a27–b13; cf. III 2, 753b25–29; V 1, 778b20–779a11). First the embryo acquires its vegetative faculties, then the sensory ones. In humans the mind *(nous)* is added last and from outside *(thyrathen)*. The reason for this lies in the nature of mind: given that it is incorporeal and therefore divine and eternal, it already exists in advance.

Ernst Haeckel was to develop the theory of epigenesis into the basic law of biogenetics, according to which ontogenesis, the development of an individual, re-capitulates phylogenesis, that is, the history of the tribe. His pupil, Hans Driesch, assumes what he calls the "E factor" for the direction of embryonal development, alluding to the Aristotelian concept of entelechy (*Philosophie des Organischen,* Leipzig 1909, 126 ff.) Aristotle himself, however, does not use this term in the context of his embryology and genetics, but instead he develops a model of hered-ity which, whilst still being mechanist, is nevertheless astonishingly modern. Ac-cording to this model, the carriers of genetic information are impulses (*kinêseis*: movements) situated in the blood, some of which are responsible for the genus, others for the species, and yet others for the gender or the shape of the individual parts of the body. As Aristotle considers blood not only the means of transport for nutritive substances, but also as the ultimate form of nourishment (*PA* II 4, 651a14 f.; *GA* I 19, 726b1 ff.), he supports the theory of haematogenous sperm based on Diogenes of Apollonia (fifth century B.C.E.). According to this, male sperm is produced as the surplus *(perittôma)* of processed ("cooked") nutriment in the blood. At procreation it transmits its impulses to the female counterpart, in the same way in which a carpenter transmits certain impulses to his tools, which in turn transmit them to the material (*GA* I 22, 730b4 ff. and b11 ff.). According to this pattern, the male contribution, sperm, is effective not through its bodily substance—which evaporates, becoming pneuma—but merely as immaterial form. The female, on the other hand, contributes matter only (*GA* I 21). Even though individual aspects of this view may be outdated, the *telos* of procreation, that is, a new living being of the same species and with its parents' hereditary fac-tors, is to be considered as preprogrammed in a literal sense. Thus, Aristotle does not need a mysterious entelechy, or an "E factor," as a directive element.

In a short text prefacing his main work, namely, in the *Historical Sketch of the Progress of Opinion on the Origin of Species,* Darwin says that a passage in Aristotle's *Physics* II 8 (198b23–31) preempts the theory of evolution or, more precisely, its principle of natural selection. And indeed, Aristotle cites the view that only those organs survive that are useful for a purpose by chance (*apo tou automatou*/on their own: b30). He does not, however, make this view his own, so that it is the very absence of a theory of evolution that distinguishes him from modern biology. He may be moving toward it with his hierarchy of nature, but, on the other hand, he believes that the programs of the different species are given in an unalterable way—even though he concedes that new species can result from hybrids and that there are species overlapping with each other (*GA* II 1, 732b15 ff.). He does not know of a transmutation of species.

8.3 THE SOUL

The term *soul* no longer plays a part in modern natural science or even psychology, and the fact that Aristotle uses it at all arouses skepticism. What is more, he speaks of a soul not only in the case of humans, but also for animals and even plants, and criticizes the philosophers who have only the human soul in view (*de An.* I 1, 402b3–5). There is good cause for skepticism not so much concerning Aristotle's theory of the soul but that of his predecessors, particularly the kind of soul-body dualism that had been known in the West since the Orphic mysteries and the Pythagoreans, was endorsed by Empedocles and, in particular, Plato (e.g., in the *Phaedo*) and had been prevalent since in different varieties. However, Aristotle rejects it vehemently (on the Pythagoreans' difficulties with dualism, see *de An.* I 3, 407b2 ff.; the refutation of Empedocles: I 4, 408a18 ff.) and thus offers an alternative approach for various kinds of dualism until the present day. In the same way he opposes the "physicalist" attempts to define the soul as something merely physical (against Hippo and Critias: I 2, 405b2 f.).

With the argument that in living beings neither the soul nor its affects, such as anger or fear, exist separately from matter (I 1, 403b17–19), Aristotle assigns the soul to the concern of the natural scientist (*physikos*: a28 f., b7 and 11; also *PA* I 1, 641a22 and *Metaph.* VI 1, 1026a5 f.). One might say that this matter-of-fact attribution is one of his greater philosophical achievements. However, in this case natural science is to be understood not as empirical science but as a fundamental discipline. While the *Physics* examines the fundamental concepts and principles of all natural things, the *On the Soul* discusses those of all living things. It is not psychology in the modern sense, since it does not investigate mental matters (consciousness, intentionality) as such but the organic (from plants to humans by way of the animals) as opposed to the inorganic. By discussing the philosophical foundations of all of biology, including human biology, Aristotle presents something like a fundamental philosophy or metaphysics of living beings. Inasfar as he deals with humans in this context, he considers them living beings, that is, higher animals.

Needless to say, some aspects of the soul are not tied to corporeality. These are therefore not the natural scientist's concern but—in the case of mathematical objects—that of the mathematician and—in the case of pure spirit—that of the first philosopher (*de An.* I 1, 403b15 f.; cf. *PA* I 1, 641a32–b10). Furthermore, there are cross-connections—with biology of course, but also with ethics. The explanation of the soul as moving force in the *de Anima* overlaps with the theory of action in the *Ethics* (see ch. 13), while the examination of the mind (*nous*: III 3–8) connects with the theory of the epistemic faculties (*EN* VI). (On the interpretation of the *de Anima*, cf. Barnes-Schofield-Sorabji 1975, Cassirer 1932, Furth 1988, Lloyd-Owen 1978, Theiler 1986[7].)

The starting point of Aristotle's conception of the soul is that—with the exception of special cases of incorporeal beings—it discusses its subject only with regard to a body endowed with soul. The body, on the other hand, is not only concerned by what happens in the soul, but it also plays an essential part in these events. In order to make it clear that the processes of living beings (from the nutrition of a plant to human perceptions and even to lack of self-control: *EN* VII 5, 1147a16) do not occur incidentally but within the unity of body and soul of these beings, Aristotle falls back upon a pair of concepts which he generally uses to oppose ontological dualisms, namely matter and form. An actual living being consists of the body *(sôma)* as matter and the form that turns mere potential life *(dynamei zôê: de An.* II 1, 412a20) into an actual living being. What the term *soul* refers to is not a special, corporeal or incorporeal thing, but rather that which distinguishes a dead body from a living one. The soul is what makes a living being alive; it is its principle of actuality. Just as, according to Aristotle's ontology, form does not exist separately from concrete things (see ch. 11. 2), the soul does not exist separately from the (living) body *(de An.* II 1, 413a4). It keeps the body together and provides its unity; without the soul the body would perish and rot (I 5, 411b8–10). In this sense the soul is defined first as the principle of living beings (I 1, 402a6 f.) and later, more precisely, as the cause and principle of the living body (II 4, 415b8 ff.). In conformity with the theory of the four causes (see ch. 7. 3), it is a cause in every sense, that is, form, purpose, and principle of motion. The only thing lacking is the material cause, which is provided by the body.

In contrast with artifacts, living beings are natural objects that carry within themselves the principle of motion and rest; the principle inherent in the living being itself is the soul. In order to explain, Aristotle uses an analogy between a tool, the axe, and a part of a living being, the eye (II 1, 412b10 ff.). If the axe were a living being, its soul would be the ability to split wood; where this ability is absent, it is only an axe by name. The analogous task of the eye lies in its capacity to see; what is left if the latter disappears is no more an eye than a painted or sculpted eye is.

The actualization achieved by the soul is called entelechy (I 1, 402a10; II 1, 412a10 ff.; II 5, 417a21 ff.). The frequently misunderstood concept designates the moment in which something arrives "in its goal" *(en telei)*, that is, reaches its completion. The term is almost synonymous with *energeia* (realization, act), but Aristotle prefers "entelechy" when he wants to emphasize the moment of fulfilment or completion, while he prefers the term *act* for emphasizing the moment of activity. In the same way in which he posits the entelechy of the axe in the splitting of wood and that of the eye in seeing, he equates the entelechy of a living being with its aliveness. The soul is not something a living being "has," but its full reality, its being-alive. Since a living being can be either awake or asleep, one needs to distinguish between two meanings. The relation of sleep to awakeness in life is the same as in the case of science that of the capacity *(epistêmê)* to the realization of this capacity, namely contemplation *(theôrein)*, in science. Both in sleep and in awakeness

the soul is the entelechy of life, but in the former it is so only in the sense of the capacity for certain processes of life, while in the latter it is their actualization.

Given that the soul is not an independent substance and even less a property (accident) but rather the entelechy of a body-soul totality (II 2, 414a14 ff.; cf. I 1, 403a3 ff.), it cannot have an existence disjoined from the body. The single faculties of the soul are linked to respective organs, on the basis of something like a hypothetical necessity. Just as an axe can fulfil its task only if it is made from a hard material (bronze or iron), so a body—or an organ—fulfils its purpose only if it is "constructed" in an appropriate way (*PA* I 1, 642a9–13; cf. for the eye: *Sens.* 2, 438a12–16).

The only exception from the body-soul unity is the spirit *(nous);* it is not connected with any organ (*de An.* III 4, 429a24–27). However, one needs to distinguish between the transient element that is linked to the body and perishes with it, and the other, which is incorporeal and therefore imperishable and at the same time divine as well as impersonal (II 4, 413b24–29 and III 5, 430a22–25). The view that only the impersonal spirit is immortal was to prove problematic for Christian Aristotelianism: Aristotle excludes the immortality of the individual soul. He is also critical of the Pythagorean dogma of the migration of souls (I 3, 407b21–26; cf. II 2, 414a17–25). Nevertheless, every animate being, even a plant, "participates in the eternal and the divine" by its "most natural achievement," that is, through the reproduction of a being of the same species (II 4, 415a26–b1).

The definition of the soul as principle of being alive only designates its essence "in outline" (*typô:* II 1, 413a9). The more detailed definition occurs only by way of the various vital functions, or faculties of the soul (cf. II 3, 415a12 f.). It is in this context that Aristotle speaks of the *scala naturae,* that is, the sequence plant-animal-human, represented as the ascent toward ever richer and more complex vital processes (II 2–3; see ch. 8. 1). Some Pre-Socratics, for example, Empedocles (Diels-Kranz 31 B 110) and Anaxagoras (Diels-Kranz 59 A 117) attribute perception, feeling, and desire to plants; according to Plato's *Timaeus* (77b), too, they have desires as well as the perception of pain and pleasure. According to Aristotle, however, the vegetative soul ("plant soul") is limited to nutrition, growth, and reproduction (*de An.* II 4). Only at the stage of the animal soul perception (II 5–III 2), combined with pain, pleasure, or desire, becomes possible. The three animal faculties are connected in such a way that Aristotle can reduce them to two—perception *(aisthêsis)* and appetence *(orexis)*—and declare them identical (III 7, 431a9–14). Occasionally he even characterizes animals, *pars pro toto,* by perception alone (II 2, 413b2; cf. III 9; 432b19 f.). The third kind of soul, the human, is in charge of the mind and the *logos* (III 3–8).

All three vital functions—vegetative, animal, and human faculties of the soul—are discussed at length but, given that the treatise is about natural philosophy, it is perception that is given the most thorough treatment (II 5–III 2). In opposition to Democritus, Aristotle demonstrates that there are only five senses (III 1), devoting a separate chapter to each of them (II 7–11). The sense of touch is considered elementary because, together with taste, it makes nutrition possible (III 12, 434b10 ff.), while the "higher senses," that is, those serving well-being (*eu:*

b24), are more differentiated. On the whole, the sequence is ordered in such a way that higher living beings dispose of the respective lower vital functions and adapt them according to their higher vital functions. Thus, nutrition, perception, and reproduction are not the same in humans as in the other living beings.

Let us focus on one topic, namely, the distinction—important for the epistemological side of psychology—between passive intellect *(nous pathêtikos)* and active intellect *(nous poiêtikos/apathês)*. The chapter discussing this, III 5, is "infamous for its opacity and brevity" (Theiler 1986[7], 142); these few (sixteen) lines probably belong to the most commented on passages in all of ancient philosophy. Aristotle's, initially barely intelligible, distinction results, on the one hand, from the conceptual pair "potentiality" and "act" and, on the other, from the parallelism, and at the same time difference, between thought and perception (III 4 and 8). To mention a common point in advance: a relation to the self is present not only in thought but already in perception. When we see or hear, we perceive by the same faculty *that* we see or hear (III 2, 425b12–25; cf. *EN* IX 9, 1170a29 ff.); this consciousness of the self includes a moment of self-affirmation.

According to the common points, central to the distinction between passive and active reason, perception and thought each have a capacity of reception which is activated by something else. In the case of perception, this is activated only when objects appear in the field of perception; the moment triggering reality comes from outside *(exôthen:* II 5, 417b20). Thought, on the other hand, is not dependent on external objects, and therefore the difference between passive capacity for reception and its activation (in modern terms, of receptivity and spontaneity) is situated within thinking itself. Like an empty writing tablet *(de An.* III 4, 429b31 f.), the passive intellect has unlimited receptivity, which is made to achieve reality by the active intellect just as light makes colors actually visible.

9

FIRST PHILOSOPHY, OR METAPHYSICS

The discipline Aristotle places at the top of the hierarchy of forms of knowledge was to be considered the "queen of sciences" for many centuries, but it was to be treated with "the greatest contempt" (*Kritik der reinen Vernunft,* preface of the first edn.) in Kant's times and again, later, by Nietzsche and, in a different way, by the Vienna Circle. This discipline is metaphysics. It is often expected to provide information about the supernatural: if not about angels, then at least about gods or the god, as well as about the immortality of the soul and freedom. Not infrequently, these expectations are combined with the belief that the meaning of human existence cannot be decoded without these elements. Philosophers, in particular since German idealism, have been anticipating a system that would be a framework for all knowledge and allocate a place in the whole to every fact.

Such expectations are for the most disappointed by Aristotle. Nevertheless he postulates, at least implicity, something that is doubted in the analytical and hermeneutic critique of metaphysics, namely, knowledge that is independent of language and history. This situation, in which a claim on metaphysics is combined with an understanding deviating from many conceptions of metaphysics, is worth noting. In his theology Aristotle does not ponder about a hereafter, which would give meaning to our existence in this world, but about the explicability of the latter. Neither in doing so nor anywhere else does he make any claims for having a system comparable to those voiced by German idealism. For both these reasons his attempt is still of interest today: the former makes it of interest for a metaphysics in the age of (natural) science, the latter for a metaphysics that is post-idealist because of its more modest systemic claim.

The term *metaphysics* was not coined by Aristotle but by the editor of his works, Andronicus (see ch. 1. 2); it refers to the part of the œuvre coming after or beyond *(meta)* the natural things *(physika)*. Aristotle himself uses other expressions: he calls the necessary intellectual competence *sophia,* wisdom (*Metaph.* I 1–2), the practice of this competence *theôria* (*EN* X 8; *Metaph.* XII 7, 1072b22 ff.), and in some of the texts he uses what was to be Descartes's preferred title for the discipline (cf. *Meditationes de prima philosophia*): first philosophy (*prôtê philosophia: Metaph.* VI 1, 1026a16; XI 4, 1061b19; *Ph.* I 9, 192a36 f.; II 2, 194b14 f.; *Cael.* I 8, 277b10. In *de An.* I 1, 403b16 he even speaks of the "first philosopher").

In Greek the word we translate as "wisdom" does not designate something like a venerable life experience combined with particularly sound judgment, but rather an ability developed to mastery, the kind of know-how that, *qua* expertise, is the object of high esteem. "Wisdom" in this sense is attributed to master craftsmen, such as to "Phidias as stone-mason and Polycleitus as sculptor" (*EN* VI 7, 1141a9–11). In the introductory chapter of the *Metaphysics* (I 1) this term of everyday language is transferred to the sphere of cognition, and it is only thus that *sophia* becomes a mastery of knowledge in general, an epistemic superlative belonging to the realm of philosophy. Those who, like Thales and Anaxagoras, desire to know "the astonishing, difficult and divine" (*EN* VI 7, 1141b3 ff.) are considered as paragons. In contrast with the penultimate stage, that is, ordinary science and philosophy, it is a matter of principles common to all the sciences; Aristotle speaks of the ruling science (*archikôtera:* Metaph. I 2, 982a16 f.) and the science in command of everything (*epistêmê kyria pantôn: APo.* I 9, 76a18). First philosophy is understood as fundamental science or philosophy.

It is tempting to think of the post-Aristotelian title *Metaphysics* as a merely external designation chosen for reasons of editorial technique, which is given an interpretation relating to the subject matter only in the commentary on the *Physics* by the Neo-Platonist Simplicius. In fact, however, Kant was right when he said in a lecture about metaphysics that the name had not "emerged by chance, given that it fits the science itself so well" (Akad. Ausg. XXVIII/1, 174; for a philological confirmation, albeit controversial, cf. Reiner 1954 and 1955). Considering Aristotle's two ways of cognition, it is defensible to have two adequate designations for the one science of principles. As for the way leading toward the principles, the science represents itself as the way leading from nature beyond nature and thus as metaphysics—although the term is not documented for Aristotle. According to its material weight and the way leading from the principles, it is first philosophy.

The fact that the reflections on the topic are collected in one volume suggests a homogeneous text, but in truth what we have is a collection of relatively independent individual treatises, compiled some time after they were written. They not only discuss various aspects of questions of fundamental philosophy, but they also apply different conceptions. Aristotle speaks also of the "searched-for science" (*zêtoumenê epistêmê: Metaph.* II 2, 996b3, 33; XI 1, 1059b1, 13, 22; XI 2, 1060a4, 6); this could imply that, while his predecessors searched for it, he presents it as a finished discipline, perhaps even developed in detail. Nevertheless, the texts collected in the *Metaphysics* reflect various beginnings or new beginnings and, in any case, the twisted paths by which Aristotle endeavors first to spell out the concept of a first philosophy and then to turn it into reality.

Often the books are numbered consecutively with Greek numbers, that is, book I = Alpha, II = (lower-case) alpha, III = Beta, etc. No fewer than the first six of the fourteen books (albeit only part of IV) are of an introductory nature. Of the nine books most emphatically devoted to first philosophy, roughly the same number—about four-and-a-half books—are taken up by the search for a program and preparation (I, III, IV 1–2, V, and VI) on the one hand and the three-part main discussion (IV 3-8, VII–IX, and XII) on the other. It is, however, possible to consider VI 2–4 part of the main discussion. Although, therefore, an astonishing amount of effort has gone into preliminary discussions, Aristotle's *Metaphysics* as a whole cannot be called aporetic (paradoxical) or merely zetetic (searching) (see above, ch. 6. 3). While the author is aware of the difficulties, he harbors no fundamental doubts about the feasibility of a first philosophy. In this respect Aristotle would have disagreed with the pre-*Critique* Kant who said: "Metaphysics is without doubt the most difficult of all human insights, except that no one has written a work on it yet" (*Untersuchung über die Deutlichkeit der Grundsätze der natürlichen Theologie und Moral,* Akad. Ausg. II 283). Although Aristotle leaves a variety of questions undecided, he nevertheless defines and elaborates various aspects of first philosophy.

Let us first acquire a general idea: book I of the *Metaphysics* deploys the idea of the highest knowledge absolute (I 1–2) and then traces a history of fundamental philosophy so far (I 3–9), from Thales to Plato and the Platonists Speusippus and Xenocrates, by way of Heraclitus, Empedocles, Anaxagoras, Democritus, the Pythagoreans, and Parmenides. In the early modern period, in Descartes and, in a different way, Kant, a new metaphysics responds to a crisis, or even the failure of all old metaphysics. Aristotle, too, encounters various types of metaphysics—as does Plato—and discovers deficiencies in his predecessors. Even though he does not speak of a radically new beginning, his fundamental philosophy nevertheless contains something we would not expect before early modern times: it is—partly—metaphysics presented as a critique of metaphysics.

The second passage to contain preliminary discussions is the so-called book of aporias or problems (III, cf. XI 1–2). In a survey of the tasks of an elementary science of principles Aristotle introduces fourteen difficulties (aporias or problems) as well as one additional difficulty. He discusses the pros and contras of suggested alternative solutions, often hinting at his own solution. The first problems continue from the introductory book (I): 1) whether the discussion of the causes is the task of one science or several sciences; 2) whether the task of such a science lies merely in the discussion of the first principles of substance, or in the examination of the axioms as well. Furthermore, Aristotle asks (problem no. 12) whether the principles are general or something like individuals, also (problem no. 13) whether they exist potentially *(dynamei)* or according to reality *(energeia)*. The catalogue of problems introduced in the introduction (III 1) closes with the question (no. 14) whether numbers, lines, figures, and points are substances *(ousiai).*

Given that book III is a continuation of book I, book II appears to be an interpolation to be read as an introduction to the study of philosophy in general. It treats three themes: philosophy as a science about truth (ch. 1), the finiteness of every sequence of causes (ch. 2), and questions of method, such as the request not to expect mathematical rigor in every science (ch. 3).

Book V, "On the multiple meaning of concepts" *(Peri tôn posachôs legomenôn)* is the oldest philosophical encyclopedia available to us. It introduces no fewer than thirty main and about ten subsidiary concepts, including principle *(archê),* cause *(aition),* element *(stoicheion),* nature *(physis),* the necessary *(anankaion),* the one *(hen),* being *(einai),* substance *(ousia),* the false *(to pseudos),* and the accident *(to symbebêkos).* They do not belong to any individual discipline but, being concepts common to all disciplines, they are of the rank of philosophy, even fundamental philosophy. The highly developed ability to differentiate is worth noting, while the almost laconic concision suits the note-like character.

Finally, book VI, too, contains preliminary discussions. It opens with the distinction between theoretical, practical, and productive reflections and the division of the theoretical sphere into physics, mathematics, and theology. The secondary modes of being are excluded from the main discussion by a reference to the multiple meaning of being.

To give merely an outline of the further topics: books VII–IX, not quite homogeneous in themselves, examine the concept of substance; book X discusses the one *(hen)* and related concepts (identity, non-identity, similarity, and opposite); book XI first summarizes (chs. 1–7) passages from books IV and VI and then (chs. 8–12) from parts of the *Physics,* thus discussing fundamental problems of both first philosophy and natural philosophy. Besides a further outline of Aristotle's natural philosophy, book XII contains the famous theology. The final books, XIII and XIV, supplement the "history of the pre-Aristotelians" contained in I 3–9, by introducing pre-Aristotelian theories of nonsensory substances and connecting them with Aristotle's own thoughts on the theories of ideas, numbers, ideal numbers, and principles.

In the course of the fourteen books, first philosophy is given a threefold definition and is realized in three forms: (1) fundamental philosophy is a science of the most general principles, the axioms, which are mentioned, but not proven as to their validity, in the *Posterior Analytics.* This conception is realized in IV 3–8 and in chapters 5–6 of book XI, the authenticity of the latter being controversial. (2) Fundamental philosophy is a science about the being *qua* being *(on hê on),* that is, it is the ontology that, in contrast with the individual disciplines, examines the structures and principles common to all being. The program is introduced in IV 1–2 and—after some reflections about what is to be excluded in VI 2–4—discussed in detail in the books on substance, VII–IX (cf. *Cat.* and parts of the *Physics).* Given that the material is not entirely homogeneous, one can distinguish between two topics within the books on substance: (2.1) on the one hand, Aristotle asks for being absolute, that is, *ousia,* substance in its proper sense, (2.2) on the other, he deals with the four causes and the dual concepts *potentiality* and *reality.* In *Metaph.* XIII–XIV (2.3) he adds a theory of mathematical objects. (The fact that the third topic, too, belongs to first philosophy reminds one of the redrafting of philosophy at the hands of logicians and theoreticians of mathematics such as Frege, Russell, and Whitehead.) (3) Finally, according to the program of book I 2 (983a5–10; cf. VI 1), realized in book XI, it is a divine science in a double sense. Being the science of the highest-ranking topic, namely, the eternal *(aei),* unmoved *(akinêton),* and separate *(chôriston),* which is identified with the divine, it is philosophical theology. Furthermore, it appears as the science that is "practised" by the divine itself. One could, however, ask oneself whether in fact Aristotle realizes the program of *Metaph.* I 2 and VI 1 in book XII or whether in the latter he envisages ontology as well. Scholasticism was to call philosophical theology *metaphysica specialis,* that is, a metaphysics that discusses a special subject; ontology was to be called *metaphysica generalis,* since it examines the structural characteristics and principles of all that exists.

The three varieties need not be seen as competing forms; on the contrary, there are sundry systematic connections. Thus, for example, the theory of axioms raises an ontological claim (*Metaph.* IV 3, 1005a23 f.), and through the dual concepts of act and potentiality, ontology points to the theory of the Prime Mover (*Metaph.* IX 8, 1050b5). (On the interconnections according to subject matter, see, e.g., Inciarte 1994.)

Aristotle not only sets up aporias, he also gets caught up in them himself. A first difficulty lies in the question what exactly first philosophy should be dealing with. Another—as we shall see (see ch. 11. 2)—hides in the question whether the true substance is the individual thing or its *eidos,* or species. A third difficulty ensues from making precision a criterion of fundamental philosophy. Given that the fewer presuppositions a science makes the more precise it is, mathematics should also be of a nature that belongs to fundamental philosophy, but this is contradicted by the fact that its subject matter is achieved through abstraction. A further difficulty: since being is examined by ontology as being, but as something existing naturally in the *Physics,* the precedence of ontology appears to be uncontroversial. However, wherever ontology and the *Physics* investigate the same concepts—e.g., act and potentiality or matter and form—the *Physics,* rather than presupposing the discussion in the books on substance, performs its own independent analysis.

Where ethics is concerned, matters are different again. Surprisingly, the two fundamental practical concepts, namely the goal *(telos)* and the good *(agathon),* are absent in the program of a threefold fundamental philosophy. Given its self-imposed task of investigating all fundamental principles, fundamental philosophy ought to deal with both the sphere of theory and that of the practical. Indeed, the book of aporias takes into consideration a theory extended to include the two aforementioned fundamental concepts (*Metaph.* III 2, 996b10–13), but in fact the *Metaphysics* leaves aside the fundamental concepts of the practical, with the exception of a few remarks (e.g., *Metaph.* XII 7, 1072a2–4). Thus, there are four tasks altogether, of which Aristotle's *Metaphysics* tackles only three: 1) Being a theory of axioms, responsible for both the theoretical and the practical, it is fundamental philosophy absolute. 2) As a theory of the highest being, that is, theology, and 3) a theory of being as such, that is, ontology, it is only a theoretical fundamental philosophy, albeit in two forms. It *de facto* leaves its 4) practical counterpart to ethics; thus, the latter merits the rank partly of a common ethics, partly of a first philosophy of the practical, a practical fundamental philosophy or practical metaphysics.

Many interpreters consider the three books on substance the core and climax of the *Metaphysics.* However, given that the other two conceptions are neither part of the theory of substance nor without justification in claiming to be a science of principles, it is better to speak of three parts of essentially equal rank: 1) the theory of axioms, which is of ontological importance without, however, being turned into the appendix or preface to the books on substance; 2) ontology (of substance);

and 3) natural theology. To this one needs to add 4), the part of ethics that is fundamental philosophy.

According to Werner Jaeger (1912), the difference between theology and ontology mirrors the development from a phase of closeness to Plato toward one of distance from him. In the former, according to Jaeger, first philosophy is understood in the sense in which metaphysics would be understood later, namely, as the science concerned with a divine world that is beyond the empirical world, transcendent or supernatural, while in the latter it is understood as a general ontology. It is correct that in the entirety of the *Metaphysics* there are different layers, or at least different parts, as well as emendations and additions, but this is no proof for competing conceptions, which in turn warrant conclusions about differing phases in Aristotle's thought. After all, Aristotle poses himself the question concerned and in his answer he takes up both conceptions, that is, the theory of unmoved substance, directed toward a philosophical theology, and the "general" science, which examines being *qua* being (*Metaph.* VI 1). There is a relatively high systemic claim being made in this programmatic remark: the difference between *metaphysica generalis* and *metaphysica specialis* appears to be canceled; first philosophy becomes theology, which as such has the value of an ontology; theology, and ontology not only overlap, they even become one.

It could be possible to consider this onto-theology as a conception close to Plato and the ontology without theology as one distant from him, but even so, important doubts arise regarding Jaeger's developmental hypothesis. For example, the critique of ideas in I 9, the version supposedly close to Plato tallies to a large extent, partly even verbatim, with the version of XIII 4–5, supposedly distant from Plato. Secondly, neither does the use of "we" in the first critique of ideas suggest an affinity with Plato nor does the use of "they" in the second suggest detachment from him. Judging from the surviving writings, it would seem that Aristotle never acknowledged Plato's theory of ideas and had been looking for an alternative fundamental philosophy right from the beginning. Furthermore, the cardinal point of his ontology, namely, the theorem of the multiple meaning of being, appears both in book VI (2, 1026a33), in which the onto-theological conception is developed, and in the ontology free of theology (VII 1, 1028a10). Not least, the supposedly Platonizing theology already criticizes Plato's theory of ideas and at the same time the current understanding of metaphysics. God is not conceived by turning away from the empirical world but by passing through it. Although he is not perceptible, he nevertheless constitutes the condition that makes the perceptible world possible (see ch. 10.2).

The various conceptions have four characteristics in common, each of which confers rank and attractivity to the respective science of principles (*Metaph.* I 2). Firstly, it is distinguished by precision, which in this case is to be understood neither in a quantitative sense (as measurements that are exact down to the fifth decimal point) nor according to the theory of proof (as a stringent argumentation), but according to the theory of principle, as the ability to make do with the smallest possible number of preconditions. In this sense, by thinking about preconditions instead of making them, fundamental philosophy is the most exact of all sciences (*Metaph.* I 2, 982a12 f. and a25–28).

Secondly, those who know the principles know everything—with one reservation: as far as that is possible. This, and only this, would appear to be the way out of the fragmentation of disciplines deplored today: not the homogeneity of a world view that could only be oversimplified, but in a unity mediated through principles. While the common sciences deal with special facts or with the special aspects of general ones only, (first) philosophy leaves behind all that is specific, dealing with the general, which at the same time is the fundamental.

Although in the entirety of his treatises Aristotle gives proof of near-encyclopedic knowledge, he considers extensive knowledge no more a sign of fundamental philosophy than a unified world view. Instead, he searches, therefore, for a qualitatively new, higher-ranking knowledge which, according to a third characteristic, neither constitutes a preliminary stage of the actual sciences (the philosopher is not a "stand-in" for great individual scientists) nor represents the embodiment of all knowledge that diminishes the value of the ordinary sciences. In that way fundamental philosophy can surpass the knowledge of the individual sciences without taking their place. On the one hand, only the fundamental philosopher familiarizes the concepts and principles common to all the sciences; on the other, only the individual scientist investigates the concepts and principles specific to his discipline. Consequently, Aristotle opposes both the idealistic self-conceit of philosophy and its empiricist disdain: neither does fundamental philosophy render the individual (philosophical and scientific) disciplines superfluous nor is fundamental philosophy made redundant by them.

Fourthly, an existential weight that has become alien to us belongs to the profile of fundamental philosophy. From the epistemic point of view, it results from the interplay between a natural desire to know and the intention of its immanent fulfilment; from the practical viewpoint, it is true that those who devote themselves to metaphysics perform a free and at the same time happy activity.

COSMOLOGY AND THEOLOGY

10.1 META-PHYSICS

The original, Homeric image the Greeks had of the gods was anthropomorphic; it was refined by philosophical influence in two ways. The natural philosophers Thales (*c.* 600 B.C.E.), Anaximander, and Anaximenes (sixth century B.C.E.) discarded the Homeric myths altogether, developing a cosmology instead. Xenophanes (*c.* 500 B.C.E.), on the other hand, undertook a sublimation of the image. The many gods were replaced by one god distinguished by perfection, and no longer by the immorality chastized in fragment B 11: "Homer and Hesiod have attributed to the gods whatever is ignominious and reproachable among men: stealing, adultery and defrauding each other." Xenophanes followed the cosmological turning point insofar as he considered God an unmoved being that moves everything by the power of its mind (Diels-Kranz 21B 23–26).

Book XII of the *Metaphysics,* also referred to as "book *lambda,*" follows this form of monotheism with cosmological intent (on Aristotle's theology, cf. Krämer 1967[2], Elders 1972, Owens 1978[3], Oehler 1984). This homogeneous treatise realizes Aristotle's program of fundamental philosophy more clearly than any other. In accordance with the conditions set up in *Metaph.* I 2 and *Metaph.* VI 1 (cf. XI 7, 1064b1 ff. and *EN* VI 7, 1141a34 ff.), it treats of the highest-ranking subject, the eternal *(aei on),* unmoved *(akinêton),* and independent *(chôriston),* as well as of the divine and what the god does. According to the first conditions, what is later called "metaphysics" proves to be a chapter of ontology, and according to the last two conditions, as philosophical theology; by this combination metaphysics becomes onto-theology.

One expects theological treatises to provide discussions of the characteristics of God, such as his omnipotence, infinite goodness, and omniscience as well as a proof of his existence, that is, a proof of God. Both expectations are fulfilled only in a limited way by book *lambda* because the Aristotelian god does not possess the characteristics mentioned here. Besides, the book contains much more than a mere doctrine of God; it offers a résumé of Aristotle's theoretical philosophy.

The first chapter names substance *(ousia)* as its subject matter and then goes on to introduce three types of substance, or three spheres of being. The genuine subject matter of mathematics, numbers and geometrical figures, is absent because—according to Aristotle's theory of mathematics (see ch. 7.4)—substances do not feature in it (cf. XII 8, 1073b7 f.). Within the framework of the perceptible *(aisthêton)*, the (1) transient substances of the world this side of the moon (the sublunar world) are distinguished from the (2) eternal substances, that is, the stars. The former are subject to birth and death, inconsistency and decay, while the latter know only the perfection of circular motions. These first two kinds of substances belong to nature (they are *physikai:* XII 6, 1071b3) but they also differ radically from each other; one could therefore term the former, that is, the theory of transient natural objects, "physics 1" and that of eternal natural objects "physics 2." Aristotle distinguishes both spheres from (3) the substance that is neither visible nor moved, the unmoved mover who takes the place of Plato's Demiurge. Even here theology plays only a small part. Instead, Aristotle confronts Plato's "metaphysics" of ideas, refuting the hypostasizing of the general. However, he remains a Platonist insofar as he recognizes a substance that is beyond perception.

By taking its departure from physics (1 and 2), book *lambda* represents itself as meta-physics in the literal sense, that is, as reflections about something beyond physics which can be perceived only in passing through physics. At the same time it states the principle of the latter: the object transcending the visible world, the transcendent, is the condition for the existence of the sensible world. In this respect metaphysics is not a rigorously autonomous scientific discipline, but a liminal reflection pertaining to a coherently conducted physics.

Surprisingly, because of this connection between the first part, belonging to natural philosophy, and the second, metaphysical, part there is no caesura distinguishing physics as "second philosophy" from first philosophy. Although the genuinely metaphysical part of *lambda* constitutes the highest degree of knowledge, it is dependent upon other steps and is not given any attention extending markedly beyond natural philosophy. The first five chapters deploy the natural objects by which one is led toward the super-natural object. Conversely, the following five chapters introduce the supernatural world without which the processes of the natural world cannot be explained sufficiently.

Another peculiarity is that the theological leitmotif of *lambda* is not "God" but the concept, pertaining to natural philosophy, of the unmoved mover. According to the decisive chapter 7, that which is desired and thought *(to orekton kai to noêton:* XII 7, 1072a26) has the power to move something without being moved, as well as that which is loved (b3: *kinei hôs erômenon).* The unmoved mover *(to akinêton kinoun)* is the principle of motion in the sense of the "because of which" (b2), that is, the final cause, or purpose, of all being. In the further discussion, too, it is not God who represents the apogee but the conception of *noêseôs noêsis,* the thinking of thinking (XII 9, 1074b34 f.; cf. XII 7, 1072b20 f.). The unmoved mover is spirit directed upon itself and achieving its dignity by that very fact.

Although, toward the end of the definitions, the expressions *divine* and *the god* make their appearance (XII 7, 1072b25 ff.), it cannot be said that Aristotle's natural philosophy and ontology culminate in theology; for "god" is only one among many definitions and far from being the most important one. Primarily it is the unmoved mover who constitutes the origin of all motion and, simultaneously, the cause of the unity of all natural phenomena. Characteristically, the *Physics* speaks of a mover who is not moved himself (II 7, 198b1 f.) as well as the first mover (VIII 6 and 10), but not at the same time of God or the divine. Thus, to give *lambda* the title "philosophical theology" is not only to overrate it but to misdefine it as well. The book is not concerned with theology as such, but with ontology, natural philosophy, and cosmology. Although the theology is an unrenounceable part of it, its importance is subsidiary to ontology and cosmology.

10.2 THE COSMOLOGICAL CONCEPT OF GOD

The second part of *lambda*, a beautiful example for the way toward the principles, leads from the perceptible substances known to us to unmoved substances that are unknown to us but known in the world of cognition. The argumentation, a reduction in four steps, first (*Metaph.* XII 6, 1071b5–11) leads from the entirety of perceivable motions to absolute form, to no longer transient, eternal motion. According to the decisive argument, not everything can be transient, since neither motion nor time have an origin (cf. *Ph.* VIII 1, 251a8–252b6). The continuous and eternal motion that is therefore necessary is only possible as circular motion (*Metaph.* XII 6, 1071b10 f.; cf. *Ph.* VIII, 8–10; *Cael.* II 3), which, as is said later (*Metaph.* XII 8, 1073b17–32), is in fact appropriate for the fixed stars. The planetary motions, too, are attributed to circular motions. An astronomical excursus begins by introducing the teachings of Eudoxus (fourth century B.C.E.), one of the greatest mathematicians and astronomers of antiquity: he presumes three heavenly spheres for the sun and the moon respectively and four each for the planets known at the time (Mercury, Venus, Mars, and Jupiter). This is followed by improvements suggested by the astronomer Callippus, and finally Aristotle's own view. In order to explain the motions, which appear so complicated within a geocentric world view, Aristotle assumes seven heavenly spheres each for Saturnus and Jupiter, nine each for Mars, Venus, Mercury, and the sun, and five for the moon, for a total of fifty-five.

Plato's Demiurge (architect of the world: *Timaeus* 41a ff.), who forms as yet unordered matter into the cosmos according to preexisting ideas, contains a moment of potentiality because of his relation to matter; according to Aristotle, this detracts from the perfection of a truly first principle. Consequently, the second and third step of the argumentation (XII 6, 1071b12 ff., 1072a24–26) demonstrate that eternal motion cannot exist unless its principle is constituted by a substance part of the essence of which is (pure) reality. According to the shorter, second step, there is a middle substance which moves other things and is moved simultaneously; it is identified with the first, highest heaven. As the first substance is itself moved, there has to be a further cause, and according to the third step, this leads us to the purely thought subject, spirit, and to the unmoved mover (cf. also *Ph.* VIII 5).

Given its pure actuality, mind can be related neither to the sphere of perception, which is co-determined by matter, nor to the specific forms, because (XII 3–5) they are connected with the substances perceptible by the senses. Thus, mind is directed toward the only subject that is free of matter, that is, itself. The result is paradoxical: the climax of Aristotelian cosmology, that is, the self-referentiality of the mind *(noêseôs noêsis),* lacks any kind of relation to the cosmos or the world (cf. Oehler 1984, 64–93, and 1997). The godhead thinks itself and only itself. Insofar as thinking is seen as discursive, not even that occurs and the godhead is in eternal contemplation of itself.

In chapter 7 Aristotle introduces the idea of the unmoved mover for the fixed stars only, and in chapter 8 he then does so for the fifty-five spheres of the sun and the planets. However, the resulting plurality of one and fifty-five intelligible substances is surprising both in the text (since chapter 7 gives no indication of this) and in its content. Given that the mover is not moving mechanically but teleologically or, more exactly, "erotically," one wonders why one single unmoved mover is not sufficient for the entire heaven.

The traditional, primarily theological, reading of *lambda* could attempt to combine the first three steps into one main step followed by a second main step which is the equation of the unmoved mover with God. However, what Aristotle uses to define the unmoved mover is not merely divinity but a wealth of definitions pointing to cosmological perfection. The unmoved mover is pure reality, pure contemplation and thought of the highest and best. He is highest and permanent pleasure as well as spirit, best and eternal life and immaterial (similarly in *EN* VII 15, 1154b26 f., X 8 1178b21 f.). Both the life and the pleasure of the unmoved mover are special forms—the former a matter-free noetic life, the latter motionless noetic pleasure—which nevertheless provide the model for the ordinary forms.

It is only in the context of these many definitions, almost in passing, that the unmoved mover is equated with the deity *(ho theos:* XII 7, 1072b23 ff.). In doing so, Aristotle undertakes a *metabasis eis allo genos;* he leaves behind the cosmological argumentation and enters the territory of theology. This transition is not necessarily inadmissible because the god of *lambda,* far from being the object of religious worship, remains a purely cosmic principle. At the same time Aristotle proposes a reinterpretation of the concept of God that constitutes a break with the theology of Greek tradition. The singular with the definite article—"the god"—criticizes popular belief in a multitude of gods, demigods, and demons. The many personified gods who interfere with human destiny, helpful and punishing in turn, are not sublimated into one personified god but replaced by an apersonal godhead unconcerned with human affairs. However, traditional polytheism maintains a certain justification insofar as "god" also exists in the plural. Whilst not addressing the fifty-five movers of the sun and the planets directly as gods, Aristotle considers it acceptable to equate the traditional gods with the celestial spheres (XII 8, 1074a31 ff.). On the other hand, he criticizes the supposition of a plurality of heavens. The reason is that their respective principles would be one according to form *(eidei)* but many according to number; however, for plurality matter *(hylê)* is needed, which the first unmoved mover in his pure *energeia* is lacking. Thus, Aristotle presents a peculiar mixture of monotheism and polytheism the more precise substance of which remains undiscussed. Research on the dialogues, transmitted only in fragments, suggests that Aristotle by no means rejected mythological theology.

One could feel tempted to attribute a higher rank to the one mover of the fixed stars compared to the fifty-five movers of the sun and the planets, but this is not possible because the absolute superlative determining the unmoved mover allows for no differences in rank within itself. Unless one dismisses chapter 8 as an interpolation alien to the train of thought of chapters 6–7, one has to imagine the purely intelligible sphere as a unity, to a certain degree as a plurality immanent in monotheism. Later this was to offer a point of attachment to Christian Trinitarian theology, given that the latter is inspired by a conception of the *noêseôs noêsis* mediated through Neo-Platonic spiritual metaphysics. This way of thought is simultaneously intuitive and reflective: it understands itself in its plurality not by passing through the latter, that is, not discursively, but "at once."

Since, according to *Metaph.* I 2 (983a5–10), the most divine science cognizes all causes and principles, it would appear that the divine mind cannot be limited to cognition of itself but has to include omniscience in the sense of comprehensive knowledge. However, book *lambda* leaves no room for this. As chapter XII 9, on problems, confirms, the divine mind has no knowledge of the world outside itself; being directed toward the most divine, venerable, and unchangeing, it is only concerned with itself (1074b26 and b33 ff.).

An argumentation culminating in "God" is usually called a proof of the existence of God, but given the extremely compressed representation, what we find in Aristotle is a thought model rather than a strict deduction. Most importantly, while he claims that the unmoved substance exists of necessity (*Metaph.* XII 6, 1071b4 f.), the same claim is not made about equating it with the godhead. Therefore, it is rather the case that *if* one wants to speak about the god, one *can* do so in the way that is outlined. However, Aristotle claims neither that the cosmological principle is of necessity to be addressed as God, nor that God can only be understood through a cosmology. *Lambda* develops a basic type of philosophical theology, its cosmological form (cf. Plato, *Laws* X, 890b–899d), without making claims about its exclusivity.

In detail Aristotle's cosmotheology is not causal-mechanical but teleological. The cosmic principles introduced by Empedocles, affection and strife, could have served as a model here (cf. *Metaph.* XII 6, 1072a6, but also XII 10, 1075b22 ff.). The unmoved mover works neither by magnetic powers nor by some kind of gravitation, since no impulses can issue from a substance that is unmoved by definition. For the same reason it is mind, but not some sort of world brain or cosmic control center. Rather, as the highest goal of all desire (XII 7, 1072b26–30), it effects its powers of attraction like a model that determines all of nature, albeit in decreasing intensity. The fixed stars imitate the mover by adopting his perfection for their movement in space and perform a circular motion. The substances of sublunar nature, that is, living beings, strive toward God by reproducing themselves as species eternally (*GA* II 1, 731b31–732a1).

Doubtless in *lambda* striving, the goal-oriented motion with which we are familiar in humans and which can be transferred to the movements of animals, is extended in a way that is difficult to reconstruct. While the ability to follow goals set by oneself (spontaneously) does not require consciousness, it does require an impulse *(hormê),* which in Aristotle requires a soul. According to the *De caelo,* however, the stars are inanimate and only heaven, in the singular, possesses a soul (II 12, 292a20 f. and II 2, 285a29 f.); thus, the problems of teleological cosmology are immanent in Aristotle. It becomes even more difficult to adjudicate to the stars an impulse for desiring, loving, or thinking, if one considers them as mere matter, as it has been done in modern times. At this point, at the very latest, the concept of striving becomes invalid for astronomy or cosmology. The theory of the *nous,* or spiritual metaphysics, does not become void at the same time, and Hegel still was to consider Aristotle's *noêseôs noêsis* the model for his theory of absolute spirit. The *Enzyklopädie der philosophischen Wissenschaften* ends in a quote of the relevant passage in *lambda* 7 (1072b18–30) in the Greek original, without commentary.

Although Aristotle's statements about the divine had some influence on medieval religious thought, one must not overlook the fundamental difference. In *lambda,* the perfection that God is more or less understood to have is introduced neither in its "technical" sense, as omnipotence, nor in its "moral-practical" sense, as all-goodness, that is, as giving love or sacred will. The perfection of pure mind is of a theoretical nature and there is no place for ideas of creation, a personal god, or the latter's providential relationship with humans. Nor is Aristotle's god the recipient of prayers or the object of meditation.

While a cosmological principle is the most venerable subject from an ontological point of view, it is nevertheless comparable neither with the "God of Abraham, Isaac and Jacob" (Pascal) nor with the incarnate God. Like the perfect form of *eudaimonia,* the cosmological God needs no other; who reflects only on himself needs no friends (*EE* VII 12, 1244b7–9). The mutuality presupposed in the ordinary manifestation of loving and being loved is absent here; any relation to lower-ranking entities would only limit his perfection.

In the period of the Enlightenment this kind of theology was termed deism. According to it, God is a nonpersonal being who neither interferes with the course of nature nor speaks through revelation. Under the influence of Stoicism, Christianity, and Islam, theist emendations of Aristotle's theology were to be undertaken, but they fail to do him justice; at the best they amount to re-Platonization.

Is it true that, as is said in *Metaph.* I 2, this kind of thought surpasses human capacity? If we consult the *Ethics* (X 7, 1177b26 ff.), it is a question of relative rather than absolute surpassing. Humans, too, are capable of a life of the spirit— albeit not *qua* humans but by virtue of having something of the divine in them. *Metaph.* XII (7, 1072b25) adds: man is capable of doing for a short time only what the god does continually.

10.3 AN ETHICAL CONCEPT OF GOD?

Being defined as pure mind, the Aristotelian godhead lacks the middle part of the soul that permitted the Homeric and Hesiodic gods attitudes analogous to those of humans. Thus, for example, the divine can no longer be full of envy (*Metaph.* I 2, 983a2 f.; for a critique of anthropomorphism: III 2, 997b10 and XII 8, 1074b5–10; for a critique of the mythological teachings about the gods: III 4,

1000a9 ff.). However, it is also devoid of the respective virtues, such as temperance, courage, liberality, etc. To think that, therefore, the godhead is deficient in perfection would be to overlook that the human conditions for applying these virtues are absent—both the objective conditions of "business dealings, emergencies, etc." (*EN* X 8, 1178a10–14) and the subjective ones, desires.

This deficiency even constitutes an intensification of divine perfection, which is so self-evident that to assume the opposite would be downright ridiculous (b10 ff.). The only passage one could contrast to this is the one in the discussion of justice according to which justice is unchangeable among the gods (*EN* V 10, 1134b28–30). However, the apparent contrast to *Ethics* X 8 (1178b10–12) resolves itself as soon as one expands the argument: *if* there were justice among the gods—but there is none—*then,* in contrast with justice among humans, it would be unchangeable, that is, have the characteristic that according to book *lambda* is part of the god in the first place.

A directly relevant passage cites with approval the view that the gods have a certain care (*epimeleia: EN* X 9, 1179a22 ff.) for human affairs. This could be an echo of the verse by Aeschylus: "Some believe that the deity has no care for humans. . . . Such belief is sinful" (*Agamemnon,* V. 370f.). In the popular belief in divine provident care the immorality of the Homeric gods is replaced by their morality. Aristotle does not refute the thought downright, but he acknowledges it only in sublimated form. The godhead cares neither for the material well-being of humans nor for the things some expect as the result of prayers or pilgrimages, such as improved health, longevity, or the avoidance of misfortunes. The godhead loves most those who resemble it most closely, such as the sage, the scientist, and the (theoretical) philosopher. Here we find outlined a second type of Aristotelian theology, namely ethico-theology, but it lacks the kind of ethics familiar to us. It is not the case that Aristotle has the beginnings of a moral rational religion, preempting Kant, nor does he adhere to its alternative, superstition, but instead his ethico-theology approximates a-personal cosmo-theology.

11

ONTOLOGY AND LANGUAGE

By setting himself the task of investigating being *qua* being (*on hê on: Metaph*. IV 1 and VI 1, 1026a23–33 and *passim*), Aristotle created a new philosophical discipline: a general science of being. It was not given the name *ontology* until early modern school metaphysics, when R. Göckel (Goclenius) called it by that name in his *Lexicon philosophicum* (1613/1964, art. "Abstractio"). By the *on,* that which is, Aristotle means any kind of object, things as well as persons, these "things" as well as their properties, the particular as well as the universal, and, not least, accidents. His ontology probes the general and basic form of reality—with the exception of the practical and social world.

Given that the word for being in its primary sense is *ousia,* ontology amounts essentially to a theory of *ousia,* even though, according to *Metaph*. IV 3, it includes the theory of axioms. *Ousia* is a noun derived from the verb *einai* (to be) and thus means literally "existence": *ousia* is the quintessence of that which is really there, that is, of permanent, factually given reality. Like nearly all of Aristotle's terminology, the word *ousia* belongs to everyday language, while the analogous nouns in Latin *(essentia, substantia)* are artificial creations—as is its German translation *Seiendheit.* In order to distinguish it from the essence of a thing *(ti estin),* one could fall back on the Latin translation, *substantia,* and use the term *substance.*

Ontological considerations had existed long before Aristotle, so here, too, he is able to refer to generally accepted views and the opinions of earlier philosophers. He never questions the common view (V 8, VII 2, and VIII 1) that the elements (air, water, earth, and fire), plants (and their parts), animals and humans (and their parts), and finally the parts of the heavens, are all substances. He merely specifies at *Metaph*. VIII 3 that only natural objects are substances in the true sense, while artifacts are not. However, he rejects the opinion that ideas and mathematical objects are also substances (as they are according to Plato and the Platonists), developing his own theory of substance. (For connections with the older Academy, expressed in the concept *ephexês*—successively or continuously—see *Metaph*. VI 4, 1027b24; XI 12, 1068b31 ff.; XII 1 1069a20.)

The theory of substance remained one of the most-discussed topics in philosophy until well into modern times. Although doubt was cast on its presupposition—i.e., an objectivity independent of any a priori activity of consciousness—by transcendental philosophy, it still had some importance in Hegel. Later it fell a victim to the twentieth century's general verdict on metaphysics, but recently it has attracted the attention of analytical philosophy (of language).

The theory of substance is developed in the short work *Categories*—a title not mentioned in Aristotle—and in the central ontological discussion in the *Metaphysics,* which goes from VI 2 to IX inclusive; its bulk, books VII–IX (Zêta, Êta, and Thêta), are referred to also as the "books on substance." *Metaph.* IV 1–3 and V 7 also deal with this topic. What these texts have in common is the concept of category and its subdivision into substance and accident. The more detailed books on substance treat not only substance in its various meanings (in particular *Metaph.* VII 1–17; cf. Wedin in: Rapp 1996), but also topics that are familiar from natural philosophy, such as the two principles of perceptible substances, that is, matter and form (*Metaph.* VIII and also VII 10–11), questions of coming-to-be and passing-away (*Metaph.* VII 7–9 and VIII 5), and another pair of concepts, potentiality and actuality (*Metaph.* IX; cf. Liske in: Rapp 1996). The thematic overlap could lead one to believe that natural philosophy and ontology cannot be clearly divided, but the same topics are not discussed from the same point of view: natural philosophy observes what is in motion insofar as it is in motion, but ontology investigates its constitution. Finally, the books on substance deal also with "veritative being," that is, with True and False (*Metaph.* IX 10 and also V 7, 1017a31–35 and VI 4).

The relation between the ontology of the *Categories* and that of the *Metaphysics* is controversial; in the nineteenth century the former was considered spurious by the majority of scholars, but it has increasingly come to be considered as a genuine Aristotelian work since Zeller (1921[4], 67–9). While other authors assume two mutually contradictory positions in the two works (cf. Graham 1987), there is no substantial difference according to Owens (1978[3], 329) and Leszl (1975, 359 ff.). According to Kapp (1965, 50), the *Categories* are "far removed from the supple finesses of the fully developed metaphysics," but the work is a thoroughly well-thought-out version, compared to which the *Metaphysics* in general contains a differentiated, partly modified, doctrine, but not a radically new theory. Whether the two are compatible or not depends on how one explains the differences (see ch. 11.2). Incidentally, the books on substance can hardly be said to contain a theory free of breaks and contradictions.

11.1 CATEGORIES

Like the *Topics* (I 9, 103b22 f.), the treatise of the above name also lists ten categories, but it lacks a meta-reflection about the function of the concept itself. The expression *katêgoria* is taken from the language of the law court, designating the charge or accusation (cf. *Rh.* I 10, 1368b1). Since in Latin the verb *katêgorein* is rendered as *praedicare,* the categories are also called predicaments. Via Aristotle the term entered the terminology of philosophy and, as a foreign word, everyday language as well as technical terminologies in most European languages.

Before speaking of categories, Aristotle distinguishes between that which is said in combination, for example, "the man is running" or "the man is victorious," and what is said without combination, for example, "man," "ox," "run," or "victorious" (*Cat.* 2, 1a16–19). Belonging to the second group, the categories are parts of propositions inasfar as they are considered on their own without combinations; categories can be neither confirmed nor denied, they are neither true nor false (*Cat.* 4). However, not all parts of propositions belong to categories: the logical terms (all, some/one), the copula *is* and conjunctions (not, and, or, if-then) do not. What remains are the elementary signifying expressions—either subjects or predicates—that signify *(sêmainein)* something without being composite. The term *white horse,* for example, has two components ("white" and "horse") and therefore belongs to two categories. The complete list of categories in *Cat.* 4 is as follows:

1. *ousia:* essence or substance; elsewhere (*Metaph.* VII 1) Aristotle uses, on the one hand, *tode ti* (a determinate this), on the other *ti estin* (What is it?);
2. *poson:* how big, how long, i.e., quantity (e.g., two cubits long);
3. *poion:* of what kind, i.e., quality (e.g., white);
4. *pros ti:* in relation to what, i.e., relation (e.g., double);
5. *pou:* where, i.e., place (e.g., on the market);
6. *pote:* when, i.e., time (e.g., yesterday);
7. *keisthai:* to lie, i.e., position (e.g., he is seated);
8. *echein:* to have (e.g., he is wearing shoes);
9. *poiein:* to do, i.e., effect (e.g., the doctor is cutting);
10. *paschein:* to suffer, i.e., being affected (e.g., the patient is being cut).

The first six categories are formulated as questions, while the remaining four can easily be understood as the reply to a question. The first four are explained in detail, categories 7, 9, and 10 only briefly and the remaining three not at all. Instead, these are followed by reflections about four kinds of contrasts and five types of priority, which were to be called the theory of post-predicaments and which originally formed a separate section (*Cat.* 10–15). The philosophical lexicon (*Metaph.* V) explicates the categories of substance, quantity, quality, relation, and having.

While Aristotle appears to be certain of the number of categories, he makes use of shorter lists according to expedience. At *Metaph.* XII 1 (1069a21) he lists three, six in the *Ethics* (I 4, 1096a24–7), and eight in the lexicon (*Metaph.* V 7, 1017a25–7). The decisive factors are the plurality and the difference in rank between the first category and the others. One can speak directly of substances such as "man" or "ox," but accidents such as "white," "runs," or "heavy" can be spoken of only in connection with substances. Within the first category, Aristotle distinguishes the first from the second substance, the former being a particular individual, for example a human or a horse, while the latter refers to the respective genera and species. This results in altogether three classes of beings: 1) individuals (first substance), 2) genera and species (second substance), and 3) properties (accidents).

Only individual objects possess the criterion of substance, that is, autonomy, in its proper sense (*Cat.* 5, 2a11–14). Unlike the property "white-haired," a particular person, such as Socrates, is neither part of another nor is it predicated of another: with the exception of artificial sentences, Socrates is always the subject and never a possible predicate. Genera and species, on the other hand, only fulfil the first of the two autonomies. The definition of the human—a rational living being—can be applied to Socrates, but, being akin to the accidents, it is not a true substance but only the quality (*poion:* 3b15f.) of a true substance. As far as the second substance is concerned, the species has a greater claim to reality; it is therefore more of a substance than the genus. Within the species, on the other hand, there are primarily no differences in rank: a human is no more a substance than an ox, but both individuals are richer in substance than the respective species, and in turn the latter are more so than the genera of living beings. It may appear that this gradation is based on zoology, because in it the species is the smallest unit, but in its quality as fundamental philosophy ontology is not dependent on zoology.

The theory of categories performs at least four functions: 1) In the sense of a descriptive ontology, it spells out the multiple meaning of that which exists and thus the richness of reality. The constructive achievement of categories is to draw up as complete as possible an inventory of the whole of reality. 2) From the point of view of an ontology that creates hierarchies and is critical in the literal sense of the word, they make it possible to express what "being" means in its primary and full sense (see ch. 11.2). 3) A further critical task of categories lies in the discovery and avoidance of ontological misinterpretations (cf. *APo.* I 22, 83a30–33; *SE* 22, 178b24 ff.). They can be used as a tool for the critique of Melissus, Parmenides (*Ph.* I 3), Plato (e.g., *APo.* I 22, 83a24 ff. and *EN* I 4), and for a critique of language in general. 4) Finally, their subsidiary effect is to be a guideline for determining the plurality of meanings of basic concepts, for example, in the case of the four classes of motion (*Ph.* V 1, 225b5–9; *Metaph.* XII 2, 1069b9–13) and of the good (*EN* I 4, 1096a11 ff.).

For the purpose of a pure activity of intelligence free of experience, the most important doctrine of categories in early modern times, the *Critique of Pure Reason,* distinguishes between two faculties of cognition, namely, sensibility and understanding, as well as between a sphere that is dependent on experience and thus empirical and an a priori one that is independent of experience. According to this subdivision, Kant assigns the categories to the a priori part of understanding; the categories are the basic concepts that cannot be deduced any further, the "true fundamental concepts of pure understanding." Kant believed that his original intention was the same as Aristotle's, but that the "keen-witted" Aristotle, lacking a criterion, had chosen his categories "rhapsodically, . . . at random." Nevertheless, he concludes, "among them there are some *modi* of pure sensuousness" (when, where, position, the same as before, simultaneously) as well as one empirical mode (motion) and some derived concepts (action, suffering), while some pure concepts are completely absent (*Akad. Ausg.* III 92 ff. = B 105 ff.).

However, Aristotle's intentions are more modest. Satisfied with a moderate theoretical claim, he is looking for certain common denominators in the bewildering wealth of possible statements about an object, calling the highest class genera *(genê)*, or forms *(schêmata)*, of propositions (*Top.* I 9, 103b20f.; *Metaph.* V 7, 1017a23). He is searching for elementary forms of propositions that, like the classes of causes, all have the same origin because of the absence of a common higher category, and at the same time he discovers a novel type of unity. Objects can be identical according to the three forms—number, species, and genus—but in addition to numeric, eidetic, and generic unity, Aristotle introduces unity according to category (although he does not name it specifically), and thus, according to Heidegger, sets "the problem of being on to a fundamentally new basis" (*Sein und Zeit,* 1927, § 1).

Since even in Kant space and time, being true forms of intuition, cannot be deduced from other elements, Aristotle is right in making them part of his list of categories. Kant's other rebuke would only be justified if it were possible to subsume "action" and "suffering" under other categories. On the other hand, Kant's distinctions between sensibility and understanding and between empirical and pure achieve higher differentiation.

Neither for Aristotle nor for Kant is the concept of category based on direct attention to the world or to humans, but it is a concept of reflection. Unlike Kant, Aristotle does not derive the concept by deducing from a principle, but by a kind of induction, or an abstraction from observable linguistic behavior. Therefore, his categories have a linguistic as well as an ontological component: they concern language as well as truth (see ch. 11.4). Departing from an individual object, for instance, Socrates, they designate different forms of propositions on the one hand—here we are talking about the standard predicative proposition "This S is P"—and, on the other, of that which is stated, that is, the being itself: Socrates is 1) a man, 2) of a certain length, 3) educated, 4), older than Plato, etc.

11.2 SUBSTANCE

Aristotle's probing of reality begins with the observation of an elementary multiplicity of meaning (*to on legetai pollachôs:* e.g., *Metaph.* IV 2, 1003a33; VI 2, 1026a33, and VII 1, 1028a10). The lexicon lists four meanings (*Metaph.* V 7; similarly *Metaph.* VI 2, 1026a33–b2), or rather, four kinds of a respectively complete multiplicity of meaning of being. One could say that the distinctions current now are missing—i.e., "is" as copula, "is" in the sense of identity, and "is" in the sense of existence—although at least the first two are familiar from Plato's *Sophist* (251a-c). However, Aristotle is not dealing with the verb "to be" but with being. Firstly, the latter is stated per se or "accidentally" (Tugendhat 1983 demonstrates that this is not the usual distinction between essential and accidental attributions). Secondly, within being there is the multiplicity of meaning of the categories, which in turn (thirdly) are differentiated into the alternatives of possibility and reality, that is, potentiality and actuality. Finally, in the third place the text has being as true or false, that is, "veritative Being" ("It is true/false that . . ."). The books on substance begin with the second meaning whilst dealing essentially with the first category. In addition, *Metaph*. IX investigates the pair of concepts potentiality/actuality and in its final chapter (IX 10) veritative being.

Anyone who, like Aristotle and unlike Parmenides (*Ph*. I 3, 186a22–25), recognizes multiplicity of meaning without seeing it as mere homonymity (*Metaph*. IV 2, 1003a34), must ask himself about unity. Aristotle answers this question with a hierarchical system, the relation of *pros hen*, within which he deals mainly with the first-order object, namely, that which truly is *(alêthôs on)*, which is of great interest to Greek thinkers in general. According to the *pros hen* relation, the various meanings of being align with an exemplary meaning, that is, a preferred first—one *(pros hen)* and *one* nature (*mian tina physin: Metaph*. IV 2, 1003a34; similarly at VII 4, 1030a35 f.). At the same time Aristotle disputes that the various meanings can be subsumed under a higher genus; he sees no points of content in common, neither between the first category and the remaining nine nor among these nine categories.

Aristotle's answer to the question of what is the one in relation to which everything else is considered as being is tripartite. The first two parts can be found already in the *Categories,* but the third appears only in the *Metaphysics*. Exemplary being is firstly the substance, secondly the first before the second substance, and thirdly a distinguished class within the first substances. The fact that each of the three answers corresponds to a ranking raises the suspicion that what we have here is not descriptive, but revisionary or axiological ontology, but Aristotle nowhere distinguishes between essential being and apparent being:

1. Neither in the *Categories* nor in the *Metaphysics* does Aristotle give the discussion a theological twist and posit the highest being, the deity, as the ultimate point of reference. With ontological sobriety he first distinguishes the substance (with its genera and species) from its properties, the accidents. Substances are due the absolute priority, because one predicates only these on their own and everything else in relation to them. Only humans, animals, plants, etc., "are" in an absolute sense, while colors, sizes, relations, etc., only have an inherent ("adhering to something") existence. According to *Metaph*. VII 1 (1028a32 f.), substance even has triple priority: it is the first according to definition *(logô)*, to cognition *(gnôsei)*, and time *(chronô)*, thus, (onto)logically, gnoseologically, and chronologically.

A reproach often raised against the theory of substance is its rigidity and its hypostatizing of the changeable and the conventional (e.g., Quine 1950). According to Russell (1975[8], 212), "substance" is a metaphysical error, which results from the transferring of the structure of subject-predicate propositions on to the structure of the world. However, the argument for the ontology of substance is that it (alone) explains how something (a person or an object) can remain identical despite a change in characteristics (cf. Wiggins 1980, Rapp 1995b). Socrates is Socrates before he starts to philosophize, and he would remain Socrates even if he lost his ability to philosophize in old age.

2. The second *pros hen* relation is about the priority, within the substances, of the first over the second substance. There is the underlying difficulty that the cognition of the real is directed toward the general, while it is the individual thing that is real and not the general. The resulting ontological question is: how can the two claims—the cognizability and definability of what is on the one hand, and its independence on the other—be made compatible? Aristotle expresses the autonomy as *chôriston* or *chôris*, that is, "separated," or by *tode ti*, "definite this," and the cognizability and definability first by *ti esti(n)*, "what is it," and later by *ti ên einai* (*Metaph.* VII 4–6; 17; cf. Liske 1985, II; Weidemann in: Rapp 1996). The first component of the second, and more difficult, of the two latter phrases, *ti* , takes up the Socratic-Platonic question of the older *ti estin*. The second component—*ên* ("was")—is to be understood as a philosophical preterite; what it means is not "what the thing was from the beginning," but "what one says that it was."

The intricate construction of *ti ên einai hekastô* shows (*Metaph.* V 18, 1022a9 and 26) that in this phrase the question "what?" refers to an individual, Socrates, for example, so that, literally, it means "that which being was (for Socrates)." What it expresses is whatever gives an object its identity, albeit not an individual but an essential identity. The *ti ên einai* of Socrates is not the being of Plato's teacher who was condemned to drink hemlock, but that of the rational living being. In the sense of this similarity in essence captured in the definition, the *ti ên einai* is simply equated with *eidos*, that is, the form or species concept, in *Metaph.* VII, from chapter 7 onward. It would seem that by the concept *ti ên einai* Aristotle advocates an altogether feasible "essentialism." He does not claim that there is a relation to the thing that is independent of description (an objection to essentialism current since Quine). He does claim, however, that, apart from a derived, accidental description, there is an essential description in the sense that it is presupposed, as its conceptual measure, in every other description.

Let us return to the question of the compatibility of independence and cognizability: if one starts from the first criterion, autonomy, the primacy is due to the individual, but the latter lacks cognizability. If one starts from the second criterion, cognizability, priority is due to the lowest grade of the general, namely, the species *(eidos)*, which, however, lacks full autonomy (cf. the eighth *aporia: Metaph.* II 4). In the *Categories*, the tension between two aspects of reality—the priority of the individual (Socrates is a substance) on the one hand, and the priority of *eidos* (being human is a substance) on the other—appears to be resolved in favor of autonomy: it addresses as a substance in the primary sense the genuine individual that is one by number *(hen arithmô)* and a determined "this," that is, the singular term. The genera and species, the general terms, are substances only in a secondary sense.

However, the priority of the individual allows for another reading, too. According to this, it is about an individual, but the individual only becomes such by being addressed within its species concept: without the species concept "human" the individual "Socrates" loses its essential individuality. By the combination of the cognizability of a substance with its autonomy the aforementioned tension is resolved. This reading refutes, even for the *Categories*, the occasionally voiced interpretation of Aristotelian ontology as naïve realism. The prototype of being, that is, the first substance, signifies not an object dependent on knowability, but the individual inasfar as it can be recognized via the species concept.

The *Metaphysics* could constitute a radical revision compared to the *Categories,* and indeed the books on substance open with their basic thesis, the multiple meaning of being (VII 1, 1028a10), and continue with a distinction between the "what" and the "definite this," which is reminiscent of the distinction between second and first substance. On the other hand, the accidents are not mentioned at all, and there is no discussion of first and second substances. Aristotle queries the substantiality of substance and looks for a unified theory that would modify the difference between first and second substance. It remains the task of this theory to remove the aforementioned tension between cognizability and autonomy; according to Zeller (1921[4], 312), this is not achieved, leading to an "extremely incisive contradiction in [Aristotle's] system." Indeed, according to the criterion of cognizability, the *eidos* has the priority; in contrast with the *Categories,* it appears to be the true substance, while the individual object is only a subordinated substance. On the other hand, the *Metaphysics* and the *Categories* agree that the substance is the substratum for all other definitions, without itself being a definition of anything else (*Metaph.* VII 3, 1028b36 f.). It is to be a "definite this" as well as autonomous, so the individual object is given priority. According to the criterion of substratum, one may feel that matter *(hylê)* should have priority because it is the truly final substratum (VII 3, 1029a13), but it is neither a "this" nor autonomous.

The apparent contradiction could be overcome by following Jaeger in positing a hypothesis about development, according to which the earlier part of *Categories* advocates the priority of the individual object, while the later books on substance support the priority of the species *(eidos).* However, Aristotle uses both criteria in the *Metaphysics,* even in the same chapter (VII 3). A closer interpretation of *eidos* decides the question whether there really exists a contradiction. According to the ideal type, there are three possibilities (cf. Steinfath 1991): 1) One can maintain the ontological basis of the *Categories,* the priority of the individual object, attaching the *eidos* as a predicate of substance, and declaring *eidos* as first substance because of the criterion of cognizability and definability (Leszl 1975). 2) According to the "Platonic" solution, the *eidos*—the first substance—has priority as being the lowest general term (Reale 1968 and Krämer 1973; for the same solution without accepting the genuineness of *Cat.*, see Schmitz 1985). 3) The eidos is seen as something individual, more precisely as an organizational form of the individual (Frede/Patzig 1988, I 48 ff; cf. Frede 1987 a/b and the earlier Albritton 1957 and Sykes 1975). This interpretation does justice to Aristotle's critique of the general *(katholou)* and of the ideas (VII 13–16). According to this critique, that which makes a horse a horse, that is to say its "horse-ness," obtains reality only in individual horses and not "beside" *(para)* them as "horse-ness" on its own. However, the assumption of an individual *eidos* contradicts the other thesis that two individuals—Socrates and Callias—are distinct only numerically but are identical according to the *eidos* (*Metaph.* VII 8, 1034a6 ff.).

Aristotle's supposed contradiction disappears if one distinguishes between two functions of the *eidos* (Rapp 1995a). When the species is taken as individual substance, a specific individual is designated, for example, "this human," whereas with the "species as generality" it is the respective class of individuals, for example,

"Socrates and Callias are human beings." Within the framework of the standard predicative proposition ("S is P"), in the former case—i.e., in the individualizing use or concrete generality—the species usually appears as subject. In the latter— the classifying use—it appears as predicate. In the case of the individual human being something is stated about the species, while in the latter case it is that which is being stated, the common characteristic of different human beings. In accordance with the criterion of the *Categories,* the species behaves like a quality (*poion: Cat.* 5, 3b20 f.); it is not a "definite this" (*tode ti*) but rather a "such" (*toionde: Metaph.* VII 13, 1039a1 f.). If it is understood in this way, the *Metaphysics* remains faithful to the view of the *Categories* on the first substance, but unlike the latter it specifies that substance in the true sense is an individual, whose essence and peculiarity are tied to the concept of species.

3. Aristotle assumes differences in rank within the individual things or substances; in particular in book XII of the *Metaphysics,* substance becomes a comparative concept. According to the ontological concepts of potentiality and actuality (*Metaph.* IX 1–9; cf. XII 6), actual being is considered higher ranking than potential being. In consequence man may be superior to plants and animals, but they all belong to the lowest class of transient and changeable being. The eternal and changeable being of the fixed stars has a higher rank, while the highest belongs to pure actuality, the Unmoved Mover or deity. For this reason not only natural philosophy but ontology, too, culminates in philosophical theology (cf. VI 1, 1026a19 ff.). In accordance with Plato, spiritual being has absolute priority over sensuous being. Together the two "spheres of being" of the perceivable world form a "derived" world in the sense that they depend for their reality on a reality that is not perceptible itself but purely intelligible.

To sum up the tripartite unity of ontology: the One in relation to which all is considered as being is firstly, within the scope of the categories, the substance as opposed to the accidents. Secondly, it is the "species as individual substance" over and above the general concepts, and thirdly, it is the intelligible substance over and above the perceptible substances. For the third *pros hen* relation Aristotle suggests the analogy of a household the members of which contribute to the common good in differing ways (*Metaph.* XII 10, 1075a19 ff.).

11.3 ARISTOTLE'S CRITIQUE OF PLATO'S IDEAS

The way in which Aristotle deals with Plato, his most important predecessor, displays an extraordinary variety of themes and facets. Several aspects have already been addressed, such as the differentiation of what is ultimately *one* philosophy into a plurality of relatively autonomous individual disciplines such as topics, syllogistics, and biology, as well as the reevaluation of perception and the greater epistemic tolerance; furthermore, the different evaluation of poetry, the critique of the doctrine of anamnesis and of the cosmology involving the Demiurge. Further aspects will be discussed in the chapters on ethics (see ch. 14.1) and on political philosophy (ch. 16); here we cast a glance at the doctrine of ideas.

DETAIL (PLATO AND ARISTOTLE) FROM RAPHAEL,
The School of Athens (Rome, Vatican, Stanza della Segnatura)

In his famous painting *The School of Athens* (1508–11), the painter Raphael places the two great men of antiquity, Plato and Aristotle, in the center. That way, "the esteem for both is balanced" (Goethe, *Materialien zur Geschichte der Farbenlehre*, 3. Abt.: "Zwischenzeit"). Raphael has Plato pointing emphatically upward, toward the sky, while Aristotle's hand is turned toward the ground in a moderating gesture. This contrast expresses a popular view: given that Aristotle nearly always takes experience as his point of departure and refers to current opinions, and in particular because he rejects the core of Platonic thought, the doctrine of ideas, it is generally believed that the idealist Plato was followed by Aristotle the empiricist and realist of common sense. To use Goethe's words again, "Plato's attitude to the world is like that of a blessed spirit whom it pleases to reside in it for some time. . . . Aristotle, on the other hand, relates to the world like a man who is a master builder."

Such views do not do justice to the relation between Plato and Aristotle. Even the critique of the doctrine of ideas is more subtle than a mere contrast between idealism on the one hand and realism or empiricism on the other. This interpretation is refuted by the fact that Aristotle, no less than Plato, acknowledges the priority of pure thought over the perceptible. More radically than the German

Idealists Fichte, Schelling, or Hegel—and no less than Plato—Aristotle considers the intelligible the protoype of being.

Aristotle's critique of Plato—for which the way may have been paved in the Academy—is about the question in which way the general concepts contained in all cognition and discourse exist. For Plato they exist as ideas, that is, as entities that 1) are eternal and unchangeable, 2) exist separately from the individual objects, and 3) provide the original image *(paradeigma)* for the objects, which in turn 4) achieve their "being" through participation *(methexis)* in the idea. The ideas are those ideal prototypes of individual objects that possess not only their proper reality but essential reality.

Aristotle rejects this interpretation as being a hybrid construction and superfluous hypostatizing *(Metaph.* I 9, VII 14, XIII–XIV; also *SE* 22, *EN* I 4, etc.). General objects, he says, are logically necessary, but their necessity for thought (and this can be compared with Kant's critique of the ontological proof of the existence of God) does not justify the conclusion that they exist independently. Furthermore, given that the ideas are supposed to be the condition that makes science possible and that there are also negative judgments in science, negative ideas would have to exist, a hypothesis rejected as nonsensical by the representatives of the Academy. Ideas of what is past are considered as similarly absurd, but they need to be assumed since general statements about what is past do exist. Nor are there ideas of the unworthy, such as dirt or dung, a problem already considered by Plato *(Parmenides* 130c f.). The doctrine of categories, too, contains a critique of Plato: the fact that the verb "is" has fundamentally different meanings that cannot be attributed to each other contradicts the view that all being participates in the ideal being of the ideas.

Finally, there is the problem of the "third man." The argument is mentioned often, but only briefly and in many different versions so that it is difficult to decode. It is to be understood as follows: if, on the one hand, the perceptible man owes his essential characteristics to his participation in the idea of man and, on the other hand, the idea is supposed to be a full substance, a "definite this," then man exists in two substances—perceptible man and his idea—between which there is a relation of similarity. According to the doctrine of ideas, similarity exists because of the participation in a common idea, so that a further idea is needed for the relation of similarity; this is also a substance, the "third man." (Plato himself introduces two varieties of this objection in the *Parmenides,* 132 ff.; it remains unclear, however, up to what point he considers it as valid.)

All these points of critique amount to the rebuke of a partly contradictory, partly unnecessary, reduplication of reality: it is nonsensical to treat general concepts as a proper reality. Aristotle avoids the reduplication by linking the criterion of cognizability with that of independent reality and furthermore (in accordance with pre-philosophical convictions) by considering the substances as independent realities. Only by doing both does he become able to diagnose precisely the errors of the doctrine of ideas and replace them with the notion of generalities and the concepts of species and genus, which exist in and with the individual objects.

The popular saying that Aristotle brought Plato's ideas down from the heavens is justified only if it does not imply that Aristotle rejects the ideas, or general concepts. It is valid only if it signifies that he concedes to them a new existence that is no longer beyond the objects. (Medieval scholastic philosophy would speak of universals existing *in re* and not *ante rem*.) Health exists only as the characteristic of concrete living beings that are healthy; being human—although there is a concept only of human-ness but not of the individual human—exists only as something through which concrete humans distinguish themselves from other concrete living beings. Thus, Aristotle disputes that the general when separated from the concrete has the character of a substance, that is, that which constitutes reality in its full sense (cf. Fine 1993).

11.4 ON LANGUAGE

Since Wittgenstein's words "The limits of my language signify the limits of my world" (*Tractatus Logico-Philosophicus* 5.6), the philosophy of language has frequently been considered the only form of fundamental philosophy still feasible. Compared to the latter, ontology appears to be hopelessly passé. However, from the onset Aristotle sees being in its relation to the *logos*—by which he means both reason and its articulation, that is, language and its meaning, the elucidation of the basic structures of reality. The *logos* addresses being as what it is and why it is; its task lies in the obtaining of truth understood as the appropriate putting into evidence of being and its causes (*alêtheuein: EN* VI 3, 1139b15). Inversely, being is from the onset oriented toward knowability, truth and its scientific investigation, an aspect addressed in the fourth meaning of being, veritative being. Given the reciprocity of reality and language, the observation of the way we talk about the objects can provide some information about their actual structure. It is the nature of the *logos* to disclose being, and therefore Aristotle's ontology concerns reality as well as the language that depicts it. Just as natural philosophy and ethics do in their respective ways, ontology uncovers the fundamental concepts that constitute both thought and speech and the world, as well as the multiple meaning and essential connections of these concepts. However, Aristotle does not recognize the philosophy of language as a separate discipline along with logic, rhetoric, poetics, natural philosophy, ethics, and politics. Nevertheless, his influence can be strongly felt in the more recent, Oxford-based philosophy of language (see ch. 18.2). Its critique of language makes use not only of his philosophical practice but also of important principles, which are introduced in particular in the *Sophistical Refutations*. The fallacies introduced and resolved there have, along with seven nonlinguistic forms *(fallaciae extra dictionem)*, six forms related to language *(fallaciae dictionis)*: homonymty, amphiboly, conjunction *(synthesis)*, division *(dihairesis)*, pronounciation, and form of language *(schêma lexeôs)* (*SE* 4, 165b27; 166b10; for the strategies for counteracting the respective fallacies, see *SE* 19–23).

Let us explicate the first two possibilities only: "amphiboly" means a syntactic ambiguity: the sentence *boulesthai labein me tous polemious* (*SE* 4, 166a6 f.) translates both as "wishing to capture the enemies" and "wishing for the enemies to capture me." The "homonymity" examined by Aristotle designates the not merely fortuitous sameness of name (equivocation), the specific plurality of meaning of objects belonging to different species but having the same name. For example, the "eye" is the organ of vision but also the blind eye and the sculpted or painted eye (*de An.* II, 412b20–22); the Greek word for "key" *(kleis)* designates the key for opening the door as well as the clavicle (*EN* V 2, 1129a29 f.). As ontology proves, there can be *one* science in the case of terms with several meanings but not for homonymous expressions.

An important aspect of the critique of language is the distinction of three relations between objects and their designations (*Cat.* 1). Besides the aforementioned homonymity, Aristotle mentions synonymity, albeit in a sense unfamiliar to us: synonyms are objects that have the same name and belong to the the same genus but to different species, for example, "human" and "ox" insofar as they belong to the genus "living beings." Paronymous objects are those the name of which is derived from something else, for instance, the grammarian from grammar or the brave man from bravery. There is a fourth type of semantic relation: "anonymy" (namelessness), or, the absence of corresponding names, which is mentioned in many passages (e.g., *de An.* III 2, 426a14 f.; *HA* I 5, 490a13 f.; b31 ff.; *EE* II 2, 1221a3). Further tools at Aristotle's disposition for the analysis of meaning are the distinction of meanings, the *pros hen* relation, and the sequence of concepts (*systoicheia*: e.g., *Top.* II 9), so it is altogether a rich instrumentarium.

However, Aristotle's philosophy of language is not limited to elements of critique of language and semantics or some general remarks about the value of linguistic analysis for cognition (cf. *SE* 7, 169a30–35; 16, 175a1 ff.; 33, 182b22 ff.). A wealth of further reflections, scattered throughout four groups of writings—1) zoology (*HA* IV 9, II 12) and psychology (*de An.* II 8), 2) the *Organon* (*Cat.* 1–4; *Int.* 1–4; *SE* 1, 4–6, 19–23), 3) *Poetics* (19–22) and *Rhetoric* (III 1–12), and 4) *Politics* (I 2, 1253a7–19)—outlines the three disciplines of present-day philosophy of language: semiotics (the theory of signs), semantics (theory of meanings), and pragmatics (theory of language use).

Rh. I 3 (1358a36 ff.) is worthy of note: there Aristotle sketches the communication triangle of speaker, subject, and audience, introducing the advisory speech, the courtroom oration, and the ceremonial speech as its expressions (on the communicative perspective, see also *Int.* 3, 16b20 f.). In the *Poetics* he adds a grammar consisting of three main parts: investigations of the elements of language (ch. 20), the types of words (ch. 21), and the form of language, or, stylistics (ch. 22).

Within the framework of biological and psychological reflections, Aristotle makes a distinction that allows him to place man in the continuum of nature and to recognize his special position concerning language, although humans are not alone in being attributed the capacity for language. On the first of four degrees, beginning at the bottom, is the acoustic part of language, the sound *(psophos)*. The first degree of linguistic communication is the voice *(phônê)*, which serves the communication of pain or pleasure (*Pol.* I 2, 1253a10–14); *phônê* is merely affective language. The *De anima* (II 8, 420b5 ff.) defines it as the sound made by an animated being with the help of certain organs, and—in contrast with, for example, a cough—it has the task of designating and meaning something *(sêmantikos)*. According to this passage, even animals appear to be capable of sounds that convey a meaning; thus, one sound could "mean" pain, another pleasure. This may be contradicted by the *De interpretatione*, where designating is connected with a convention *(synthêkê)*, which does not exist in animals. While the moment of convention is not valid for every kind of voice conveying meaning, it is so for the *logos*. According to Aristotle, even the third degree, articulated speech *(dialektos)*, is not characteristic of man alone: certain birds, too, have this faculty (*HA* IV 9, 536a20–22). Only humans, however, possess the highest degree, *logos*. Its elements—words— differ from mere affective sounds by the fact that the latter have their meaning by nature and the former by agreement (*Int.* 2 and 4). Furthermore, elementary sounds (vowels, consonants) can be combined to make complex sounds (syllables, words, sentences) (cf. *Po.* 20). According to the *Politics* (I 2, 1253a14–19), language serves not only cognition but also pragmatic and political and social—and thus moral—purposes.

Language is discussed in particular detail in the work transmitted with the misleading title *Hermeneutics* or *De interpretatione* (cf. Weidemann 1994). In this treatise, Aristotle is not dealing with the exegesis or interpretation of texts, but with the logical structure of propositions or statements. Against the background of the theories of language developed by the sophists and by Plato, he begins by introducing his semiotic starting point. These few lines (*Int.* I, 16a3–8) constitute not only the most important passage in Aristotle about semantic theory, but also the "most influential text in the history of semantics" (Kretzmann 1974, 3). Linguistic utterances are considered as signs *(symbola)* that are determined by four moments: writing, sound, accidents of the soul, and the objects. The smallest unit of true and false is the "declaratory statement" (*logos apophantikos*: ch. 4 ff.). By distinguishing the proposition from the request (*Int.* 4, 17a3 f.)—and, in *Po.* 19 (145b8–19), from the order, the report, the threat, etc.—Aristotle refers to the different uses of language that are now called pragmatic dimension or speech acts; in the *Poetics*, Aristotle uses the term *schêmata tês lexeôs*, forms of expression or speech.

By modern understanding the *Hermeneutics* combines grammatical and logical considerations. According to Whitaker 1996, it is mainly a treatise about the various forms of contradictory pairs of statements, for the purpose of bolstering the practice of dialectic dialogue (see ch. 4.2). In this context, chapter 9 debates a problem much discussed in modal logic, that of contingent statements about the future *(contingentia futura)*, with the subsequently famous example of the sea battle. If one man asserts: "There will be a sea battle tomorrow" and another disagrees, does one of them necessarily have to be right? In other words: do statements of this kind about the future have any truth value in the present; are they already true or false? According to Aristotle, it seems that at the present point in time one can say only that of necessity one of the two statements is true and the other false, because the sea battle will either take place or it will not (cf. Weidemann 1994, 223 ff. and Gaskin 1995, as well as earlier D. Frede 1970).

Many of these remarks make Aristotle appear decidedly modern; it is clear that his relation with language is not naïve. He makes clear distinctions between linguistic entities, words *(onomata)*, and objects that are designated by words *(pragmata)*, rebuking the sophists for disregarding these distinctions (e.g., *SE* 1,

165a6 ff.). However, in the course of the individual investigations he does not always make it sufficiently clear whether he is talking about the different meanings of a word or about different objects. Possibly this may be based on a certain naïvety concerning the philosophy of language, and Aristotle may assume that he can treat the two terms of a proposition—subject and predicate—in an entirely analogous way, and not (like the Stoa and later Frege) attribute semantic priority to the combination of the two terms, that is, the proposition or sentence.

PART IV

ETHICS AND POLITICS

12

PRACTICAL PHILOSOPHY

We expect to find a world alien to us in Aristotle's ethics and political philosophy, because we assume that the subject matter treated in it—morals, right, and politics—has changed radically since antiquity. We also expect outdated theoretical premises such as a teleology of nature, theories about the cosmos, and other "metaphysical" elements. In reality, it is here, in the sphere of practical philosophy, that the conversation with Aristotle proves to be particularly stimulating.

For example, he developed a model of human action, the model based on desire—with its important distinction between *poiêsis* and *praxis,* that is, production and action—which would lose its importance only through later ethics of will such as that of Kant, and even then was not merely replaced. Similarly, Aristotle's political theory was modified in modern times, but it was not simply devaluated; his statements about man as a political being and about the various forms of government remain worth considering to this day. Despite the distance in time, the reflections on justice, friendship, weakness of the will, or pleasure still invite philosophical discourse. The reason for this is simple: the questions that are dealt with are not tied to any particular area, and in general the arguments are not so closely linked to pecularities of the Greek *polis* that they would a priori resist transcultural, universalist discourse.

12.1 THE AUTONOMY OF ETHICS

By "ethics" we mean a normative discipline, the philosophy of moral action that as a foundation asks mainly for the moral principle. While Aristotle develops this kind of ethics, he does not stop there. It needs to be explained that the word *êthos* has a triple meaning: the usual place where one lives one's life, the habits lived in that place, and finally, the way of thinking and disposition, that is, the character. Given the first meaning, Aristotle deals also with social and political institutions; politics is part of his ethics in a wider sense. Because of the second meaning, his ethics takes on the characteristics of ethology, a doctrine of *ethos* (habit, custom) which is etymologically related to *êthos* (cf. *EN* II 1, 1103a17 f.). However, Aristotle does not merely examine the customs of his own time: in contrast with empirical behavioral sciences or empirical sociology, he deals primarily with the foundations of human behavior as such. Finally, in keeping with the third meaning of *êthos*, he develops a normative ethics, concerned with far more than just a moral principle.

Three treatises dealing with ethics in a narrow sense have come down to us. This textual situation, "which is unique in the whole of Hellenic literature" (Schleiermacher 1817), the "enigma of the three ethics" has not been resolved to this day (cf. Dirlmeier 1983[5], 93 ff.). In comparison with the *Eudemian Ethics* and in particular the *Great Ethics* (the *Magna Moralia*, the authenticity of which is disputed), the discussions in the *Nicomachean Ethics* are usually the most detailed, and they have by far the greatest effect. For these two reasons (and not as a refutation of Kenny's [1978] thesis that the *Eudemian Ethics* is the more substantial work), in the following we shall be referring mainly to the *Nicomachean Ethics*, or, for short: *Ethics*. Incidentally, the question why the name features in the title cannot be answered; it could refer to Aristotle's father, his son, or some other Nicomachus.

The *Nicomachean Ethics*, a mature work, is to a large extent based on a well-considered composition. Book I quickly approaches the topic, "the aim of human action," identifies the goal as happiness *(eudaimonia)*, and goes on to develop its concept in several approaches. This results in two kinds of practical competence, virtues of the character and of the intellect, which are explained successively in books II–VI. The subsequent books continue with "related" topics: weakness of the will (VII 1–11), pleasure (VII 12–15 and X 1–5), and friendship (VIII–IX). The climax and conclusion (X 6–9) is constituted by the discussion of the two ways of life that lead to happiness, theoretical and moral-political existence. (For a more detailed interpretation of the individual parts, see the anthologies by Rorty 1980 and Höffe 1995).

Three elements, which are already hinted at in the introductory chapter, give Aristotle's *Ethics* its profile: the concept of desire, the question of the good life, and the three qualifications of the so-called excursus on method, from which we shall begin. According to these, ethics belongs to politics, its claim is practical and even existential, and it is characterized by a doubly specific knowledge (*EN* I 1, 1094a7–1095b13; further reflections on method can be found at I 2, I 7, I 8–9, II 2, and VII 1, 1145b2–7).

By the first definition, Aristotle aims for an interpenetration of ethics and politics (1094a27–b7, etc.), but he does not concede politics superior importance, as it has been assumed after Hegel. On the contrary, the basic concepts the two have in common—happiness, virtue, justice, and friendship—are developed in the *Ethics*. Therefore it is more adequate to use the other more encompassing title, *hê peri ta anthrôpina philosophia* (*EN* X 10, 1181b15). Without one or the other side being given priority, ethics and politics together constitute a "philosophy of human matters," a genuinely philosophical anthropology. Within the latter's framework the *Ethics* discusses—apart from the common normative basic concepts—the actions of the individual, leaving the investigation of institutions and constitutions to the *Politics*.

The call for an "ethics without metaphysics" (Patzig) has been going around for some time. If it is only a question of general basic concepts transcending many individual disciplines, it would seem that even nowadays ethics still contains "metaphysical" elements. If, however, "metaphysics" is understood as the theory of a highest being or that of another world, the program of "ethics without metaphysics" is realized by Aristotle already. Even in the cross-references to the *Metaphysics,* for example, in the critique of Plato's theory of ideas (*EN* I 4) or the reference to the divine in the *bios theôrêtikos* (*EN* X 6–8), the decisive arguments are taken from ethics. Furthermore, while there is a teleology, it is not a teleology of nature alien to ethics, but one that is derived from the concept of action. Finally, where Aristotle mentions the function characteristic of man (I 6, 1097b24 ff.), he does make statements on essence, but they contain a very cautious "essentialism" and make do without metaphysical assumptions along the line of the *Metaphysics.* Most clearly, he develops a theory of the highest good, designating it as "practicable good" (*to pantôn akrotaton tôn praktôn agathôn:* I 2, 1095a16 f.) as well as "human good" (*anthrôpinon agathon:* I 1, 1094b7), what is obviously a pointed remark against the prototype of metaphysical entity, Plato's idea of the good (cf. I 4, esp. 1096b 33–35). When Thomas Aquinas (for example in the *Summa Theologiae* I–II, quaestio 3, art. 4 ad 4) combines the theory of desire with the teleology of the *Physics* and the doctrine of the Divine Mover from the *Metaphysics* (XII 7 and 9) into the concept of natural desire *(desiderium naturale or appetitus naturalis),* not expecting perfect happiness *(beatitudo perfecta)* until the afterlife, he systematizes too rigidly the statements present in Aristotle.

Aristotle develops his ethics as a matter of course practically without metaphysical premises. The relation appears to be rather the inverse, since the question "Why metaphysics?" is a practical, even existential, question. Ethics and metaphysics are largely independent of each other as philosophical disciplines, but the justification of a life dedicated to mere cognition, and ultimately to natural philosophy and metaphysics, belongs within the scope of ethics. Incidentally, there are connections with other disciplines as well: the final chapter of the first book of the *Ethics* develops the main features of a theoretical psychology; the sixth book treats the theory of various forms of knowledge together with their perfect form, science; *Topics* (book III) and *Rhetoric* (esp. I 4–7, 11 and II 2–11) are a mine of viewpoints relevant to ethics.

12.2 THE GOAL IS ACTION

It goes without saying that ethics and political philosophy are concerned with practice; what is not so evident, is that their purpose is action, not knowledge (*to telos estin ou gnôsis alla praxis: EN* I 1, 1095a5 f.; similarly at II 2, 1103b26 ff. and X 10, 1179a35–b2). In his *Principia Ethica* (1903, § 14), a work that greatly influenced anglophone ethics, G. E. Moore sustained the opposite thesis: "The direct task of ethics is knowledge, not practice." However, Aristotle does not seek this practical intention by way of moral admonitions or political actions either, but through concept, argument, and the determination of principles (*EN* I 2, 1095a30 ff.; cf. I 7, 1098a33–b8). Also, it is not true that, as has been said again and again since Teichmüller (1879, § 2), practical philosophy originates from practical reason, *phronêsis* or prudence. Oriented directly not toward action, but toward its cognition, it belongs to theory by modern standards. However, as a "practical theory" it has no end in itself, in contrast with "theoretical theory," but it is in the service of another—practice.

Its practical character begins with its ability to pinpoint difficulties with orientation and legitimation in its own time. Nevertheless, the three types envisaged by Aristotle are still relevant today in an only slightly modified form. A moral-practical difficulty is that there are competing ways of life (*bioi:* I 3), and therefore humans do not know how best to reach their goal which, according to Aristotle, is happiness. The second, ethical, difficulty is that there is such difference and vagueness *(diaphora kai planê)* about the subject matter—the good and the just—that everything appears like the mere work of humans or statute *(nomos),* lacking any kind of supra-positive moment *(physis:* nature) (I 1, 1094b14–16). The third, epistemological, difficulty is that the subject matter lacks the consistency that would make exact cognition possible (I 1, 1094b16 ff.).

In order to counter the practical difficulty, Aristotle elucidates the concept of happiness in the first book, demonstrating at the end which way of life satisfies the concept (book X 6–9). Without repeating the antithesis of *nomos* and *physis* at each occurrence, he establishes supra-positive moments in order to overcome the second difficulty: happiness as an unrenounceable goal, the theoretical and political lives as the forms of life appropriate for happiness, as well as conscious and free actions, moral and intellectual virtues, and, not least, friendship as the decisive elements of these forms of life.

In his sober way, Aristotle does not rely on the power of mere words; he even excludes explicitly the possibility that the insights of moral philosophy could be of use to young people (I 1, 1094b27 ff.; 1095a2 f.; cf. Shakespeare, *Troilus and Cressida,* II 2, 166 f.: "Unlike young men, whom Aristotle thought / Unfit to hear moral philosophy"). While a young person can be a mathematician, this still does not make him prudent (VI 9, 1142a11 ff.), since he lacks practical experience and in particular the "moral maturity" achieved through education and habit, because of which a person has found a firm position in rational life, no longer following the passions of the moment. Thus, practical philosophy in itself is not able to bring about the intended practice. It can, however, provide insights about itself when faced with the aforementioned difficulties and, in doing so, develop a remarkable critical potential.

Aristotle does not limit himself to a commonsense ethics in the sense of a hermeneutics of the world he lived in (see ch. 6.2). To name just one example: faced with the competition of alternative forms of life, he objects both to the morals of the many, the life devoted to enjoyment *(bios apolaustikos:* I 3, 1095b17), and to the widespread view that what mattered ultimately in the (moral and) political existence *(bios politikos)* was honor *(timê:* b22–31). On the other hand, unlike Plato, he is not aiming at a profound and radical reversal. Beyond the smooth alternative "mere hermeneutics or fundamental critique," he chooses a third way, namely, a qualified commonsense ethics competent also for critique. By clarifying in superior style the initially vague and tangled views—partly superficial (concerning honor), partly misleading (regarding the life of enjoyment), but somehow already correct—he sets out the aim of human life, happiness with all its elements and conditions, so clearly for man to see that he can hit it like an archer (I 1, 1094a22–24).

This ethics not only elucidates practice about itself, but it also improves it morally. He who recognizes the principles of his actions on the basis of a primary morals acquired through habituation, no longer acts merely from habit, but also from insight and conviction. Any initially merely external accordance with what is right—referred to as legality since Kant—is expanded by an internal assent opening up toward morality.

One misunderstanding needs to be avoided: to modern ears "practical knowledge" has entirely positive connotations; at last, one tends to think, philosophy is stripped of its uselessness, acquiring a practical value. However, according to Aristotle, only what is pursued for its own sake is truly valuable; utilitarian gain contains human disadvantage (see ch. 3.3). Given that practical philosophy directly only aims at knowledge, it comes close to knowledge sought for its own sake, that is, genuine theory. It retains practical relevance, though, if one takes notice of it not as an unconcerned observer, in the third person so to speak, but from the position of the first or second person, as someone who is affected. The fact that it is the addressee and not the author who decides on this results in something that Aristotle does not realize: it does not lie in the hands of the philosopher alone whether ethics in fact becomes a practical philosophy or not.

One remark on the import of the thought of a practical philosophy: at the core of the thought is neither a precise research program nor a definite method, but only a research intention. This intention remains valid until modern times, even to the present. Moral philosophers from Kant to Nietzsche's philosophical critique of morals and from critical theory to Rawls have been looking for an elucidation about practice for the sake of practice. In this aspect they are therefore Aristotelians whether they like it or not—and those philosophers who are not have to find a reply to the question whether they are not taken in by an intellectual glass bead game.

12.3 OUTLINE KNOWLEDGE

Because of the third, epistemological, difficulty, Aristotle introduces a specific form of knowledge (*EN* I 1, 1094b11–27; cf. I 7 and II 2). Scientific character is often measured by a standard measure, the deductive proof of mathematics, and as a result ethics and political philosophy are usually considered lacking in scientificality (even Rorty 1980, 2). However, Aristotle remains true to his flexibility concerning the theory of science, without abrogating the ideal of scientific proof. Referring to the corresponding situation among craftsmen (a blacksmith is permitted a degree of imprecision that is not acceptable in a goldsmith), he develops, with a downright methodical strictness, a principle of precision to suit the subject matter (*EN* I 1, 1094b12 ff.; cf. Höffe 1996[2], Part II).

The principle has two very different consequences, because the subject matter of ethics lacks constancy in two respects. Given that goods such as courage and even wealth contribute to human happiness, objective statements concerning happiness are possible and not only subjective advice, as Kant believed. Since, however, these goods are not always conducive to happiness—wealth may generate envy or attract thieves, and courage may endanger one's own life—ethics on the one hand is satisfied with statements that are valid in most cases but not always (*hôs epi to poly: EN* I 1, 1094b21; III 5, 1112b8 f.; V 14, 1137b15 f.; cf. *APo.* I 30, 87b20; *Ph.* II 4; and *Rh.* I 3, 1374a31). On the other hand, for its concrete application it challenges the capacity of a sensitive as well as creative form of reflection, the deliberation (*boulê: EN* III 5).

This capacity points to the second lack of constancy, that is to say, the dependence of concrete action from the variety of situations as well as forms of society. In order to deal with the resulting task of combining supra-positive ("natural") liabilities with varying concretions, Aristotle introduces the concept of *typô* knowledge, that is, of an outline or summary knowledge. The term is used in two ways. Understood in a relative way, it designates a provisory statement that is explained in more detail later or elsewhere (e.g., at *EN* V 1, 1129a6–11; *Top.* I 1, 101a18–24; *Metaph.* VII 3, 1029a7 f.; *HA* I 6, 491a8). The "absolute" sense used in the excursus on method in the *Ethics,* on the other hand, designates a final, if incomplete, information. *Typô* is used in this sense for example at *Ethics* I 11, 1101a24–28 or III 5, 1113a12–14.

In the former case the principle of subject-appropriate precision leads to a range characteristic of the ethics: its statements are usually, but not always, valid. In the latter case it denotes a precision appropriate to the matter. The *typô* statements are not concerned with objective or subjective probability, but rather they lay claim to the truth (*talêthes:* I 1, 1094b20). However, while in fact they hit upon the essence of a thing (happiness, the virtues, etc.), they leave the concrete action open. In order to prevent the main matter becoming swamped by minor matters (I 7, 1098a32 f.) because of superfluous details (I 11, 1101a26), Aristotle provides only a kind of (normative) structural grid for correct actions instead of complete descriptions. In the first place this designates the essence that remains unchanged, in the second it takes into consideration that concrete realization is part of the essence of a thing, and in the third it deliberately leaves open what is pertinent. (cf. X 10, 1179a34). The latter depends on the situation and the various abilities and resources as well as on the variations in what is usual in society. Needless to say, what is left open is not the normative side—the demand for virtuous actions and the determination of the concepts of these actions are of unlimited validity—but the partly individual, partly social context.

Thus, the ethics that makes the proud claim of being a "practical philosophy" is self-critical with great modesty on several accounts. Aware that it can only achieve its practical goal where the moral life has already been established, it is content with being of secondary and subsidiary use—and even so it limits itself to statements for most cases and to a knowledge about normative structural grids, an outline knowledge.

13

THEORY OF ACTION

Because of its normative guiding concept—*eudaimonia,* happiness—Aristotle's ethics is considered as belonging to eudaemonism, which has been discredited since Kant, but recently attempts have been made to rehabilitate Aristotle against Kant. These are stated in part in the name of the power of judgment, in part in the name of the habits of a community, partly from anti-Enlightenment skepticism and generally as a doctrine of the good life distinguished from Kantian theories of justice. However, power of judgment and the good life feature in Kant as well; justice is of importance in Aristotle, too, while one would not find pleading for mere common practice there; it goes without saying that he already has the basic ideas of what would later be called the "Enlightenment." Any "re-Aristotelizing of ethics" aiming for more than a secondary shift in accent needs to go deeper. Not even the concept of the (moral) good is sufficient for this because, while both Aristotle and Kant define this concept as the unlimited good, they nevertheless combine it with differing theories of action respectively, and only for this reason reach different moral principles. Aristotle, taking the concept of desire as his starting point, advocates the principle of happiness, but Kant, starting from the concept of will, that of autonomy (on the relation between Aristotle and Kant, see Höffe 1995, 277–304).

13.1 THE BASIC CONCEPT OF DESIRE

Aristotle bases the basic concept of the theory of action on an observation (*EN* I 1, 1094a1–3; cf. I 2, 1095a14 f.). Typical human actions strive for an end that is considered as positive or as something good *(agathon).* It would appear that this connection, the link often overlooked by moral philosophers, between the normative basic concept "good" and the basic principle of the theory of action, that is, the goal-oriented desire *(orexis)* in this case, goes back to Eudoxus of Cnidus (cf. X 2, 1172b9 f.).

Of course, desire only designates the first general kind of movement of living beings (cf. *de An.* III 9–11; *MA* 6–7). In his characteristic way, Aristotle does not define man in his pure singularity, but rather first places him in the continuum of nature by means of his concept of desire and then, by means of the *logos* (reason), concedes him a distinctly special position (cf. also *Cael.* II 12, 292b1 ff.). Desire need not necessarily be determined by reason, it can also be subject merely to perception (*ê logistikê ê aisthêtikê: de An.* III 10, 433b27–29). For this reason there are two alternative forms for both the good and desire (see *EN* I 1, 1095a7–11; III 6, 1113a16; cf. *de An.* III 10, 433a28 f.; *Rh.* I 10, 1369b22 f.). Where perception is determinant, man lives only according to passion *(kata pathos)*, strives for the only apparently good *(phainomenon agathon)*, and in doing so lives "in the manner of a slave" *(andrapodôdeis:* I 3, 1095b19 f.), that is, subject to appetite *(epithymia)* and affections *(thymos).* If, however, he follows reason *(kata logon),* he strives for the good without reservations, the simple (and at the same time true) good *(tagathon:* cf. *Rh.* I 10, 1369a2–4). The other driving forces are not suspended but guided; the urge and energy for action remain (cf. *MM* II 7, 1206b17 f.). Like Kant, Aristotle, too, recognizes a fundamental alternative, but in contrast with Kant's dichotomy of duty and inclination, the idea of pure reason that is practical only for itself is alien to Aristotle's dichotomy of reason and passion.

Within the scope of rational desire, Aristotle makes a distinction that was to leave a mark despite the brevity of his explanations (*EN* I 1, 1094a3 ff.; VI 4, 1140a1–5, which refers to the exoteric writings; VI 5, 1140b6 f.; cf. also *Pol.* I 4, 1254a1–8). With desire in a technical sense, that is, with production or making *(poiêsis),* what matters is the final result and not the performance of the action. Scholastic philosophy would succinctly call this an *actio transcendens,* an action that points beyond itself, to an independent goal. Action in a narrower sense, *praxis* or *actio immanens,* on the other hand, does not have a goal that is not already reached in the completion of the action. Not all the examples are of a moral nature. Thus, according to *Metaph.* IX 6 (1048b23 f.), those who see have already seen (on hearing and perception in general, cf. *De sensu* 6, 446b2 f.); those who deliberate have deliberated; those who think have already thought. In these cases and in those of the actions of courage, temperance, or justice the goal of the action coincides with the performance. Therefore the quality of these actions is not measured by the result; the good action *(eupraxia)* itself is the goal (*EN* VI 5, 1140b7).

In the way in which he develops his ethics, Aristotle expresses the thesis that, while the various forms of production are indispensable for humans, life as a whole is to be understood in terms of action and not of production. What matters in the end is not an isolated task but the mere completion, simply life *(zên)* as well as the successful outcome called *eudaimonia,* happiness or well-being. This difference, namely the improvement from simple life to the good life, is characteristic of humans.

We are indebted to Aristotle for the analyses of many themes in the theory of action, but what is lacking is a concept for one of the most elementary human activities: labor. This deficiency is all the more astonishing as Aristotle treats economy, the science that deals with work, as a relatively autonomous discipline (*Pol.* I 3–11). We can find elements of the concept of labor, such as the moment of production *(poiêsis)* and that of laboring *(ponein: Pol.* VIII 3, 1337b38–40), but these moments are not combined and expanded by the moment of the transformation of nature for the purpose of satisfying one's needs. This absence, which can be observed in antiquity in general, can be explained by the aristocratic leisure society of the times, in which only noneconomical activities—science, politics, theatre, games, sports, and art—counted, while even the virtue of the typical "working professions," craftsmen and day laborers, is questioned (*Pol.* III 5, 1278a 20f.).

13.2 DECISION AND POWER OF JUDGMENT

Prohairesis, decision. A person who sees different possible actions, ponders the possibilities against each other and takes one for himself acts on the basis of a choice or decision. For this Aristotle uses the term *prohairesis*, explaining it quasi-etymologically as *pro heterôn haireton*: something that is "chosen before others" (*EN* III 4, 1112a17). Decisions result in a historical reality that, being attributable to an individual or a group, merits praise, blame, or forgiveness. Conversely, in order to judge the character of the acting person one must pay attention to his decision and not merely to the external action (III 4, 1111b5 f.; cf. *Rh.* I 13, 1374a11 f. and b14). Aristotle's investigations into this topic are such a paragon of thoroughness (*EN* III 1–7, esp. 4–7; *EE* II 6–11; cf. also *EN* VI 2, 1139a17–b13; *Rh.* I 10) that Hegel could praise them as "the best thing up to the most recent times" (*Vorlesungen über die Geschichte der Philosophie,* in: *Werke* 19, 221; for secondary literature, see Loening 1903, Sorabji 1980, chs. 14–18, and Meyer 1993).

Decision is defined as a "desire determined by deliberation" (*bouleutikê orexis: EN* III 5, 1113a10 f.; cf. *MA* 6, 700b23). According to this definition, two moments—one volitional and one cognitive—interlink (*EN* III 4–7 and VI 2). This dual nature is one of the reasons why decision does not coincide with spontaneity: children and animals act spontaneously, but not on the basis of a decision (III 4, 1111b6–9). It also needs to be distinguished from a variety of related phenomena (III 4, 1111b10 ff.): from appetite *(epithymia)* and anger *(thymos),* which irrational beings also have, as well as from wishing *(boulêsis),* which can be directed toward something that is unobtainable such as immortality or something that is in the power of others. These three phenomena also lack the moment of judging. On the other hand, the decision is not an opinion *(doxa),* the latter being responsible for the distinction between true and false, not between good and bad; it also lacks the moment of desiring, while mere thinking does not move anything (VI 2, 1139a35 f.)

According to the volitional moment (III 1–3 as well as V 10, 1135a15–1136a9), that which occurs as the consequence of a decision is not happening by coercion *(bia)* or through ignorance *(di' agnoian),* but rather voluntarily and knowingly. The person acts willingly *(hekôn)* or voluntarily *(hekousion).* On the other hand, those who do not know all the details of their actions act unwillingly; thus, for example, Oedipus voluntarily slays a man, but involuntarily his father. Because the origin of the motion lies in the acting person (*EN* III 1, 1110a15–17; III 3, 1111a22 f.), Aristotle uses the succinct term *aitiasthai* (III 1, 1110b13). The person involved is culpable in the neutral sense of authorship, and can therefore be held responsible, including civil liability and criminal guilt. Aristotle's examples include criminal cases of his times, for example the charge brought against Aeschylus for having betrayed the Eleusinian mysteries in one of his tragedies, and several trials for manslaughter (1111a9–11).

This criminal-law background—together with the fine differentiations of everyday discussions—explains why the more detailed problems are examined with an almost casuistic accuracy. Speaking about actions performed in drunkenness or anger, Aristotle says that they are not done through ignorance *(di' agnoian)* but in ignorance *(agnoôn:* III 2, 1110b25–27). Nevertheless, they are imputable and not to be excused, since it is within the individual's power not to get drunk (III 7, 1113b32 f.). Following willing *(hekôn)* and unwilling *(akôn),* the *Ethics* introduces a third modality of action, non-willing *(ouch hekôn:* 11108b18-24); this term designates actions that are performed through ignorance but not repented later, so that there is a lack of virtue of character *(pace* Kenny's critique of Aristotle: 1979, 169). Speaking of actions that a person rejects per se, but then chooses because of special circumstances, as accepted side effects, he says that they are "mixed, but resembling more the voluntary ones." For example, one may commit an unjust deed in order to save one's parents or children from the hands of a tyrant, or throw valuable objects overboard in a storm (III, 1110a4 ff.).

According to the other, cognitive, moment, decision making calls for a certain form of rationality, a pondering and planning, the deliberation leading to a judgment *(bouleusis;* cf. *Rh.* I 4, 1359a30–b1). This is compared to the construction of a geometrical figure, thus to an act that is creative as well as methodical *(EN* III 5, 1112b20 f.). To deliberate something means to construct an action—one that can be realized and about which one "knows with the greatest certainty that it is good"—leading to an already given goal (III 4, 1112a7 f.). Thus, the deliberation is not about ends but about the means and ways *(ta pros to telos:* III 4, 1111b27) leading to the goal (or goals: III 5, 1112b12). However, in the sphere of intermediate goals the goal of one deliberation can be the means of another; only final goals are devoid of deliberation. Aristotle's examples are: the physician knows that he should heal, the orator that he should persuade, and the politician that he should create a good order for the state (b13 f.). In fact, deliberations about the final goal are not called for where the task is already given by the profession, the role, or the office, but it is possible to abuse one's competence or one's office.

Only where deliberation encounters several possible ways does it search for the fastest and most beautiful (III 5, 1112b 16 f.). In many cases the goal cannot be reached directly, but only through lengthy chains of actions; deliberation follows these chains of actions backward from the goal until it reaches the origin, the acting person; this, too, constitutes a geometrical construction. An important part of this consists in the analysis of the situation (Aristotle lists its most important aspects); ignorance of it entails, at times partial, involuntariness (III 2, 1111a2–6). The points that need to be deliberated about are: 1) who is acting; 2) what he is doing; 3) toward what or whom the action is directed; 4) by means of what he is acting; 5) for what purpose; and 6) how, that is, gently or violently. Elsewhere the *Ethics* also adds the further points 7) when (II 2, 1104b26); 8) how much, or to what extent (II 9, 1109a28); 9) how long (II 9, 1109b15); and 10) where (IV 2, 1120b4).

Given that the rational side of decision, deliberation, does not extend to final goals, it looks as though Aristotle limited responsibility to the dimension of the instrumental. However, in the case of one of the fundamental strategies of life, the life of pleasure, he also mentions deciding (*prohairesthai:* I 3, 1095b20; cf. *Metaph.* IV 2, 1004b24 f.). Although he only says so in passing, in a certain sense he anticipates Kierkegaard's existentialist ethics, namely, its exhortation to make a choice between fundamental forms of leading one's life. On the other hand, he provides criteria for the choice of direction in life, following from the *telos* "happiness" (cf. *EN* I 3 and X 6–9); this is not possible in Kierkegaard. Consequently, *prohairesis* is ultimately a pragmatic choice committed to happiness.

A further argument against an instrumental understanding is the responsibility that one has for the goal in the form of preliminary determination, which is not innate but in our power (III 7, 1113b6 ff.; cf. III 8, 1114b32 f.). Here a datum makes its appearance as the third moment of decision; it consists in the virtues of the character, which guide the acting person toward the right goals.

Altogether Aristotle knows three areas of choice and responsibility, which are only outlined: 1) the choice of the fundamental form of life, explained in some detail; 2) the responsibility for the goals, contained in the virtues of character; and in particular 3) the explicit decision. In the latter, three factors work together: preliminary determination, moral virtue, combined with deliberation and with the voluntary employment of means appropriate to the situation. Since this basic structure still appears valid, the types of theory prevalent in modern times, decisionist and rationalist theories of decision, contain a problematic diminution. According to the decisionist theories, there are no sufficient reasons, especially in essential decisions, for supporting one of the alternative possible actions; taken with complete arbitrariness, the decisions have a purely volitional character. In contrast with this de-rationalizing of decisions, according to Aristotle decisions possess a special form of rationality, deliberation, even though they cannot be calculated in a scientific way (*boulê:* cf. *EN* III 5). It also contains more than the task with which the rationalist theories of decision content themselves, that is, the maximization of utility or the expectation of utility in view of already given possibilities for action. While this plus cannot be resolved with scientific accuracy, as the task of maximization can be at times, it increases the overall rationality of the decision. To put it succinctly: an interplay of competences of the character with rational competences and the volitional moment of voluntariness, the decision is neither purely arbitrary nor a purely rational task.

Phronêsis, prudence. If one wants to rely on the rational part of decision, it needs to be developed into a competence and disposition, an intellectual virtue with power leading to action (*praktikê:* VI 8, 1141b21 and *passim*). Aristotle calls it *phronêsis,* best translated as "prudence" rather than "moral insight" (Engberg-Pedersen). Animals that possess the capacity of making provisions are also considered prudent (VI 7, 1141a27 f.), for example, ants and bees gathering provisions (*HA* I; cf. *Metaph.* I 1, 980b22) or cranes taking precautions when a storm is approaching (*HA* IX 10, 614b18 f.). Prudence is examined in the sixth book (VI 5 and 8–13), which deals with the five intellectual virtues: art(fulness) *(technê),* science *(epistêmê)*, prudence, wisdom *(sophia)*, and spirit or intellect *(nous)*. Again, Aristotle proves his *esprit de finesse,* his sublime art of subtle differentiation.

As far as prudence is concerned, he concedes that there is "Machiavellian prudence," the prudence of the snake or the cunning of the fox. It even exists in two forms: as a morally indifferent and merely instrumental power of judgment—he calls it *deinotês,* cleverness—and as a power of judgment with amoral tendencies—*panourgia,* knavery or craftiness (VI 13, 1144a23–27). Prudence *qua phronêsis* is also directed toward the good and the useful for the person involved, but it differs from merely interested cleverness in its commitment to moral presuppositions. Aristotle states emphatically that those who are not at the same time good, used here in the sense of virtuous, are not prudent (VI 13, 1144a36 f., a8 f. and a30).

The mean between knavery and simpleness *(euêtheia: EE* II 3, 1221a12; *EN* VI 5, 1140a24 f.), prudence is concerned only with means and ways, but not with a view to arbitrary goals, not even a self-evident partial goal such as health. It is part of the definition of prudence that from the start it is directed toward the goal, in the singular and with a definitive article *(pros to telos),* that consists in *eu zên holôs,* the well-lived life in its entirety (VI 13, 1145a6 and VI 5, 1140a27 f.). The character virtues are responsible for the basic direction toward the *eu* or happiness, while the intellectual virtue, prudence, on condition of this basic orientation, takes care of its concretization in a way appropriate to the situation. A person who possesses prudence is capable of deliberation directed toward the leading goal, happiness. What matters in this deliberation is partly the good of the individual, partly that of the household, of legislation or consultative and judicial statesmanship (VI 8, 1141b29–33).

The exact concept has been the object of several misunderstandings. For example, it is assumed that prudence is competent not merely for moral deliberation, but also for moral philosophy. However, the theory of *phronêsis* (and that of all the other subjects in Aristotle's ethics) is different from the completion of *phronêsis.* In the former prudence is only analyzed, in the latter it is put into practice; in the case of the former, the competence for individual cases is discussed, in that of the latter, something that is common to all individual cases, something universal. Furthermore, there is no instrumental reason, but it is pragmatic or eudaemonistic, directed toward happiness. Finally, prudence has a practical rather than a theoretical character insofar as, in contrast with understanding *(synesis)* and good understanding *(eusynesia),* it not only makes judgments, but also commands that they be enforced. By stating what one should and should not do (VI 11, 1143a8 ff.), prudence has the power to determine action. It is, however, incapable of restraining the powers that obscure the view of the correct goal, the passions, and therefore has to depend on a cooperation with the virtues of character. To give an example: in the case of courageous behavior, virtue assures that one reacts to dangers neither in cowardly fashion nor rashly, but fearlessly, while one uses prudence in order to deliberate on the course of action. Thus, there is no genuinely moral power of judgment, but not a morally indifferent one either. *Phronêsis* is no more, but also no less, than a moral and practical power of decision; only Kant was to deal with a genuinely moral power of judgment (cf. Höffe 1990).

13.3 WEAKNESS OF THE WILL

At the beginning of the *Ethics* the alternatives are simply "according to passion" or "according to reason," but in the discussion of *akrasia*—weakness of the will or incontinence—the situation looks more complicated. Aristotle does for these complications what he had not done for prudence: he devotes a relatively independent discussion to them (*EN* VII 1–11). It is one of the best-composed, but also one of the most difficult, parts of the *Ethics*.

If one looks at the phenomena discussed in this section, its topic is—taking up a mention in the introduction (I 1, 1095a7–11)—the power and powerlessness of practical reason. As far as powerlessness is concerned, we find, along with weakness of the will, softness or moral weakness *(malakia)* and intemperance *(akolasia)*; as for the power of practical reason, we find self-control *(enkrateia)*, endurance *(karteria)*, and temperance (*sôphrosynê*, which had already been discussed, together with intemperance, in III 13–15). There are therefore six possibilities altogether.

It would be possible to criticize Aristotle (with Davidson 1980) for not recognizing weakness of the will as a problem preceding moral matters and belonging to the theory of action, but here, as elsewhere, the *Ethics* is not concerned with a morally neutral theory of action. Since Aristotle is dealing only with weakness of the will in the face of morally good habits, his concern is a particular form of moral pathology, moral weakness. Two other forms are *kakia,* badness or vice, and *thêriotês,* brutality (VII 1, 1145a16 f.).

Aristotle develops his views in three questions: does the man without self-control act knowingly or not (VII 5)? Does he refer to every kind of pleasure or displeasure (VII 6–7)? And finally: how do the different forms of the strength and weakness of practical reason relate to each other (VII 8–11)? For the first, systematically most important, question the decisive interlocutor is Socrates, who "struggled against the concept of incontinence altogether, stating that it did not exist, for nobody acts against his better knowledge, only from ignorance" (VII 3, 1145b25–27). Socrates' position is known by the key words "virtue is knowledge." Aristotle accepts it insofar as he recognizes the phenomenon of weakness of the will, but explains it as a specific lack of knowledge (VII 3, 1145b23). In the *Divine Comedy,* Dante, a great admirer of Aristotle, takes weakness of the will to mean certain sins—gluttony, greed, and anger—and therefore habitual misdemeanor (Canto V, V.56 f.: "She became subject to wantonness to such an extent / that her law permitted desire"). Aristotle, however, means it to signify only occasional badness. He is not calling incontinent a man who follows morally bad habits, but one who allows himself to be deflected from good habits by anger, desire, pleasure, or, where the reason is pain, softness (VII 8, 1150a9–16).

According to the essential definition, the weak-willed person is one who acts without or against a decision (III 4, 1111b13 f.; VII 9, 1151a7). Given that three moments make up the decision (see ch. 13.2), there are three possibilities for defining weakness of the will, although Aristotle does not say so here: there is a lack of either moral datum, rational deliberation or voluntariness. The decisive chapter 5 operates with the so-called "practical syllogisms," which relate to actions, thus discussing weakness of the will as a problem of knowledge. Although the term *practical syllogism* appears only elsewhere (VI 13, 1144a31 f.), in this passage Aristotle lists the elements of a syllogism, the premise (VII 5, 1147a1 and b9) and the conclusion (a27), as well as stating that they guide action (b10). The explanatory value of practical syllogisms is controversial. In the discussion of weakness of the will they serve the theory of action and not action itself. Aristotle does not intend to deduce (moral) decisions and actions mathematically, but rather to make comprehensible the structure of non-moral actions, and indirectly of moral actions as well. For this purpose he introduces three conceptual distinctions in knowledge, complementing them by a "scientific" *(physikôs)* reflection. These four elements could amount to four autonomous solutions (Robinson in: Höffe 1995, 188), but it is more plausible to see them as four building blocks that result in Aristotle's solution only when combined.

In the background of the first distinction—the use or non-use of some knowledge *(theôrounta / mê theôrounta)*—one can see the pair of concepts potentiality and actuality. With the help of this distinction it is possible to see weakness of the will as an epistemic deficiency without imputing insufficient knowledge to the weak-willed person. In fact, he "has" sufficient knowledge, but it is a dead possession. According to the second distinction (VII 3, 1146a35 ff.), the major premise of the two premises designates the universal, while the minor premise designates the individual. Insofar as moral virtue is responsible for the universal orientation and prudence for individual concretion, the practical syllogism as if in passing shows the aforementioned structure of action, the interplay of character and intellectual competences. Furthermore, two kinds of moral pathology become transparent: those who lack "knowledge" of the universal are evil; those who lack knowledge about the individual case are imprudent or foolish. Lack of self-control constitutes a third pathology, which becomes apparent only in combination with the first distinction. According to this, despite "having" knowledge about both premises, it is still possible to act against it *(para tên epistêmên:* VII 5, 1147a2) by not actualizing this knowledge in the individual premise *(chrômenon . . . mê:* a2 f.; *ouk energei:* a7).

The third distinction serves for specifying the nonactualization: a person may possess knowledge like a "normal," awake person or like one who is asleep, mad, or drunk. In the latter case he might be able to recite difficult things such as proofs and sayings of Empedocles (a19 ff.; cf. b12), but he would not be speaking for himself, being merely a mouthpiece for another's thoughts. According to a fourth reflection—no longer an analysis of concepts, but "natural science"—there are two competing major premises, for example, "it is forbidden to taste the sweet" and "the sweet is pleasurable," the latter (directed toward the sweet) prevails because of an actual desire.

Since desire as well as anger can be overcome in two ways, a further distinction is needed for a precise concept of weakness of will. This distinction is no longer in the context of the practical syllogism (VII 9, 1150b29–36): those who follow the wrong major premise habitually and without remorse, suffer from a chronic and incurable badness, intemperance *(akolasia)*. Those, on the other hand, who are still capable of remorse and therefore in principle acknowledge the right major premise—albeit not in their actual action—suffer only from an intermittent and curable badness, namely, from weakness of the will. This fifth element explains why only humans can be weak-willed. Since it is not merely the individual minor premise that matters but also the right universal major premise, and animals have no access to the universal, weakness of the will is fundamentally alien to them (VII 5, 1147b3–5).

With the help of these five elements it is now possible to specify the sense in which the weak-willed person acts "without or against a decision." Inasmuch as the weak-willed man resembles a drunk, he acts voluntarily with respect to the first, volitional, moment of the decision—because he knows what he is doing and why (VII 11, 1152a15 f.)—but within the restrictions of ignorance. With regard to the second element, deliberation, both possibilities are open: "Incontinence is at times rashness, at times weakness. Some deliberate, but in consequence of passion do not stick to their deliberation; others are led by their passions for lack of deliberation" (VII 8, 1150b19–22). Finally, with respect to the character conditions, those are weak-willed who, unlike the intemperate, possess moral traits, which, however, have not yet taken roots in them sufficiently (VII 5, 1147a22).

To review the complication mentioned at the beginning of this section: according to the discussion of weakness of the will, there are three possible relations with regard to the desires. If one lines them up directly, the guiding concept becomes sufficiently clear: while the temperate man (sôphrôn) possesses a harmonious soul that is free from violent and, in particular, bad desires (VII 3, 1146a11 f.), the intemperate man (akolastos) gives way to his "harmoniously" bad desires in principle. The self-controlled and those capable of endurance have good as well as bad desires and a soul that is torn in this aspect, but the self-controlled man (enkratês) is fundamentally stronger than the desires, while the man capable of endurance (karterikos) can resist merely the pain resulting from desires. The morally weak, or "soft" (malakos), man on the other hand, avoids this pain, and the incontinent man (akratês) is overcome by the desires. Again and again, albeit not in principle, the desires emerge victorious from the contest between reason and desire. The intemperate man is completely evil, the weak-willed man only "half-evil" (hêmiponêros: VII 11, 1152a17). An overall sequence becomes evident: in the first position regarding goodness is 1) temperance, followed successively in order of decreasing goodness by 2) self-control, 3) endurance, 4) moral weakness, and 5) weakness of will; intemperance 6), is worst.

13.4 DOES ARISTOTLE KNOW THE CONCEPT OF WILL?

The question whether the concept of will, of such great importance for modernity, is developed only in Christian thought, in Augustine, or whether it can be found in Aristotle, is controversial among modern historians of philosophy. Convinced that according to Aristotle the good life depends only on two factors, the striving for the good and the deliberation of the appropriate means, Gauthier/Jolif (1970², II 218), Dihle 1985, MacIntyre (*Three Rival Versions of Moral Enquiry,* 1990, 111) and Horn (1996) give a negative answer, as had, albeit concerning antiquity or at least the Greeks in general, Hume (*An Enquiry concerning the Principles of Morals,* App. IV) and Kierkegaard (*Die Krankheit zum Tode,* 2. Abschn., ch. 2). The affirmative answer is both older and more widespread. Its advocates include the Greek commentator Aspasius (XIX, 27–32) and, later, Thomas Aquinas, who renders Aristotle's *boulêsis* by *voluntas* (*Summa theologiae* I q. 80 a.2; *De veritate* q. 22 a.3–4). Hegel, too, believes that Aristotle knew the concept of will; Kenny 1979 and Irwin 1992 also assume this.

On the basis of the preceding interpretation, the disputed question can hardly be answered with a simple yes or no. The basic concept in theory of action seems to point to a clear no, because desire consists in reaching for a preset goal, ultimately for happiness, while from the point of view of will the goal is not given but is to be chosen. An essential component of will is the possibility of knowing the good and yet doing evil. Furthermore, the concept demands the "mustering of all means as far as they are in our power" (Kant, *Grundlegung,* Akad. Ausg. IV 394). Although his starting point in the theory of desire differs clearly from that according to a theory of will, Aristotle brings certain volitional elements into his theory through the characteristics by which he distinguishes human propension from prehuman propension. These become necessary because there are driving forces that are contrary to happiness, and therefore the alternatives of life according to reason and life according to the passions open up.

The first characteristic of human desire, voluntariness, merely designates a volitional prerequisite; it does not reach as far as the dimension of will. Even in the case of children and animals the acting individual can be held responsible; furthermore the nonrational impulses of desire and anger remain active; these are excluded by will, which assumes a rational impulse. Unlike Thomas Aquinas and Irwin as well as Gigon (1991), I do not see a clear indication of will in a further attribute of humans, *boulêsis.* Given that *boulêsis* can also be directed toward something that only a foolish person could want, such as something unobtainable, it moves between wishing and genuine willing, even though it contains a rational moment (*de An.* III 10, 433a22–25).

Aristotle's third volitional characteristic is contained in the decision. Whilst being directed only toward means, by doing so it is directed also toward the entire area of whatever belongs to the good life, therefore also toward goals, even final goals. The only exception is the final goal of the second degree, happiness. However, even the latter is not given in such a way that a failure to obtain happiness would be due to cognitive deficiencies. On the contrary, happiness as a goal of the second degree in a way challenges the volitional moment. Aristotle is justified in considering happiness a pure datum; given that happiness is understood as the condition for the suitability of goals (see ch. 14.1), it is hardly possible to decide for or against it. However, decisions are called for in the sphere of actions, attitudes, and even forms of life from which one expects happiness. The fact that in these cases one can live against a better decision amounts at least partly to a decision for or against the good.

One passage in the *Rhetorics* (I 10, 1368b6 ff.) even comes very close to the full concept of will: it is said there about wrongdoing that it means acting badly not only willingly *(hekonta)* but even from a considered decision *(prohairounta)*. Bad is defined as contrary to law *(para ton nomon),* and law explicitly includes the unwritten law common to all humans which comes close to the moral law. In this sense Aristotle knows injustice done with knowledge and will, on the basis of a decision. Nevertheless, he does not take the consequences as far as moral theory is concerned, that is, to the point of modifying the principle of happiness in favor of a new principle, autonomy of the will.

The virtue of character responsible for the orientation toward happiness also contains a volitional part, since Aristotle defines it as a competence that is neither cognitive nor prerational (see ch. 14.2), stating emphatically that doing good as well as doing evil are within our power *(EN* III 7). Not least, the volitional character of action becomes evident in the treatment of *akrateia,* moral weakness. Kierkegaard's words about the "intellectual categorical imperative" of the Greeks *(Die Krankheit zum Tode,* 2. Abschn., Kap. 2) fits Socrates—about whom it was coined—because according to it humans cannot offend against the good against their better knowledge. With the thought of a practical syllogism Aristotle, too, interprets moral weakness as a deficiency of knowledge; however, this is based on an impulse competing with the good—desire or anger—so that in fact there is a deficiency of will and not of knowledge.

Even this brief survey shows that Aristotle does know elements of the concept of will, understood as the responsibility for goals that are neither cognitive nor prerational. In its essence, however, it remains within the limits set by the concept of desire. Only occasionally—for example, in the aforementioned passage from *Rhetorics* as well as in a certain modification of the concept of happiness (see ch. 14.4)—does it go beyond those limits. Otherwise, the full concept of will, the free decision for good or evil, is not present.

Augustine uses the example of fallen angels in order to introduce the full concept of will with particular clarity. One could exonerate Aristotle of this conceptual deficiency by pointing out that the *theologoumena* belonging to this sphere—ideas of Creation, Fall, and theodicy—were unknown to him. One could even add that this deficiency is advantageous for a moral philosopher, since it distinguishes the theory of morals aiming at universality from Christianity, which is peculiar in this respect and furthermore bound to a theology of revelation. On the other hand, the question arises whether the absence of a full concept of will is a moral deficiency or one of moral philosophy. Does a culture lacking the full concept of will have a less developed moral consciousness or at least a less developed theory of a fully developed moral consciousness? Aristotle's theory appears to be sufficient for "common" cases of morality or immorality, for questions of good or bad and strength or weakness of will. It may even allow room for the experience that Kant expresses in the concept of radical evil—not in the sense of extreme but in that of completely or thoroughly—that is, the propensity of humans to do wrong, which can hardly be entirely overcome. One need "only" form a relative rather than absolute concept for temperance and self-control. However, what about the "occurrences of unprovoked cruelty in scenes of murder" among some primitive tribes which, according to Kant, show man to be "evil by nature" *(Religionsschrift,* Akad. Ausg. VI 33)?

The systematic question, going beyond the limits of an interpretation of Aristotle, can only be decided in the face of phenomena of this kind. A more in-depth examination may point to an (admittedly small) area of extremely immoral behavior that is not taken into account in Aristotle's theory of action. Or could he refer to animal-like brutality *(thêriotês)*, in which the good has not been destroyed, but had never been present (*EN* VII 7, 1150a1 ff.; cf. VII 1, 1145a17; VII 6, 1149a1), and even more to the depravity in which a person decides *(prohairounta)* to do harm and do evil in a way contradictory to the law (*Rh.* I 10, 1368b12–14)? For Kant, too, defines evil as nothing other than lawlessness having become a motive (*Religionsschrift*, Akad. Ausgabe, VI 20).

14

THE GOOD LIFE

14.1 THE PRINCIPLE OF HAPPINESS

Aristotle uses several expressions for the conceptual field of the good. He calls *agathon* something that is good for someone. In the singular and with the definitive article—*tagathon,* the good—and even more so the superlative—*ariston,* the best—it comes close to the morally good. It amounts to the moral good if understood as obligations that are valid without reservations, not only toward others, but toward oneself as well. *Dikaion,* the right and just, singles out a certain sphere of responsibilities toward others; *prepon,* the appropriate, refers to habits and customs of one's own culture; *deon,* the befitting, has a genuinely moral element; and *kalon,* the good-in-itself, the fine and beautiful, which leaves behind any consideration of utility, is the concept that corresponds most to the morally good. (However, *Top.* I 5, 102a6 equates *kalon* with *prepon.)*

It is within this conceptual field that Aristotle develops his leading concept from its beginning in the theory of action. From the viewpoint of the concept of desire, what is called "moral principle" today, the final measure of human action, desire, consists in a highest goal absolute, the most elevated of all practical goods: *eudaimonia,* happiness. Given that Aristotle takes the concept of desire as his point of departure, his ethics becomes a theory of the good—or more precisely, the best—life, which, however, contains a genuine moral. The customs of one's own community only play a subordinate role.

In the search for a well-defined concept, Aristotle refutes both the too-small happiness, in the sense of "being fortunate" (*EN* I 10, 1099b10 ff.; *Pol.* VII 1, 1323b26 f.), and the excessive happiness, the bliss *(makariotês)* reserved to the deity (*EN* X 8, 1178b21 f.). Unlike the happiness of yearning, the happiness that one does not await passively and that one neither owes to a gift of the gods but is to be striven for actively, the happiness of desire, consists in a perfection inherent in life *(eu zên)* and action *(eu prattein).* The term *eudaimonia*—literally, being animated by a good spirit—contains some echoes of the presence of blessing and salvation. While the concept of happiness has been suffering from great uncertainty since Kant's epistemological objection (*Grundlegung,* Akad. Ausg. IV 418), Aristotle succeeds in giving a well-defined and also objective definition.

Forms of life. The *Rhetoric* (I 5, 1360b19–24) answers the question in what happiness consists with a long list: "noble lineage, the affection of many and righteous friends, wealth, well-bred and numerous children, a happy old age, physical advantages such as health, beauty, strength and aptitude for physical exercise, as well as a good reputation, renown, the favour of fate *(eutychia)* and finally virtue with its parts such as prudence, courage, justice and temperance." The *Ethics* takes up practically all these elements common in Greek thought, at the same time emphasizing them in a characteristic way.

First, it discusses happiness along the lines of *bioi* (I 3 and X 6–9). What this means is alternative forms of leading one's life overall, as well as definite ways of being human. This beginning already contains three statements. First, it hints at the well-known difficulty that everyone strives for happiness, but cannot intend it directly, given that it is transmitted via forms of life. The utterance attributed to Voltaire—"therefore I decided to become happy"—is as impossible as the attempt, undertaken by the Utilitarian Bentham, to calculate happiness by a "hedonistic calculus." The question for happiness calls for an answer comprising at least three steps: 1) look for a strategy of life appropriate for happiness; 2) within its framework develop certain fundamental attitudes ("virtues") or rules of action of the second degree, principles; 3) it is only by taking the latter as a point of departure that concrete actions can be determined. Second, given that the form of life is chosen, as Aristotle suggests (*EN* I 3, 1095b20; cf. *Metaph.* IV 2, 1004b24 f.), man owes his happiness not so much to external powers as to himself. To use the analogy of music, the instrument—here external goods—matters, but the ability to play it is more important (*Pol.* VII 12, 1332a25–27). Finally, happiness must be equated neither with a (transitory) state of the highest well-being nor with an outstanding single achievement, such as the heroic deeds of an Achilles or an Antigone that count for so much in archaic Greek society. What can be achieved reliably and is open to many, in something like a "democratisation of happiness" (*EN* I 10, 1099b18–20), is the happiness that can be expected from a certain conception of life.

At the beginning of the *Ethics* (I 3), Aristotle offers a competition between the three forms of life primarily discussed—the life of pleasure, the political, and the theoretical lives, as well as a fourth option, the life oriented toward gain. Since the political life appears in two forms, there are five competing versions altogether, three of which are eliminated.

According to the views of the sophist Thrasymachus (cf. Plato, *Politeia* I, 343b ff.), those who act justly make themselves unhappy; the ideal of the happy man is the tyrant who acts only according to his own judgment. Without referring directly to this view, Aristotle rejects it entirely. It is true that the life corresponding to it, the *bios apolaustikos,* or life devoted to enjoyment, is chosen not only by the masses but also by powerful rulers such as Sardanapalus (Assurbanipal). However, far from being in control of their lives, they become subject to sensual desires and passions or affects, thus living in the manner of slaves *(andrapodôdeis)* and like animals (*EN* I 3, 1095b19 f.; III 13, 1118a25, b4, b21; on pleasure and displeasure as the causes of morally bad actions and attitudes, see *EN* II 2, 1104b9–11; cf. VI 5, 1140b17 f.).

Although a mere life of pleasure fails to achieve happiness, pleasure *(hêdonê)* constitutes an integrating part of happiness (I 5, 1097b4 f.). To define it exactly is the task of the two discussions of pleasure (*EN* VII 12– 15 = A; X 1–5 = B; cf. Gosling/Taylor 1982; Ricken in: Höffe 1995). Strangely enough, they define the subject in different ways. While A equates pleasure with unhindered activity (VII 13, 1153a14 f.; VII 14, 1153b10 and 16), B sees it as a perfection that is added to perfect activity, comparable with the beauty that comes with the flower of youth (X 4, 1174b33). Furthermore, pleasure is evaluated in different ways. Thus, only B rejects the hedonistic view of Eudoxus of Cnidus that pleasure is the highest good and that any pleasure is worth choosing; however, in contrast with strict antihedonism, some forms of pleasure are acknowledged as intrinsically choiceworthy. A and B agree on one point: both consider pleasure not a motion *(kinêsis)* but a reality *(energeia)*. The basic tenor in particular is the same: understood as the free assent with what one is doing, pleasure brings an enhancement of that activity (X 5, 1175a30–36 and b14 f.) and at the same time of the good life. However, given that one of the virtues, courage, comprises the readiness to face wounds or even death, the good life is not necessarily connected with pleasure (III 12, 1117b7–16).

Even less appropriate for achieving happiness than the pure life of pleasure is the form of life that Max Weber was to describe as the basis of capitalism—the existence oriented only toward financial gain *(chrêmatistês bios)*. Aristotle does not despise wealth; on the contrary, he counts the possession of external goods among the conditions for happiness (e.g., *EN* X 9, 1178b33 ff.), and great wealth can increase the virtue of generosity to make it magnanimity (IV 4–6). What he condemns is merely the perversion that turns a means such as wealth into an end for its own sake (cf. *Pol.* I 9–10 and VII 1, 1323a36 ff.). This leads to heaping up money without limits, in a way reminiscent of the process of accumulation of capital. He condemns also the political life *(bios politikos)* if it is aimed at *timê,* renown and glory. Here Aristotle is not criticizing the, typically Greek, desire to secure oneself a place in the memory of future generations, but he considers honor as merely an external sign of what one is actually seeking.

Only two forms of life remain in the contest for happiness: the political life, if excellence matters *(aretê:* I 3, 1095b22 ff.; cf. IV 7, 1124a22 f.), and the theoretical existence. However, before the competition can be decided, a plethora of other questions needs clarifying, first of all the more precise concept of happiness. Aristotle defines it in three lines of argumentation: a critique of Plato (*EN* I 4, cf. *EE* I 8), a formal, semantic, reflection (I 5) and an anthropological consideration concerning its contents (I 6).

The critique of the idea of the good. What Plato calls an "idea" is a common form that provides the model and measure for the diversity constituting it; ideas are ideal archetypes. As far as ethics is concerned, they could be refuted with the relativist argument that there is no universal thing that has normative meaning. Nevertheless, Aristotle rejects moral relativism by orienting his entire ethics toward one leading concept, happiness. What he criticizes in Plato is not the idea of normative universality, but the precise concept and its magnitude. The first five arguments—concerning the developing series (I 4, 1096a17–23), categories (a23–29), science (a29–34), hypostatization (a34–b3), and eternity (b3–5)—counter the assumption that the manifoldness of the good can be subsumed under one idea. In the terms of the argument about categories, in truth there is no single universal common for the different meanings of the basic ethical predicate "good," just as there is none for the different meanings of "being" (cf. *EE* I 8, 1217b25–35). According to the subsequent argument, if there was a common idea, there would be only one science of the good, but in fact there is a plurality, represented by the art of the military commander, the medical art, gymnastics, etc. Indirectly, this argument limits also the claim of philosophical ethics, given that it is concerned with any form of the good. Furthermore, Aristotle objects to the reification of universal concepts that results from the separation of a "good itself" from the individual goods (cf. ch. 11.3).

The subsequent three arguments (1096b8 ff.) first introduce a conceivable retort by Plato and then proceed to refute it. If one assumed that the doctrine of ideas related not to any good, but only to one that is desired for its own sake, it would be concerned with the goods that are the basis of the aforementioned forms of life—thought, certain pleasures, and honor. However, there is no common idea for these either. Only the idea itself is considered worth striving for for its own sake, but that makes it an *eidos mataion,* a concept that is as devoid of content as it is superfluous (argument 7). Finally, Aristotle assumes by way of trial that the "ontological" critique up to that point is unfounded. This still leaves the objection—a practical one—that the good, when seen as an idea, is unattainable. Aristotle does not see the idea as an overambitious goal or as a beautiful but illusory model. Referring to the craftsmen, doctors, and generals who attempt to do their job as well as possible without, however, being interested in the idea of the good, he says that if the idea exists separately, it can have no influence on practice (cf. *Metaph.* I 9, 991a8 ff. and XIII 5, 1079b12 ff.).

The critique of ideas continues on this point in the investigations into individual problems in the *Ethics*. For example, the often-repeated thesis that one becomes just by just actions, or prudent by prudent ones (*EN* II 3, 1105b9–11, etc.), indicates that what matters is acquiring a habit by practice and the way one leads one's life rather than the insight into an idea of the good. A further critique is implicit in the structure of the *Ethics*. In Plato the theory of ideas and principles constitutes the zenith at which the dialogues *Phaedo* and *Politeia* are aiming. The functional equivalent in a certain sense in Aristotle—the concept of happiness—provides the criterion for forms of life, and it also forms the bracket connecting the beginning of the treatise with its end, but the similarity ends there. Neither the semantics of the concept of happiness in chapter I 5 nor the discussion of the two forms of life guaranteeing happiness in chapters X 6–9 amount to an acme that would be the focus of the other investigations, the relatively autonomous discussions of voluntariness and decision, moral virtues, intemperance, friendship, or pleasure.

The absolute highest goal. In order to convey the extraordinary character of happiness as an end, Aristotle forms two concepts, *via eminentiae,* of the farthest and ultimate for which one can strive (*EN* I 5). For the first concept he constructs a formal hierarchy of goals *(telê)* in three grades: 1) mere intermediate goals, which are chosen, like wealth, for the sake of other things, 2) goal-like goals *(telê teleia)* such as pleasure, honor, and reason, which are chosen for their own sake, and finally, 3) the "most goal-like *[teleiotaton]* end," for which one strives "always as such and never for the sake of another," the absolutely highest goal, happiness (I 5, 1097a15–b6). By being the highest goal, happiness is akin to the Unmoved Mover. In order for natural processes in the case of the latter and action in the former not to be unfounded, it is necessary to assume a final purpose: for nature this is the Unmoved Mover and for action it is happiness.

There are two interpretations of the highest goal both in the debate about Aristotle and in that about the subject mater. Happiness is seen either as something monolithic, a dominant goal excelling over all others (e.g., Heinaman 1988; Kenny 1992), or as something multiple, an inclusive goal that comprises all others (Ackrill in: Höffe 1995). Both definitions apply to the *polis* at the same time, because in its relation to the household and the village it not only outclasses the other communities, but includes them as well (*Pol.* I 1, 1252a4–6). Both definitions apply for the concept of happiness, too, albeit in both cases only with certain reservations. Insofar as Aristotle defines happiness as being logically on a higher level than the ordinary final goals, he makes it dominant in character. However, given that it does not constitute an alternative (happiness *or* pleasure, happiness *or* knowledge, . . .), the usual concept of a dominant goal does not really apply; reason is dominant compared to honor within the same level. Happiness has an inclusive character inasmuch as it connects several "final goals"; pleasure, as a moment of perfection, is always involved. In the course of the *Ethics,* Aristotle takes up practically all the elements of Greek notions of happiness listed in the *Rhetoric.* Nevertheless, he does not claim that only those who realize all the elements are happy: on the contrary, the *bios politikos* makes do without some of these elements, the *bios theôrêtikos* without many of them.

Aristotle's concept of happiness is reminiscent of the ontological definition of God. What Anselm says concerning being *(ens)*—God is that beyond which nothing greater can be thought: *id quo maius cogitari nequit*—is applicable here regarding the good or the goal. Being the *telos teleiotaton,* happiness is represented as an end that constitutes the goal at an unsurpassably high level. As this end is on a higher level than the ordinary goals and can be realized only "within" these goals, its character is transcendental. While Aristotle does not prove a synthetic a priori, as Kant would demand, he nevertheless fulfils the postulate to indicate a "fundamental condition of the possibility of . . .". Happiness is the condition that decides the appropriateness of all ends.

For the second criterion of happiness, self-sufficiency *(autarkeia:* I 7, 1097b6), Aristotle again forms a superlative, this time of "choiceworthy" *(hairetos).* To counter the attempt to tone down the singularity of the concept, he adds *mê synarithmoumenê* ("without being reckoned among the rest"). While, as he says later, a life of pleasure becomes more choiceworthy when combined with prudence (X 2, 1172b29–31), happiness is choiceworthy to the absolute degree, because nothing can be added to it (I 5, 1097b17; cf. 1172b31 f.; cf. *Top.* III). Virtues such as justice are praised, but happiness, an end in itself in the absolute sense, is extolled as something divine and better (I 12, 1102a1–4).

Human self-realization. Nowadays we distinguish between universalist ethics and the ethics specific to a certain culture or era. Aristotle's critique of the doctrine of ideas as well as his semantics of happiness fall under the former category, demonstrating that it is greater than is generally assumed. The same is true for the third succession of argumentation, the search for a significant concept, which becomes necessary because a purely semantic definition could result in a truism. Again, Aristotle refers not to the peculiarities of the Greek *polis,* but rather to a consideration, anthropological in this case, that transcends culture (*EN* I 6; cf. I 13). Therefore, the basic pattern of his normative ethics is: theory of action plus (constructive) semantics plus anthropology.

Although we are now sceptical about anthropological considerations, it would seem that Aristotle's way of proceeding is still convincing. He asks for a function characteristic of the human being (*ergon [tou] anthrôpou:* I 6, 1097b24 f., 1098a7, cf. a16), thus equating happiness with self-realization, albeit understood in an objective way. One realizes one's true self in a life lived according to the *logos.* Aristotle evades the resulting danger of attributing too great an importance to the intellectual sphere by, on the one hand, emphasizing the moral and practical character of reason in the *Politics* (I 2, 1253a9 ff.) and, on the other, in the *Ethics,* considering reason as present in two ways, "essentially and in itself" as well as "obedient to reason as to a father" (I 6, 1098a f. and I 3, 1103a3). Essential reason is present in the scientific and philosophical life, "obedient reason" in the life according to the virtues of character.

According to Solon, a man can be called fortunate only at the end of his life, but then what should be called happy—i.e., life—is over (I 11). Aristotle replies to this paradox by remarking that happiness needs to last "a complete life" (I 6, 1098a18); those who, like the Trojan king Priam, are befallen by a great misfortune in their old age cannot be called happy (I 10, 1100a5–9). This terse remark is reminiscent of the Jewish experience of Job that even a man who works righteously toward his happiness remains at the mercy of a superior power. However, the secular thinker Aristotle perceives this power not in a theological way, but as the embodiment of contingent accidents.

The view that reason does not guarantee the meaning of rational life, that is, happiness, because even a form of life appropriate for obtaining happiness does not liberate one from the insecurities and risks of life, reads like an anticipated critique of the Stoic thesis, according to which the sage can be happy even when suffering from poverty and illness or even when being tortured. It would seem that everyday experience supports Aristotle. On the other hand, in the evaluation of the theoretical and the political life at the end of the *Ethics* it does not matter that, despite the best efforts that humans need to undertake, happiness remains a fragile good. Aristotle does not arrive at the radical consequence that humans are responsible only for their worthiness to be happy but not for happiness itself, and it is true that it would modify his principle of happiness too much. Instead, he states rightly that no human activity has the amount of constancy that activities according to virtue have (I 11, 1100b12 f.). Even though the path of moral righteousness does not protect one from misfortune, any other path is even more likely to lead to the abyss.

14.2. VIRTUES OF CHARACTER

While prudence is orientated toward man's goal, happiness, it is not prudence itself that is in charge of this orientation but its necessary complement—*aretê êthikê*, virtue of character. Only the man who possesses both prudence and virtue of character, the excellent man *(spoudaios)*, lives in accordance with himself. He does the good merely because it is good, thus corresponding to Kant's concept of morality. At the same time he serves his own happiness as well: unlike the vicious, he does not suffer from inner conflicts; he has pleasant memories and hopes and need not regret anything later *(EN* IX 4, 1166a1 ff.).

Virtue of character is defined in the classical way, by genus and species. By its genus it is an attitude or habit *(hexis),* by its species a mean for us *(meson pros hêmas).* The former concept complements that of *bios.* Those who act from habit act as they do not by chance or from a happy mood, but on the basis of a firm component of their personality and therefore reliably. Here Aristotle points out the importance of a gradation that is again reminiscent of Kant's concept of morality. As he says emphatically, those who act rightly with a certain regularity do not possess virtue, but only those who rejoice in doing the right thing (II 2, 1104b 4 ff.; cf. III 11, 1117a17).

There is a natural predisposition to this kind of attitude (VI 13, 1144b1 ff.). Virtue itself needs to be learned, but this is not a matter of theorizing. Aristotle does not tire of emphasizing, against misunderstandings concerning this matter, that one only becomes just through just actions, temperate through temperate actions, and in general virtuous through virtuous actions, that is, through practice (II 3, 1105b9–12, etc.). This learning process is completed successfully when a person has found the right kind of relation to his affects and therefore pursues the right aims spontaneously (II 4, 1105b25 ff.).

The second element in the definition of virtue, the concept of mean, had considerable impact, while it is now considered obscure or empty. Thus, for example the legal theoretician Kelsen *(Reine Rechtslehre,* 1960, 375) believes that here Aristotle is, inadmissibly, giving the moral good a mathematical and geometrical definition. However, the text speaks of a mean "for us" *(pros hêmas),* explicitly rejecting mathematical definability or the objective mean *(pragmatos meson:* II 5, 1106a29–31). Kant, too, succumbs to a misunderstanding when he objects to Aristotle's "middle way between two vices" that virtue and vice are different not merely in gradation but also in quality *(Tugendlehre,* "Einleitung" XIII; § 10). In antiquity the mean was understood not only in the mathematical sense of a point that is at an equal distance from two given points of lines; the mean also indicated something perfect. In this sense Aristotle defines virtue through superlatives; he considers it the best, the ultimate, and the highest as far as excellence and goodness are concerned (II 2, 1104b28; II 5, 1106b22; II 6, 1107a8 and a23; cf. IV 7, 1123b14, etc.; cf. Wolf in: Höffe 1995).

Let us take the example of the right course of action in the face of danger. The fact that *andreia,* bravery and courage of one's convictions, is defined as the mean between rashness and cowardice (II 9–12) means also that the rash man has too much and the coward too little courage. However, what is more important is the fact that both follow a natural predisposition, the former not shrinking from any dangers, while the latter shirks all danger. To be "brave," on the other hand, means to be fearless and steadfast in the face of dangers and thus able to master them with confidence. However, it cannot be said in a way unrelated to the person involved what exactly constitutes this attitude; that is what Aristotle means by the addition "(a mean) for us." The attitude to be expected will be different depending on whether a man tends to shrink from danger or to "dash forward blindly"; furthermore, the kind and magnitude of the danger will also be important.

The brave man takes an intermediate attitude insofar as he neither faces all dangers nor recoils from all of them. He can achieve the appropriate attitude only by having the correct relation to his affects. One could also say that he organizes them in a rational way; the virtuous man has a well-considered and superior position toward his affects. Since that way he suspends mere affectivity, he excels by absence of affects in a qualified sense (*apatheia*: II 2, 1104b24–26).

The situation is analogous for the other virtues. Where bodily pleasures are concerned, the natural inclination consists in intemperance or, more rarely, apathy, while temperance (*sôphrosynê:* III 13–15) is the moderate practice. In monetary matters the attitude befitting a free man *(eleutheros),* liberality (*eleutheriotês:* IV 1–3), avoids both wastefulness and avarice; only he who does not cling to his wealth nervously is free in a personal sense. Aristotle even introduces a new virtue for generosity on a large scale: magnificence (*megaloprepeia:* IV 4–6).

The arguably most impressive section of the discussion of the virtues portrays the man whose sense of honor *(timê)*—that is, renown, recognition, and reputation—goes far beyond the common measure of *philotimia:* the magnanimous man (*megalopsychos:* IV 7–9). In the background one can see the class consciousness of an aristocracy. However, while the aristocracy bases renown on descent, Aristotle severs the connection; hereditary nobility is, so to speak, replaced by moral aristocracy. The right to renown is based exclusively on a person's achievement; honor is considered the prize of virtue (IV 7, 1123b35), because "in truth only the good man deserves honour" (IV 8, 1124a25). Again, Aristotle differs from what the Stoa will present as an ideal. In his view the superior moral person does not withdraw from the world of politics and business; the magnanimous man is active, but he concentrates on a few things that are of importance. As for the rest, conscious of his own worth, he is moderate with regard to external goods such as wealth and power; he neither rejoices excessively in good fortune, nor complains in misfortune. In addition he is not rancorous and loves things that are good in themselves rather than those that bring gain or utility. In the discussion of the magnanimous man, one aspect of Aristotelian ethics in particular becomes evident: the "standard and measure" of things is "the excellent person" (III 6, 11113a32 f.; similarly at IX 4,

1166a12 f. and III 12, 1117b17 f.). The singular denotes the individual who, whilst relating to his fellow humans, does not depend on them for his moral notions.

For these and other virtues there is a typified situation that defines their respective scope of duties, resulting not from specifically Greek, but from generally human conditions. For Aristotle the virtues of character are not the emanation of the common practice of a community, but historically developed schematizations of moral practice undertaken with regards to certain types of passion and spheres of action. Here again we find a universalist element; the same is true for the natural reaction and for the virtuous reaction to the typified situation.

In Plato, and perhaps already in the Pythagoreans, a scheme of four cardinal virtues had been developed: temperance, courage, prudence or wisdom, and justice. Aristotle abandons the scheme because he discovers, on the one hand, more than four types of situation and, on the other, more than one moral attitude in the case of two types of situation, that is to say, for reasons of differentiation. Nevertheless, Western history of thought in general, while often following Aristotle in the individual definitions, was to accept the conception canonized by Plato (*Politeia* IV, 427e, 433b-c, and *passim*). Even the Aristotelian Thomas Aquinas was to confirm the canonization (*Summa theologiae,* I–II quaestio 61 and *passim*) as well as the simplification it contained.

14.3. JUSTICE, NATURAL LAW, AND EQUITY

With respect to income and wealth, Aristotle knows three virtues: along with generosity and magnificence he also knows justice (*dikaiosynê;* cf. Bien in: Höffe 1995; Williams in: Rorty 1980). However, justice is not merely about dealing with money. A typical trait of it is the characteristic that is important for an ethics of right, that is, the concept of something owed. By this Aristotle practices a division of law and moral, which is lacking in modern Aristotelians such as Samuel Pufendorf and Christian Wolff. Justice differs from generosity and magnificence in that compulsorily authorized right may intervene if something is owed, but not otherwise. Aristotle speaks of the *allotrion agathon* (*EN* V 3, 1130a3 f.; cf. V 10, 1134b5), the "alien good" that can be understood as a good to which the other person is entitled. The characteristic of what is owed no longer corresponds to the subjective concept ("a mean for us"), but to the objective concept ("a mean according to the thing") or "mathematical accuracy," which Kant also claims for the law as opposed to virtue (*Rechtslehre,* Einleitung § E).

In general the terms *just* and *unjust* have two meanings. In the objective or institutional sense they refer to rules, in particular legal rules (laws) and institutions, even the constitution of a political community; in the subjective or personal sense they refer to the attitude of persons. In his discussion of the subject matter, book V of the *Ethics,* Aristotle deals with both meanings. Regarding the former, he speaks of *dikaion,* "what is just" or general justice, for the latter of *dikaiosynê,* justice as a virtue.

Given that the second meaning provides the leading concept, it is not possible to speak of a "new" and "legalist treatment," as Dirlmeier does in his commentary

(1991[9], 438). Right at the beginning Aristotle says that justice not only enables one to be just and perform just actions, but makes one want to do so (V 1, 1129a8 f.; cf. V 10, 1135a5–V 13). This means that it comprises more than the accordance with what is just, which would be called (juridical) legality by Kant; there is also the need for a free agreement, a disposition toward justice, or (juridical) morality. Incidentally, Kant is following Aristotelian tradition (and that of Plato: *Politeia* I 331) by using the example of the deposit: Aristotle calls just in the essential sense only a man who returns a deposit voluntarily and not from fear of punishment (*EN* V 10, 1135b4–8). Similarly, Aristotle sees injustice done in the not merely fortuitous sense only where it results from the appropriate attitude (V 13, 1137a22 f.; *Rh.* I 13, 1374a11 f. speaks of a *prohairesis*).

"Just" in the objective sense is defined as lawful *(nomimos)* and equal *(isos: EN* V 2, 1129a33 f.). The first definition refers to both the written and the unwritten law, the second not to the democratic call for equality but the fact that one should not receive less, and in particular not take more, than one's due according to the law. While the unjust man in his greed *(pleonektês:* b1 f.) wants ever more, the just man takes the middle way between doing and suffering injustice. Aristotle also introduces distinctions that are not always clear as a matter of course, but—in a certain scholastic definition—came to take on an almost canonical rank well into modern times.

Aristotle's distinctions of justice

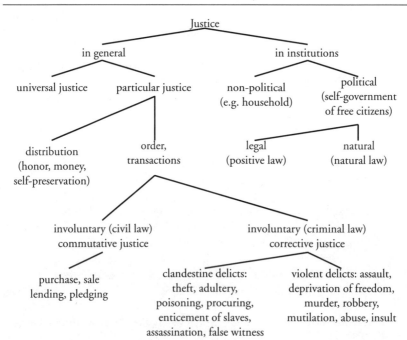

The first distinctions result from the subject matter itself. By constituting the entire virtue *(holê aretê)*—the scholastics speak of *iustitia universalis:* universal justice—justice is considered the perfect virtue *(aretê teleia: EN* V 3, 1129b26–1130a13). Given that it is easier to be virtuous toward oneself, those who are capable of being virtuous toward others as well achieve increased virtue. However, as Aristotle qualifies against Plato *(Laws* I 631c-d), justice is the complete virtue only in relation to others, but not toward oneself. In chapter V 15 he considers forbidden a typical injustice toward oneself, namely, suicide, but he interprets it as an injustice against the *polis,* considering Plato's idea of suicide as injustice against oneself as valid in a metaphorical sense only (V 15, 1138b5 f.).

Surprisingly, universal justice is equated with legal justice *(iustitia legalis:* V 15, 1138a8–10 and *passim).* This is based on the view that the laws "talk about everything" and, for example, prescribe what courage demands—not to leave one's place in the battle line—or what is part of temperance—not to commit adultery or acts of violence (V 3, 1129b14–25). Nevertheless, one need not fear that Aristotle is advocating a moralization of law and at the same time an excessive demand to be put on the legal system. In Aristotle's view the laws cannot demand the virtues but only their works *(erga:* V 3, 1129b19 f.). In addition they are *de facto* satisfied with a part of the virtues, with prohibitions of actions that were furthermore—as in the case of the prohibition of adultery—considered as a violation of the law.

Not least, Aristotle dissociates himself from the traditional opinion that in a good *polis* there is a complete correspondence between the righteousness of the citizens and the laws of the *polis:* he modifies legal justice by a second kind, justice as a specific part *(en merei aretê:* V 4 ff.). This, the *iustitia particularis,* is concerned with external goods that within the framework of political life have the status of prerequisites. The goods Aristotle defines as "basic social goods" (Rawls)—without, however, demanding their redistribution—offices and honors *(timê),* income or money *(nomisma),* and health or safety *(sôtêria:* V 4, 1130b2).

Particular justice is subdivided into 1) distributive justice *(nemêtikon dikaion),* *iustitia distributiva,* and 2) corrective or restorative justice *(diorthôtikon* or *epanorthôtikon:* 1132a18). The latter has been called *iustitia commutativa* (justice of exchange) since Thomas Aquinas, but it was not introduced with that name by Aristotle. Its measure is arithmetical proportionality ("a:b = b:c"). Corrective justice is in turn subdivided into (2.1) a "voluntary sector," that is, what is now called civil law—only in this area is there a question of justice of exchange, but only where goods are concerned—and (2.2) an "involuntary sector," or what we call criminal law, in which again one distinguishes between (2.2.1) "clandestine crimes" and (2.2.2) "violent crimes." The persistence of these legal spheres is noteworthy: Aristotle's statements (V 5, 1131a1–9) remain relevant to this day.

While for Plato money always remained suspect and no more than a necessary evil, Aristotle presents, in the context of corrective justice, the first theory of money ever written in Europe. He describes its essence and function with astonishing clarity. By making it possible to compare vastly different goods and services, money allows varied processes of exchange in a society based on the division of labor. Marx acknowledges "the genius of Aristotle," which "shines especially in the fact that he discovered a relationship of equality in the exchange of goods. It was only the historical barrier of the society in which he lived that prevents him from finding out in what this relation of equality consists 'in truth.'" (*Das Kapital*, MEW 23, 74). What Marx means is human labor. However, the fact that Aristotle uses utility value and demand value as an orientation and therefore defines money as the substitute of demand (*EN* V 8, 1133a29), can also be understood as an alternative to Marx.

The second distinction relates to the range of validity rather than the subject matter of law. In a short passage Aristotle introduces a pair of concepts that has been influential in Western ideas about law until almost the present. He speaks of natural *(to physikon or physei dikaion)* and conventional law *(to nomikon:* V 10, 1134b18–1135a5; cf. *Rh.* I 13, 1373b4 ff.); later the terms would become natural law and positive law. This distinction is based on the contrast, established at *Rh.* I 10, between a specific law and a universal, if unwritten, law common to all humans. Natural law—as well as universal law—corresponds to the moral idea of law and has two characteristics in Aristotle: universality—its power is the same everywhere—and nonarbitrariness, that is, it does not depend on people's opinions. Strangely enough, Aristotle does not discuss the possibility of conflict with positive law; this is mentioned only in the *Rhetoric* (I 13) with reference to Sophocles' *Antigone*.

While nowadays, when natural law is often considered obsolete, we tend to think of it as an eternally immutable ideal, Aristotle considers it to be changeable *(kinêton)*. It is not quite clear, however, whether it is the ideal itself that he sees as changeable or merely its always imperfect realizations. He definitely does not have in mind a finished system of universally valid legal maxims that should take the place of positive law. In the *Ethics* he does not even establish criteria, and in the theory of constitutions in the *Politics* he essentially only repeats the idea of the common good (see ch. 16.2). Natural law in Aristotle consists in a "regulative idea," the common good that is not defined in more detail—for that precise reason it contains a potential for social criticism, but otherwise he refrains from establishing certain principles. Perhaps the ideal *polis* outlined in the two last books of the *Politics* is an attempt to honor the intention of natural law concretely. However, there the realization does not, or at least not explicitly, obey the two criteria of universality and nonarbitrariness.

Aristotle's third distinction, that between justice and equity *(epieikeia: EN* V 14), is concerned with the correction of that which is provided by the law. This correction could be imagined as "improvement"; if the lawgiver has not been sufficiently careful, an amendment becomes necessary. The *Ethics* hints at this task by speaking of laws promulgated in a hurry (V 3, 1129b25). However, equity is concerned with a different correction, namely that of actual application: given that laws are by definition universal, they do not do justice to every individual case. Thus, equity is a protection against a precision that could be pedantic or merciless. Cicero can therefore refer to Aristotle when, in the *De officiis* (I 10, 33), he says that the highest justice can turn into injustice *(summum ius summa iniuria)*. It has to be said, though, that the Roman proverb quoted by Cicero is based on a double sense: its first half is about right guaranteed by the laws, while the second is about something like a moral right.

A man who acts equitably is prepared to yield even when the law is on his side (*EN* V 14, 1137b34–1138a3). Kant says with good reason (*Rechtslehre*, "Anhang zur Einleitung in die Rechtslehre") that a renunciation of this kind cannot be forced. Aristotle agrees with this insofar as he describes the instance authorized to undertake forced corrections—the judge—as animated or living justice (*dikaion empsychon:* V 7, 1132a22), but does not discuss him in the context of equity. The *Rhetoric* (I 13, 1374b19–22) makes the judge *(dikastês)* explicitly responsible for the law, allowing only the arbitrator *(diaitêtês),* a separate institution in Athens, to keep an eye on equity.

While justice and equity are introduced as two virtues, they are nevertheless not considered different attitudes (*EN* V 14, 1138a3). Situations that call for fairness are in a way test cases in which one needs to prove one's justness. Directed against mechanical subsumption, equity challenges the power of justice and in this respect complements prudence (cf. VI 11, 1143a19–24). While it disposes one to an eventual correction of the law, prudence establishes the exact correction. Since other virtues, too, need to do justice to the individual case, one would expect a corrective in them as well. However, unlike justice they are not responsible for rules and even, as "a mean for us," explicitly reject any responsibility of that kind, and therefore they already contain something that equity can provide only as a corrective: the flexibility to operate according to the situation.

Given that rules restrict justice for individual cases, it seems reasonable to want to do without rules. That is precisely Plato's opinion in the *Politicus,* when he says: "It is best when it is not the laws that have power, but the kingly man endowed with insight" (294a). In the *Politics* (III 15), Aristotle considers the same alternatives, but unlike Plato he does not consider either of the two options—the justice according to rules as present in the laws and the justice for the individual case as present in equity—renounceable. Laws are better for being free of passions, unlike men; on the other hand, man is better able to advise in individual matters (Pol. III 15, 1286a17–21). Here we have the dual task, not without tensions, that everyday language preserves in expressions such as "right and fair" and "all those who think justly and rightly." On the one hand the law, in its concern with equality, needs the general norm, on the other it needs to acknowledge the individual case in its unmistakable particularity.

14.4 THEORETICAL OR POLITICAL EXISTENCE?

The final reflection in the *Ethics* (X 6–9) decides the competition, left open up to that point, between the *bios theôrêtikos,* the theoretical life, and the *bios politikos,* the moral and political life. The semantic viewpoints of the highest goal and of autarky as well as—along with pleasure—the achievement characteristic of humans play a role in this. Given that humans differ from animals by their *logos,* the result is evident. Priority is given to the life that Aristotle sees exemplified by Anaxagoras and Thales (*EN* VI 7, 1141b3). The prototype of the excellent man is one who knows things that are extremely difficult and astounding, but also generally useless (b6–8). He is the purely theoretical scientist and philosopher, not oriented toward the application of his knowledge (*Pol.* VII 1–3, esp. 1325b14–32). According to Aristotle, the life of *theôria* fulfills the criteria of happiness, such as autarky, to the highest degree, because, unlike the political life, *theôria* has no need of external goods or of the fellow citizens and friends toward whom one acts justly, generously, etc. (*EN* X 7, 1177a29–32). Furthermore, *theôria* is free from the threat of adverse circumstances. Also, as a practice that is performed for its own sake (*Metaph.* I 2, 982b24–28), it carries its justification within itself. (The origin of the term *theory* lies in the sphere of the religious, where it means the attendance at cultic functions. In Aristotle's secularized meaning, the original concept is present only in the object of theory, the eternal.)

Two aspects of this answer catch the eye. On the one hand, the form of life chosen by Aristotle for himself is given the highest rank, on the other, this form of life is accessible only to a small number of men: the *Ethics* argues for an aristocracy of the mind. It is true that religious texts and the statements of artists use the same strategy: the former put the saint at the top, the latter the creative artist.

The thesis of the definitive superiority of *theôria* may have been even more provocative at the time than it is today. Aristotle's era did not yet have long-established and highly renowned scientific institutions; establishments resembling institutions such as Plato's Academy were viewed with suspicion (cf. the sharp criticism directed at philosophers in Aristophanes' *Clouds* or Plato's *Politeia* VII 500b; cf. also *Gorgias* 484d ff., etc.). The first sentence of the *Metaphysics* counters this attitude with an "ingenious strategy forward," namely, with the anthropological status of pure desire for knowledge. Furthermore, the *Ethics* adds (X 7, 1177a22–27), the desire for knowledge provides the greatest pleasure for humans, and it does so with marvelous purity and consistency. The *Poetics* supports this claim by saying: "Learning is the most pleasurable thing not only for philosophers but equally for the other humans, but the latter only have a share in it briefly" (4, 1448b13–15). Also, through *theôria* one approaches the divine and is most loved by the deity (*EN* X 9, 1179a30). Plato's famous claim that the philosophers should become kings so that there would be an end to misfortune for states (*Politeia* V, 473c-d; cf. *Ep.* VII 326a-b), still acknowledges the criterion, popular nowadays, of "social relevance"; Aristotle's apology of pure *theôria* rejects it uncompromisingly. In his *Six Livres de la république* (1583, ch. I 1), Jean Bodin refers to Aristotle in declaring "the highest good of the individual and that of the state" as "identical." However, the superiority of the *bios theôrêtikos* suggests otherwise. Even W. Jaeger's cautious interpretation (1954[3], I, 16 f.), suggesting the idea of a "political humanism" according to which man only develops his potential fully within the framework of the *polis*, applies to Aristotle only to a limited extent. Seen on its own, the *bios theôrêtikos* which increases reason and therefore humanity, is apolitical.

Strangely enough, while the superiority of the theoretical existence is made clear, it is not considered unqualified. The moral and political existence, too, can lay claims to happiness, given that the necessary component, the freedom of *theôria*, is possible only on a high level of economic and cultural development. Only a few people are capable of leading the appropriate kind of life, and even for them *theôria* is a condition of life that, whilst making them immortal (*athanatizein: EN* X 7, 1177b33), is possible for humans, in contrast with the deity, only for a short span at a time, in a perfectly fulfilled moment (*Metaph.* XII 7, 1072b14 f.).

To the extent to which man concentrates on the realization of the divine in himself, he rises above the moral and political life. The philosophers, who in Aristotle no longer become kings in the Platonic sense, withdraw from the *polis*. They do so not from resignation because of political hopes having been disappointed, or from a lack of political responsibility, but from an insight into their own nature. Because of his nature based on *logos*, man is destined for transcending the political life; where he does so, he is "most fully human" (*EN* X 7, 1178a7).

In his statement about the philosopher king, Plato advocates a unity of philosophy and *polis* that is not achieved voluntarily by the philosophers (*Politeia* 519b–521b). Aristotle does not oppose this relative unity by a division, the strict severing of political and theoretical existence. The transcending of the nature of the *polis* is to be understood in a more "dialectical" way, as a form of immanent transcendence: the transcending remains connected with that which is transcended. Since humans have to rely on the necessities of life and in consequence (though not merely because of them) on living with other humans, the *bios theôrêtikos* does not fulfil the semantic conditions of happiness completely. Compared with the *bios politikos,* it is the dominant goal, but is only relatively rather than absolutely choiceworthy. The theoretical life fulfils the criterion of being unsurpassably desirable only in combination with the political life. For most people, the latter represents the form in which they are capable of living for their own sake; for a small number it is the environment in which they rise to *theôria* and to which they always return because they are not pure intelligence but a combination of body and soul (X 7, 1177b28 f.). For the former, the theoretical life is an alternative, while for the latter it is supplementary. Those who dedicate themselves to the theoretical life lead a partially suprapolitical existence, but not an extrapolitical one.

A critical remark in conclusion. Given that the political life is defined by the elements that are developed in the *Ethics*—the virtues of character, intelligence, and, not least, the highest form of friendship that exists for its own sake—one leads this life not for the sake of any advantage; it is free in the Aristotelian sense. Nevertheless, one will search in vain for an indication of this in the concluding reflections of the *Ethics*.

15

POLITICAL ANTHROPOLOGY

15.1 THE RELEVANCE OF THE *POLITICS*

With all respect for other cultures' ideas about law and the state, the creation of a true theory, the combination of fundamental philosophical reflections, empirical inquiry and normative evaluation, goes back to the Greeks. While in Homer the legal system is still considered as sacral, the tragedies touching upon this subject by Aeschylus (e.g., the *Oresteia*), Sophocles *(Antigone),* and Euripides *(Orestes)* as well as the historiographers Herodotus and Thucydides, together with the Sophists, pave the way for the two outstanding theoreticians, Plato and Aristotle. Although both Plato and Aristotle treat their subject—politics including law, justice, and the state—with an unparalleled combination of analytical and speculative power, it is not until Aristotle that we get the first discursive investigation in the true sense.

Plato's leading intention, the outline of a "state according to one's wishes" (cf. *Pol.* II 1, 1260b28 f.) is still present in Aristotle: he describes in detail the size of the state, the constitution of the land and its links with the sea, the social classes, the age for marriage, education, and even the defense of the state. However, before dealing with the ideal he examines the actual *polis,* its foundations, structures, and hazards. The text on this topic, the *Politics,* a masterpiece of political science unequalled to this day, is by right studied not only by philosophers, philologists, and historians, but also by legal and constitutional theoreticians, political scientists, and even empirically oriented sociologists.

Many of the tenets remained effective throughout the Middle Ages and early modern times until the American and French revolutions and not infrequently beyond them: the central statement of a political anthropology (I 2); the beginnings of an economical theory (I 3-13), together with the influential criticism of demanding interest and of usury (*Pol.* I 10, 1258a38 ff.) and the no less influential justification of slavery; a discussion of constitution from the viewpoint of the history of problems (II); the model of a comparative morphology of the political (III–IV), including the notion of legitimate and illegitimate forms of state; the outline of a political sociology, including a pathology of the political (V); a theory of democracy that also considers the consequences (VI 1–5); not least a political utopia in the sense of the outline of an ideal polity (VII–VIII)—a remarkable number of topics and important theses either go back to Aristotle or are given a treatment by him that was to be influential for centuries.

The *Politics* is not a "work made in one casting." If its eight books can at all be said to be a homogeneous unit from beginning to end, they do not read as fluently as for example the *Ethics,* but they nevertheless represent an essentially coherent doctrine. Without doubt it contains elements that are tied to a specific time and era, beginning from the reductive size of the polities; in comparison with the city-states that formed in the limited spaces of the Aegean coast, even small modern states look like complexly large societies. In addition, the legal system of Aristotle's times shows a far smaller incidence of regulations, and there are no professional judges or lawyers. Most importantly, the degree of direct democracy present at the time is unknown not only in our representative democracies but also in the present-day model of direct democracy, those Swiss cantons that have annual assemblies of citizens. Other elements, in particular slavery or serfdom and the inequality of women, are offensive to us, but one needs to keep in mind that these were present practically everywhere at the time and remained so even in Europe and the United States well into the nineteenth century.

However, what is still the most important element of a theory of the state was known to the Greeks. Their polities were in charge of civil and criminal law; they demanded taxes, called up their citizens to military service, banished by means of ostracism *(ostrakismos),* and, as in the case of Socrates, condemned individuals to death. In brief: they knew public authority and therefore dominion in the neutral sense of the term. From a methodological point of view the *Politics,* like the *Ethics,* makes do almost without metaphysical elements. Aristotle's arguments are anthropological and based on social theory, theory of institutions or the comparison of constitutions, and occasionally on biology—when he states that the whole is by essence *(physei, ousia)* prior to the part *(Pol.* I 2, 1253a20–22) or that nature does nothing in vain (1253a9)—but they are always free of metaphysics. In its combination of theory and empiricism and its interest in the practical side of politics, too, Aristotle's *Politics* has a distinctly modern flavor.

Communitarianism, a relatively recent trend in social philosophy, likes to quote Aristotle, claiming that he was skeptical about universal principles of justice and argued for the particular forms of life of communities, and, what is more, small communities, instead. In fact, Aristotle, knowing about the diversity of the "good and just," modifies the traditions of his own society; instead of referring merely to custom *(nomô),* he champions supra-positive instances *(physei).* Nowhere does he defend customs and traditions that have not been measured against universal, or at least to a large extent *(hôs epi to poly)* acknowledged, obligations. The fact that virtues are acquired within one's own community and not in an abstract world society does not mean that one accustoms oneself merely to the peculiarities of that community. According to Aristotle, what one learns is primarily universally valid: to react to dangers neither in a cowardly way nor rashly, but bravely; to be neither wasteful nor stingy with money, but to use it generously; to be moderate as far as pain and pleasure are concerned, etc.

Where communitarians base their plea for living together with as few constraints of the state as possible on Aristotle's appreciation of friendship, they fail to see that, while Aristotle emphasizes the value of personal affiliation and relationships, he is at the same time aware that they are no substitute for a legal system, political offices, or public authorities. He is deeply skeptical about the absence of rule, recognizing in a way universal principles of justice for the legal system and order of the state that is required instead. While he does not establish a catalogue of basic and human rights, he cites legal prohibitions—such as the prohibition of theft, ill-treatment, manslaughter, robbery, and insult (*EN* V 5, 1131a5–9)—by which he supports certain basic rights implicitly: the protection of property, the integrity of life and limb, and the right to a good name. The right to political participation is beyond question in any case. The "good of a community" does not have the anti-universalist slant assumed by communitarians either. Aristotle means the notion of public good which is vague but universalist in its intent. (For a critique of the communitarian appropriation of Aristotle, see also Nussbaum in: Patzig 1990.)

15.2 "POLITICAL BY NATURE"

Aristotle is the author of the fundamental maxim of political anthropology by stating that man is *physei politikon zôon*. At the beginning of the *Politics* (I 2, 1253a2 f.), it appears in combination with three other claims: that the *polis* is the perfect community (1252b28), that it is natural (1253a2; cf. a18 f.), and also that by nature it is prior to the household and the individuals (1253a19; cf. a25). All four theorems were accepted uncritically for centuries, and it was only in early modern times that they began to encounter increasing criticism. Should these be justified, the theorems would decline to become a *via antiqua* that is replaced by the *via moderna*.

The sharpest objection is Hobbes's. Given that he considers the human less a social animal than one prone to conflict, he sees political communities as "not merely assemblies but also alliances for the conclusion of which loyalty and contracts are necessary" (*De cive*, I 1). From this fact he deduces the counterthesis that the polity is created not by nature but by art (*Leviathan,* Introduction). He believes that Aristotle makes a further error by assuming that it is the laws and not humans that rule in the state (*Leviathan,* ch. 46).

Hobbes's first objection is later followed by another, based on the theory of legitimation, that from statements about what man *is* like Aristotle derives statements about how he *should* live with his equals, thus confusing what is with what should be. Finally, man could not be a political animal, because political communities only originated at a relatively late point in history.

The last, historical, objection is relatively easy to invalidate: it imputes a static concept of nature whereas Aristotle uses a dynamic concept. As for the objection concerning legitimation, it combines descriptive and normative moments. Following the pattern of biological processes, "nature" in the context of political anthropology designates a development according to three viewpoints: the beginning and at the same time the impulse, the goal, and finally the course of the development.

According to the second meaning, nature has something to do with the essence of man and with self-realization. Aristotle does not claim that humans had always organized themselves in city-states, but that the *ergon tou anthrôpou,* the characteristic activity of humans (see ch. 14.1), is fully realized only within a *polis* community. Yet for him the modest concept of self-realization is sufficient according to which more than mere survival *(zên)* is required. And this modest concept proves to be true in a development taken for granted also in modernity: human beings are not content with living together in families and clans, but they also establish political communities.

After another objection Aristotle compares individuals as well as households with bodily organs that are capable of their characteristic activity only within the framework of the entire living organism (*Pol.* I 2, 1253a20–22). He is, however, not advocating the organological concept that declares the polity as a hierarchically structured organism in which there are qualitatively differing functions—in particular ruling and serving ones. This is clear from the fact that for Aristotle the part of the population destined to serve, the slaves, are not citizens, while the rest, the citizens, are coordinated and therefore in principle equal, given that the *polis* is defined as a community of free men (see ch. 16.2). Aristotle uses the analogy of organs in order to stress the essential importance that the relation to the *polis* has for individuals as well as for pre-political communities. As far as individuals are concerned, the relation is essential for most but not for all: there are humans who are incapable of living in a community—like a wild animal *(thêrion)*—and also those who thanks to an unusual level of self-sufficiency—like a god *(theos)*—do not need community (*Pol.* I 2, 1253a27–29).

It can also not be said that Aristotle succumbs to a "biologistic fallacy" according to which political communities develop "on their own" without any conscious human activity. Speaking about a man who established the *polis,* he calls him the originator of great goods (*Pol.* I 2, 1253a31). By doing so he goes some way toward Hobbes's position; *pace* Keyt (1987, in Keyt/Miller 1991), the two thinkers do not represent the simple alternative of *via antiqua* and *via moderna.* Aristotle would agree with Hobbes that there is a moment of art, but he rejects the notion that the political is artificial in the sense of being unnatural, by being an obstacle to the true destination of humans. At the same time it becomes evident that they have an essential point in common: both Aristotle and Hobbes object to the view that the state is a place that humans have alienated from its essence—either through luxury and decadence (as Plato says concerning the second level of the *polis*) or through the undue restriction of freedom (according to anarchist critique of the state). Rather, both consider the state a form of society that benefits humans.

Aristotle is "modern" also in the sense that he places humans in a connection with subhuman beings, given that the attribute of the political can be found among animals as well. At *HA* I 1, Aristotle distinguishes between animals living alone and those living in herds; the latter he subdivides into animals living scattered and "political" animals. As examples for "political" animals he names humans, bees, wasps, ants, and cranes, because they all perform some communal activity *(koinon ergon:* 487b33–488a10) in living together. The second of the two most important passages concerning the concept of the political, *Pol.* I 2, does not retract the biological definition, but complements it by means of comparative use. According to this passage, man is not the only political animal, but he is more so *(politikon . . . mallon)* than the bee or any other animal living in herds (*Pol.* I 2, 1253a8 f.).

The difference could be seen in purely quantitative terms, but that is not the point that matters for Aristotle, neither does what is genuinely political by modern understanding: offices and institutions, right and the struggle for power. What is important is, rather, the *koinon ergon* that is already contained in the biological concept; in this context Aristotle looks less at the reliability of cooperation—if one takes into consideration disputes and wars, it is difficult to consider humans more cooperative than bees and ants—than at quality. Essentially, animals only care for survival or simply life *(zên),* while what matters for humans is the good life *(eu zên).*

Not least, Aristotle is "modern" because he already develops a notion that has become topical recently: subsidiarity, that is, the community or society as help and support for the individual, and the higher forms of community and society as help and support for the lower forms and ultimately the individual.

Aristotle's justification of man's political nature is executed in four extremely tightly argued sequences of arguments, of which three will be outlined here. The first sequence of argumentation (*Pol.* I 2, 1252a26–1253a7) takes up the Platonic notion that the individual is not sufficient to himself *(ouk autarkês)* and needs many fellow humans (*pollôn endeês: Politeia* II, 369b). Aristotle, however, develops the thought further and, in contrast with Plato, goes beyond the economical sense of the division of labor and the facilitating of life. He assumes two forms of mutual dependence. Reciprocity contains a normative moment, which, in its modest scope of justice of exchange, again makes Aristotle appear modern. Because of an urge resembling instinct *(hormê:* 1253a30), sexuality, man and woman join together, and because of their qualitatively differing talents master and servant or slave work together. Elsewhere a third relation is added, that of children (needing assistance) to their parents. This threefold relation forms the foundation of the basic economical unit, the household *(oikos, oikia).* Since the grown-up children go on to found their own families, on the second level a community of households of the same descent—a village *(komê)* in the sense of kin or clan—is formed. Finally, several clans join together to form a *polis,* a community in which the decisive element is no longer blood ties but the interest in the good life.

While the first sequence of argumentation in favor of the *polis* takes as its starting point natural social impulses—partly biological (man-woman, parents-children) partly biological-economical (master-servant/slave)—the second refers to the gifts of language and reason (I 2, 1253a7–18). It has to be admitted that the two arguments are not entirely different from each other, since the slave is characterized by a deficiency in reason and the lack of forward-looking intelligence: *Pol.* I 2, 1253a31–34. Vice-versa, reason is something "nature makes" (a 10). Thus, the two fundamental definitions of Western anthropology—the political nature of humans and their linguistic and rational nature—are interconnected. Without his gift for reason man cannot realize his political nature; while this gift unfolds within the framework of the *polis*, it only reaches the perfection of the *bios theôrêtikos* outside the *polis* (see ch. 14.4).

Aristotle distinguishes three stages, each coupled with a level of ability of communication. Even animals possess the first level, which is a preliminary stage of practical rationality, the perception of pain and pleasure; it makes possible the political in its simple form, the survival of individuals and genera. Because of the second, the first genuinely rational stage, the ability to consider what is useful and what is harmful, the goal of survival can be differentiated into partial and intermediate goals, and the appropriate specific associations formed. Finally, the *logos* is capable of transcending the viewpoint of individual utility and thus reaches the genuinely political dimension—a community not only of good and bad, but also of justice and injustice (*Pol.* I 2, 1253a14–18).

The anthropology developed so far lays itself open to the Hobbesian reservation that it perceives the political only as a form of cooperation. However, given that this cooperation has to be organized and is threatened by conflicts as well as free-riders, there is a need for offices and institutions having the authority to coerce. Indeed, the Greek *polis* is not the extraordinary case of a polity without the elements of dominion.

The *Politics,* too, deals with laws and obedience to the laws, moreover in great detail with offices and institutions, even with the same three public powers that we know from the modern theory of the separation of powers (*Pol.* IV 14). It would be all the more surprising if, in his political anthropology (*Pol.* I 2), Aristotle said much about cooperation and nothing about the authority to coerce and rule. It would mean that the political acquired an apolitical character and that, *per silentium,* Aristotle voted for a notion that is represented explicitly only in modern times, in the era of the French Revolution: he would be advocating anarchy. Most of all, if he referred only to cooperation, Aristotle would not obtain the goal of his argumentation, the reconstruction of the *polis* from its parts; social nature alone does not make a social order with the authority to coerce, or a state.

Apart from the two considerations mentioned so far, Aristotle puts forward a third group of arguments, which is, however, missed by Hobbes and many others. He says plainly that the man who lives outside the *polis* is "a glutton for war" and a "wild beast"; not least, Aristotle says that the worst is armed injustice (*Pol.* I 2, 1253a6, a29, a33 f.). Here Aristotle anticipates something of the Hobbesian statement about "war of all against all" and of the saying that man is a wolf to man. Moreover, the concept of right and justice *(dikaion)* must not be seen from the perspective of social nature only. To put it succinctly: the Hobbesian reading that sees only man's social nature in Aristotle's political anthropology is surprisingly biased. In contrast with Hobbes, Aristotle knows more than one remedy against the threat of war; friendship is at least as important as law and justice (see ch. 15.3).

The three outlined sequences of argumentation do not appear to be entirely coherent. The first argument connects the *polis* with the more ambitious task of *eu zên,* the good and successful life, while the two other arguments are content with mutual utility and a community of right and justice. But for the first argument, as already said, a modest concept of good life is sufficient.

In the course of the *Politics* both definitions are taken up, the former, for the good life, in chapter III 9 (1280a32, b33) for example, the latter at III 12 (1282b17: *politikon agathon to dikaion*). It is, rather, the second goal that is actually redeemed. Although the *polis* takes on educational tasks as well, it is responsible neither for the perfect form of happiness, the theoretical life, nor, within the scope of political life, for the full measure of virtue. It restricts itself to the part due to one's fellow humans (see ch. 15.3), so that the "ordinary" virtue of the good citizen *(politês spoudaios)* does not coincide with perfect virtue *(aretê teleia)* (*Pol.* III 4, 1276b16 ff. and b34).

According to the first, unspecific, understanding of *politikon,* the "political nature" implies only the following: humans do not become happy alone, but only by living together with fellow humans. The second, specific, reading specifies the way of living together: man does not realize himself in sexuality or work, in economical "self-support" (cf. *Pol.* VII 6, 1326b27–30) and economical well-being, in the assistance against lawbreakers or internal and external peace, but only where he recognizes these aspects without pushing them aside and transcends them at the same time by integrating them into a demanding life. That way the "political" comprises a wide spectrum. It starts on an almost nonpolitical level with the economical relationships between households, increases in relations of kinship, the cultic and cultural community, and internal and external defense. But the *polis* is most strongly political through its community of law and justice. The meaning of the political nature postulated by Aristotle and common to the two readings lies in the following two claims: that man—on a first stage of subsidiarity—depends upon living with his fellow-humans, that is, that he is a social being *(ens sociale),* and that—on the second stage of subsidiarity—the opportunities of living together are fulfilled only in a community of the free-born and equal who organize their own living together, that is, that man is a genuinely political being *(ens politicum).*

It has to be admitted that the present has become more and more skeptical toward the polity's commitment to the happiness of its citizens, especially given Aristotle's exacting interpretation of happiness as the realization of the potential for reason innate in man, or, more generally speaking, self-realization and humanity. It is now doubted that legal and political circumstances have the power to help citizens to reach self-realization. It is also feared in particular that a legal and political system that attempts to do so nevertheless, interferes in the free play of social forces and the individual's private sphere, therefore develops totalitarian or at least illiberal tendencies, thus running counter to the true goal, humanity.

However, in Aristotle one needs to distinguish between a formal and a substantial definition of happiness. *Formaliter* happiness is not a "positive" goal for Aristotle, but one that is necessary, the horizon in which all customary goals and interests find their meaning. It is therefore possible to agree with Aristotle's formal definition even while being skeptical about his substantial concept of happiness, either in principle or within the perimeters of the debate about political legitimation. Moreover, one needs to distinguish between direct and merely indirect importance of the *polis* for the good life, a fact that Aristotle does not always take into consideration (e.g., not at VII 2, 1325a7 ff.). Furthermore, it must not be forgotten that the Greek *polis,* being a manageable location with a familiar topography and citizenry, is not merely a specific administrative unit, but also a homeland, and therefore offers far greater direct possibilities for humaneness than the present-day state with its systemic character. In addition, the latter, given its varied means for bureaucracy and policing, possesses far greater potential for abuse. Not least, the normative element in the idea of the good life must not be interpreted too emphatically. Although Aristotle does not point this out sufficiently, the *polis* is advantageous also for those who look for a life of pleasure or one of gain, that is, who are following life strategies that run counter to the substantial definition of happiness. And moreover, he is using a political, not a personal concept of good life. For, however one personally understands it, politically the good life consists in a community of law and justice.

15.3 FRIENDSHIP AND OTHER PREREQUISITES

Aristotle would not be one of the foremost political thinkers if he had only pointed out the political nature of humans while leaving aside the prerequisites and limits of the political. The most important element is friendship. Not only is it generally one of the most necessary things in life (*EN* VIII 1, 1155a4 f.), but insofar as the *polis* exists for the sake of the good life, it has to rely on "family connections, brotherhoods, common sacrifice and amusements which draw men together"; these are all "the work of friendship, for to choose to live together is friendship" (*Pol.* III 9, 1280b36–39; cf. *EN* VIII 13). Aristotle does not limit friendship to the specific case of the "romantic," very personal friendship of souls, but rather he means any kind of intentional (cf. "decision") relationship that at the same time is not institutionalized, or at least not institutionalized by the *polis.*

Friendship is dealt with in the *Ethics* (VIII–IX; cf. II 7, 1108a26–30; *EE* VII; *Rh.* II 4), because it is about noninstitutional relationships and because there is a close link with justice. There are three types of friendship among equals (*EN* VIII 3–8 and 15). It can be for mutual utility, for mutual pleasure, or—the complete form, a "friendship based on character"—for the truly good and the friend himself. In all three motives friendship shows itself to be a social reflection of man's relationship to himself, for "no one chooses to become another person" (IX 4, 1166a20 f.). By the type of friendship he chooses a man shows what ultimately matters to him in life.

Other friendships are based on inequality (VIII 8–10; also VIII 12–13 and 16). These comprise the relationships between parents and children, man and wife, and even between master and slaves; when considered as humans, the latter, too, are capable of friendship (VIII 13, 1161b5 f.). In their diversity—camaraderie, friendship among young people and personal familiarity, travel acquaintance, relations of hospitality, family, and neighborhood, as well as, to use modern terms, clubs, and networks, all the way to the rare associations for the sake of the good (VIII 6, 1157b23; 13, 1161a13–27)—the various friendships counteract the Hobbesian war of all against all. They create the kind of concord among humans that does not result from the offices and institutions of the *polis.* In that way they foster political cohesion and therefore, according to Aristotle, are of greater importance to the law-giver than justice (VIII 1, 1155a23 f.). Among friends there is no need for justice (with the exception of friendship for utility: *EN* VIII 15, 1162b16 ff.), but the just are in addition in need of friendship (VIII 1, 1155a26 f.).

Friendship calls for the ability to enter into true relationships with others without losing one's own independence. To this purpose one needs to free oneself from two kinds of affects: the importunate desire to please and calculating flattery on the one side and contentiousness and rudeness on the other. Given that the two affects are opposed to each other, friendship, too, is based on the mean (*EN* II 7, 1108a26–30; cf. *EE* III 7, 1233b30–33) as we know it already from the virtues of character, and which consists in an attitude toward the affects that is deliberate as well as superior.

The *Ethics* gives an initially surprising answer to the question whom one should love best, oneself or another: the good man should love himself (*philautos*: cf. *EE* VII 6), but the bad man *(mochthêros)* must not do so. Aristotle's argument runs as follows. The good man acts in a morally good way and thus benefits himself and others at the same time; he stands up for his friends and his country, sacrifices his money if the occasion arises, and even his life in an emergency. Since the morally bad man follows evil passions, he is harmful both to himself and to his fellow-men (*EN* IX 8, 1169a11 ff.). Thus, according to Aristotle—for the good man only, needless to say—his own happiness forms a unity with that of others; the friend is "another self" (IX 4, 1166a32; 9, 1170b6; *EE* VII 12, 1245a30). This solves a fundamental problem of eudaemonism, namely the question how one who is committed to the principle of happiness can nevertheless be altruistic (cf. Annas 1993, III, ch. 12). He can, because "in the name of happiness" he enters friendships that go far beyond his own benefit. (On the question whether the happy man needs friends, see also *EN* IX 9–11.) In this way altruism, without being specifically required, finds a natural place in eudaemonist ethics. However, this altruism is directed only at some people—not a small number, but definitely not all. A general charity as exemplified in the Good Samaritan does not feature.

Aristotle's theory of friendship overlaps with the critique of Plato's *Politeia* (*Pol.* II 1–6; see Stalley in: Keyt/Miller 1991). Opposing the anonymous relationships involved in the sharing of women, children, and property, Aristotle advocates the advantages of personal relationships: there is less argument, dispute, and violence; people take greater care of each other; not least, social relations are clearer. He protests explicitly against something that is often imputed to him: the absorption of the individual into the political community. If one is to use these labels at all, Aristotle is not on the side of communitarianism, but on that of "social liberalism" (see ch. 16.2).

A second prerequisite of the *polis* becomes apparent in the elements from which it is constructed, and to which Aristotle concedes their own justice, as his critique of Plato suggests. Not only do the economical circumstances and the relations between man and wife or between parents and children come about from pre-political reasons, but also the law of these relations are pre-political, so that a polity can only disregard but not nullify them. The *Politics*—again showing itself to be relatively modern—acknowledges these specific rights as a matter of course. The political philosophy in a narrower sense does not encroach upon the part that discusses the structure and laws of households (*Pol.* I 3–13). Science, including philosophy, also follows its own laws.

A further prerequisite is in a more complex relation to the *polis*. The virtue of character is a prerequisite as well as a consequence of the *polis* and finally also something that goes beyond it. (1) It is a prerequisite insofar as without it the existence and well-being of the *polis* are threatened. The virtuous person agrees freely with the laws, so that their coercive moment is diminished and the *polis* has no need constantly to fall back on its means of coercion—which would overtax it or lead to its perversion, the totalitarian state. Here Aristotle realizes an insight that modern liberalism has regained only gradually: the insight that it depends on correlative morals. (2) The virtues are a consequence of the *polis,* because most of them relate to social or political circumstances and are therefore practiced and learnt within the *polis*. Finally (3), they reach beyond the *polis* in the sense that the citizen's virtue comprises only part of the complete virtue; in those who rule, however, the virtue of the citizen should coincide with that of the man (III 4, 1277a12 ff.). Aristotle also concedes that the state cannot possibly consist of perfect persons only (*Pol.* III 4, 1277a 37 f.). Furthermore, the *polis* is not responsible for the good life in its entirety, but only for the communality of what is just and injust (cf. Pol. I 2, 1253a15–18, etc.). Therefore the much-quoted thesis professed in the *Ethics*—that the individual and the *polis* pursue the same good (I 1, 1094b7 ff.; cf. *Pol.* VII 1, 1323b40 ff. and VII 15, 1334a11 f.)—calls for a modest interpretation. While the *polis* provides the economical, social, and legal framework for the good life, each citizen has to define his life in this framework more closely for himself and lead it himself. In doing so, the individual good is not necessarily that of the polity.

An even more incisive limit for the *polis* lies in man's *logos*-based nature, since it serves cooperative practice neither exclusively nor primarily. On the contrary, the highest form of human self-realization, theory, belongs to *eupragia,* good actions (*Pol.* VII 3, 1325b14 ff.). Perhaps Aristotle is alluding to it when he says that the man who, because of his autarky, has no need of a community, is either evil or nobler than the man living in society (1253a4, cf. 28). At any rate, for a variety of reasons political nature is not all of man; life in a state does not coincide with full humanity.

Aristotle's argumentation still convinces, albeit only in its principles, since at least two points attract criticism. On the one hand its view of public authority is "extenuating," given that it is primarily their potential for order that is perceived, while the aspect of dominion is played down. On the other hand there is a notable deficiency. Although the Greeks had institutions common to all, such as the Olympic Games or the oracle of Delphi, as well as common coins, trade agreements, and military treaties and relations with polities outside Hellas, there were not even the rudiments of a legal community going beyond the limits of the *polis*, at least within the Hellenic world. Nor did the peace conference convoked by Philip II after his victory over the Athenians and Thebans (338 B.C.E.), which resulted in a pan-Hellenic league, find any reflection in Aristotle's philosophy. He is supposed to have developed, in a political admonition addressed to Alexander, the vision of a world state, a cosmo-polis with one constitution and one government and without war (Stein 1968). However, the fact that the *Politics* with its wealth of topics shows no tendencies in that direction, makes one rather skeptical as to whether that text, transmitted only in Arabic, is truly by Aristotle. In what concerns the "international" perspective, which is by no means disregarded (*Pol.* II 6, 1265a20 ff.), Aristotle is the child of a culture accustomed to war. Like Plato (*Politeia* II 373d-e), he sees reasons to prepare for war, but none for working toward an "international" legal system. In his *Politica* (1614³, c. 17, §§ 25–33), Johannes Althusius, an early-modern Aristotelian, would envisage the more wide-ranging units that had been developed by his time. Otherwise, he takes over the basic pattern of Aristotle's argumentation: the fundamental concept of the political is the *consociatio symbiotica,* life companionship. Marriage is its smallest form, on which the social whole builds successively and organically: first the family and the guild, then the community, the town or county or province, and finally the state. With the last two social stages Althusius goes beyond Aristotle's orientation toward the single *polis,* but here, too, the idea of a worldwide legal system is absent.

16

POLITICAL JUSTICE

16.1 ELEMENTARY INEQUALITIES

Although Aristotle defines humans by their gift of language and reason, he does not concede them elementary legal and political equality on the grounds of this gift. On the contrary, he justifies the inequalities of his times, that is, the absence of equal rights for slaves, barbarians, and women. At least part of the presented arguments is ideological in character.

16.1.1 SLAVES

The legal position of slaves—working in mines, craftsmen's workshops, private households, and on agricultural estates—is even worse than that of the helots ("bondsmen"). Helots, for example in Sparta, are excluded from owning property and political rights and are obliged to pay levies to their masters, but they live in one fixed location. Slaves, on the other hand, are bought, taken as booty in wars and sold again. The absence of sedentariness, or homelessness, is thus added on to a legally even more inferior position.

While others, such as the Sophist Alcidamas, doubt the legality of slavery (cf. Euripides, *Io* 854 ff.; *Pol.* I 3, 1253b20 f.), Aristotle asserts that slaves exist not only *bia,* through violence, but also *physei,* by nature and therefore for good reasons (*Pol.* I 4–7; cf. VII 14, 1334a2: there are people who deserve to be slaves; cf. Schofield and Kahn in: Patzig 1990; Schütrumpf 1991, I 234 ff.). In the *Politics* he assumes born slaves and born masters (I 5, 1254a23 f.), but surprisingly this notion is absent in other writings such as the *Eudemian Ethics* and the *Magna Moralia,* although these also deal with slavery.

Despite our esteem for Aristotle, the idea that there are born slaves is quite simply scandalous to us. However, upon further consideration the scandal is somewhat mitigated, given that the relationship between master and slave is supposed to serve mutual welfare (*Pol.* I 2, 1252a30–34; I 5–7 and 13) and is therefore aiming at reciprocity and, through that, justice. Those who thanks to their intellectual ability are able to provide for their own lives are masters by nature; slaves by nature are those who, in default of this ability and therefore because of a handicap due to

175

their disposition, a congenital disability, depend on someone who thinks for them; moreover they possess a body that is fit for "procuring the necessities" (I 5, 1254b22 ff.).

Extreme intellectual impairment can indeed render necessary a status of legal incapacitation that corresponds to the juridical side of slavery. Nevertheless, a number of arguments can be advanced against Aristotle: for example that intellectual deficiency can hardly be so frequent as to apply to 35 to 40 percent of the population—the percentage of slaves in classical Athens. Moreover, intellectual disability at most justifies less taxing activities and lower remuneration, but not legal and political inequality. Furthermore, intellectual disability need not necessarily be accompanied by a higher aptitude for physical labor. As for the rest, Aristotle's position is not consistent: at *Pol.* VII 10 (1330a32 f.) he recommends promising the slaves their freedom as remuneration for their activities, a suggestion that would be nonsensical if they were naturally born slaves. He also concedes that friendship with slaves is possible if one regards them not as slaves but as human beings (*EN* VIII 13, 1161b5 f.).

Aristotle's third justification for slavery, following the intellectual deficiency and physical condition of slaves—a weakness of character, the lack of courage (VII 7, 1327b27 f.)—is reminiscent of the famous chapter "Master and Servant" in Hegel's *Phänomenologie des Geistes*. There, it is not the ability for prospective thinking that decides whether someone is a master or a servant, but the readiness to fight to the death. However, the absence of this readiness does not result in a *right* to legal and political inequality, but at most the *fact* of being defeated. Incidentally, Aristotle does not regard the relationship between master and slave from the viewpoint of reciprocity but from the master's standpoint. The latter wants to devote himself to leisure activities and therefore needs, apart from the usual tools for production, "animated tools" as helpmates for action (*Pol.* I 4). Those who are too poor use an ox instead of slaves (I 2, 1252b12), but those who can afford to do so employ a steward and devote themselves to politics or philosophy (I 7, 1255b35–37). Here the situation is reversed. The deficiency is on the side of the master, who shirks (physical) work and in fact gets the greater benefit from what looks like a fair division of labor. Therefore, the *Politics* correctly concedes a deficiency of justice, albeit only in the case of those who are enslaved by force, in wars (*Pol.* I 6). On the other hand, Aristotle presents no eulogy of slavery, but on the contrary, he sees nothing edifying in the use of slaves (VII 3, 1325a25 f.); nevertheless, even the ideal *polis* is founded on this institution (VII 10, 1330a25–33). Moreover, it should not be forgotten that the first declaration of human rights, the Virginia Bill of Rights, was made in a slaveholder state.

16.1.2 BARBARIANS

The Greeks used the term *barbarians* not in a neutral way in order to designate the members of a different linguistic community, but for those who did not speak Greek, the language of high culture; the onomatopoetic word discredits those speaking a foreign language as culturally inferior. In classical times, for instance, in

Herodotus, barbarians such as Egyptians and Persians were admired for their science, wisdom, and humanity (e.g., *Histories* VII 136, where Herodotus describes the magnanimity the Persian king Xerxes demonstrates toward the Spartans). Nevertheless, Aristotle quotes with approval the words of the poet (Euripides, *Iphigenia in Aulis*, V.1400) that "[i]t is fitting that Greeks rule over barbarians" (*Pol.* I 2, 1252b8). In this passage he derives political privileges from cultural superiority, and he also reinforces the meaning of the poet's words by placing the barbarians at the level of born slaves. He justifies this by saying that "there is no natural ruler among them." The lack of prospective thinking cannot apply because the Egyptians, Persians, etc., also enjoyed periods of economical and cultural heyday and political stability.

In the *Persians* (V.181–199), Aeschylus represents the world of the barbarians and that of the Greeks as systems of life possessing equal dignity; what he criticizes is merely the attempt to force the Greeks under foreign dominion. Antiphon, a contemporary of Socrates, also emphatically denies any anthropological difference: "By nature we are all created in the same way in all respects, barbarians as well as Greeks" (Diels/Kranz 87 B 44). In this sense Alexander would treat all peoples as equal and even attempt to merge the respective élites together.

Although Aristotle does not adopt this evaluation, referring rather to the rule of free men over free men, a singularity from the viewpoint of constitutional politics which he interprets as a moral-political advantage (*Pol.* VII 14, 1333b27–29), this fact does not restrict his scientific curiosity. In the *Rhetorics* he calls repeatedly for a comparative study of political conditions (e.g., I 4, 1360a30–37), and he expresses his respect for constitutions such as that of Carthage (*Pol.* II 11, 1272b24 f.).

16.1.3 WOMEN

In Athens women were legally dependent on a guardian, usually their husband or father. The husband was not choosen freely; business was supervised by the guardian and women had no right of inheritance, but heiresses were able to pass on their inheritance to their sons. They were also legally free, had a legal claim to support and were able to sue in the case of ill-treatment. On the one hand, women are considered inferior to men even with regard to virtue (*Pol.* I 13, 1260a20–24), and the entire household, including the wife, is ruled monarchically (*Pol.* I 7, 1255b19). On the other, the *Ethics* reduces the superiority to a merely aristocratic rule and speaks also of a division of labor (VIII 12, 1160b32 f.; VIII 13, 1161a22 f.). At *Pol.* I 12–13 the relationship is even defined as "political" and therefore as a relationship between equals. By the loophole of a comparative, Aristotle reintroduces inequality, however: the male is not exclusively fit for ruling, but he is so to a higher degree (*hêgemonikôteron*: *Pol.* I 12, 1259b2).

The empiricist Aristotle could have doubted his own hypothesis about woman's inferior ability to lead, given a legal institution of his times, that of the heiress, which authorized women to "rule" the house (*EN* VIII 12, 1161a1–3; cf. *Pol.* II 9, 1270a26 ff.), as well as the fact that other peoples were ruled by women (*gynaikokratoumenoi*: *Pol.* II 9, 1269b24 f.). He does point out the active position of women in the Spartan constitution (*Pol.* II 9), and he also acknowledges that women constitute "half of the freeborn" (I 13, 1260b19). However, his statements to the contrary are more frequent and weightier, such as his quote from Sophocles' *Ajax* (V.293): "For woman silence is an adornment" (*Pol.* I 13, 1260a30). Furthermore, he speaks of the virtue not of the good person, but of the good man (*aretê andros agathou:* III 4, 1276b17), he mentions only the father in connection with children (I 3, 1253b6 f.) and only sons concerning the education of children (VIII 3, 1338a31). Thus, here, too, Aristotle follows prevalent practice: although women played a dominant role in certain cults (cf. the Delphic priestess of Apollo) and in important festivals, although great female figures feature in Homer and the tragedies—Penelope, Iphigenia, Medea—and although in vase paintings, too, we find female life represented as rich in cultural and public activities, we nevertheless encounter the Greek mainly as a citizen, soldier, head of household, and father—in short: as a man.

16.2 RULE OF THE FREE OVER THE FREE

Aristotle's political anthropology (*Pol.* I 2) operates with a minimal condition of social legitimacy, with mutual advantage for all concerned. One could speak of a *polis-legitimizing* justice: given that the political organization improves everyone's position, it is just by comparison with its absence. Aristotle's *Politics* also contains elements for a *polis-normatizing* justice. These are found in the reflections about *archê.*

Aristotle is never in doubt that society needs an *archê,* a rule or government. One reason for this may be the fact that in the term *archê* he sees less the coercive character than the moment of order and control, and therefore perceives the absence of *archê* primarily as disorder, lack of leadership, and lawlessness. Like Homer (*Iliad* II.703 and 726), Herodotus (*Histories* IX 23), Euripides (*Hecuba* V.607; *Iphigenia in Aulis* V.914), and Plato (*Politeia* VIII 558c and 560e), Aristotle, too, sees *an-archia,* absence of rule, not as a chance for freedom, but as a cause of military and political decline (*Pol.* V 3, 1302b 27–31). To him, absence of government is as undesirable as a ship—the classical simile for the state in miniature (*Pol.* III 4, 1276b20 ff.; cf. Plato, *Politeia* VI 488a ff.)—sailing without a captain; Aristotle considers rule as a fact that exists "by nature" (*Pol.* I 2, 1252a31–34). In one passage he speaks about *mê archesthai* (VI 2, 1317b15), not being ruled, but he only does so in order to ask himself whether democracy could be interpreted in such a way, and to reject the interpretation. Herodotus (*Histories* 3, 80–83) is the only ancient source to relate the story of a Persian nobleman, Otanes, who advocates a complete democracy on the grounds that he wants neither to rule nor to be ruled.

While the existence of governement is beyond question for Aristotle, the type of government is less evident to him. Legitimate rule is limited in five ways. The first limit is contained in Aristotle's differentiated concept of government. According to this, it makes a difference whether one leads a *polis,* rules as a king, is the head of a household or commands slaves (*Pol.* I 1, 1252a7–13; cf. VII 3, 1325a27–30). While the master of a household, in Greek *despotês,* the despot, rules over those who are not free, the ruler of a *polis* rules over free men. Here government is defined, and at the same time limited, using the citizen as a criterion: legitimate rule is directed at free men, and therefore those who belong to themselves and live for their own sake (*Pol.* I 7, 1255b70 f.; *Metaph.* I 2, 982b26). The free man neither assumes a subaltern position nor works for wages (*Pol.* VIII 2, 1337b5 ff.), since thanks to his wealth he can leave the care for subsistence to others, dedicating himself to public affairs. Moreover, he does not cling to his money anxiously, but, rather, distinguishes himself by his generosity.

At this point it seems opportune to digress about the conceptual field of "freedom," which Aristotle—like the Greeks in general—does not see as a unity; he does, however, know the variety of phenomena that constitute it (cf. Raaflaub 1985). While Aristotle lacks the overall concept, he does not lack awareness of the problem, which is as rich as it is differentiated. Let us point out the six most important aspects:

(1) In the theory of action the concept of the voluntary *(hekôn or hekousion)* designates primarily a person's negative freedom; a person who acts voluntarily acts neither under external coercion nor from ignorance, but rather of his own accord: from himself. (2) Aristotle uses the term *prohairesis,* deliberate decision, for the positive concept. (On points 1 and 2, see ch. 13.2.) (3) Another concept for freedom is all-round self-sufficiency, *autarkeia* (see ch. 14.1). (4) Freedom in the economical as well as legal and political sense, is *eleutheria.* According to this concept, a man is free if, unlike a slave, he is not owned by a master and therefore lives for his own sake and for the sake of the good life (cf. *Metaph.* I 2, 982b26). Subject only to the law and the succesion of public office in his life with his equals, he is politically free in a dual sense: in the positive sense by alternatingly governing and being governed (*Pol.* VI 2, 1317b2 f.), and in the negative sense by being allowed to live as he pleases (b12).

We can see that Aristotle knows three of the dimensions that are still relevant for political liberalism. According to Benjamin Constant's famous treatise *De la liberté des anciens comparée à celle des modernes* (1819), antiquity knew only the second, political, dimension and not the third, personal, one; the first is not relevant in Constant. However, Aristotle's philosophy has at its disposal economical liberty as well as positive political freedom, democratic participation, which, incidentally, goes beyond that of our democracies, and finally the negative political or personal freedom: the right to live according to one's own preferences and ideas. Admittedly, the third dimension is not guaranteed as a fundamental right and only a small part of the population is entitled to it, namely free men, as opposed to resident foreigners (metics), slaves, and women; and Aristotle does not believe that where the first dimension is lacking this must be balanced through a welfare state.

(5) According to Aristotle, those are free in a moral and practical sense who—rather than either clinging to their wealth or squandering it—are confident in their relations with external goods and distinguish themselves by liberality *(eleutheriotês).* (6) Finally, a polity is free if it makes its own laws, that is, possesses *autonomia* (cf. *Pol.* V 11, 1315a4–6).

The six viewpoints are interconnected and all play a role in the *Politics.* When government in its specifically political form is directed at free men (and equals) (*Pol.* I 7, 1255b20), when the *polis* is defined as a community of free men (*Pol.* III 6, 1279a21) and the citizen's freedom is referred to frequently, this relates mainly to aspect (4), freedom in the sense of threefold—economical, legal, and political—independence. What corresponds to it more or less on the political level is the combination of aspects (3), the autarky of a *polis*, and (6), its autonomy. The prerequisites for freedom in the sense of a person's independence are aspect (2), the capacity for decision dealt with in the *Ethics*, and (1), negative liberty, also familiar from the *Ethics*. Aspect (3), autarky, is relevant not only in the *Politics*, but also in the *Ethics*; in the former it distinguishes the form of community called *"polis,"* in the latter the principle of happiness.

After this digression, let us return to the elements that standardize rule: while Plato, in his statement about the philosopher king, pleads for the good ruler, Aristotle makes a case for the (good) law (cf. *Pol.* III 16, 1287a18 ff.). In this he is following the poet Pindar (ca. 518–446 B.C.E.), who was greatly venerated in Greece and for whom the (passionless) law was "king over all" (cited in Plato, *Gorgias* 484b; cf. *Ep.* VIII 354c). The second limitation of just rule consists in the "rule of law" (III 11, 1282b2 f.). Universal and immediately applicable regulations create the equality of rights that counteracts the danger that men easily become tyrants, because they prefer to act according to their own good (*EN* V 10, 1134a35–b2). Laws are free from all passions, and in addition they are based on considerations over a long period and therefore rich in experiences (*Rh.* I 1, 1354a–b2). However, they only guarantee a first degree of legal equality, that is, the impartial application of rules, which admits unproblematically the unequal legal position of slaves and women. Conscious of the limitations inherent in universal rules, Aristotle also adds a corrective to the laws: equity (see ch. 14.3). Greece knew neither professional lawyers nor any other professional experts, a fact that made politics both closer to the people (more "democratic") and less shaped by a strict legal form; the quasi-expert, the orator, occupied the position of the juridical expert (see ch. 4.3).

Aristotle already differentiates three public powers (*Pol.* IV 14–16). In this distinction, which anticipates the idea of the separation of powers, a *third* limitation of governance becomes evident (*Pol.* IV 14, 1297b37 ff.): the deliberative authority corresponds roughly to the legislative body, since it decides on war and peace, alliances and treaties, laws and the election and accountability of magistrates (*EN* VI 8, 1141b32 f. introduces legislations separately and distinct from deliberation). The magistrates constitute the executive and the third is jurisdiction. *De facto* there was a second, even twofold, type of separation of powers, but Aristotle does not describe it. Within Greece, power was divided between the various city-states, and these as a whole divided their influence with Delphi, the "spiritual center."

In his influential doctrine of the twice three constitutions or forms of state, Aristotle distinguishes the constitutions oriented toward the *common good (to koinê sympheron)* and those aiming at the *good of the rulers (to tôn archontôn);* he calls the former altogether just and the latter mistaken (*Pol.* III 6, 1279a17–20). (In Hobbes this criterion is lost: *Leviathan,* ch. 19.) Legitimate according to this, the *fourth,* criterion are: kingship, but not tyranny; aristocracy, but not oligarchy (rule of the rich, so it should better be called plutocracy); finally, the polity, but not democracy, which Aristotle understands as a rule of the poor (see ch. 16.3), the "most bearable" among the "worse constitutions" (Pol. IV 2, 1289b2–5). Tyranny bears no resemblance with modern forms of state such as absolutism and dicta-torship, not to speak of totalitarian regimes. A Greek tyrant's capacity for control and oppression is not even approximately like that of the machinery of modern states. Belonging to one of the leading families, he usually creates a private army, an armed following, and then attempts to legitimize his rule through public build-ings (temples, fountains, fortification), thus contributing to the common good; he also presents himself as a patron of poets, artists, and cultic festivals.

Discussing the topic at IV 10 of the *Politics,* Aristotle distinguishes between three types of tyranny. The first two—the absolute autocracy among certain bar-barians and the rule of the so-called *aisymnêtês* in archaic Greece (cf. also *Pol.* III 14–5)—correspond to the morally-politically neutral concept of tyranny desig-nating—as in Sophocles' tragedy *Oidipous Tyrannos*—an autocrat come to power by ways other than succession. In both of the cases cited by Aristotle, the rule is based on a legal foundation and (because it is chosen by the people?) is directed at men who obey voluntarily (*Pol.* IV 10, 1295a15 f.); the addendum that neverthe-less the ruler governs according to his own judgment (a17) appears inconsistent. Only the third type, tyranny properly speaking, fulfils the criterion of reprehensi-bility: (1) the autocrat rules, without being accountable, (2) over men who are his equals or betters; (3) this is done primarily for his own benefit rather than that of his subjects, and (4) no one obeys voluntarily (a 19–22).

Despite its considerable criteriological importance, the concept of common good remains curiously colorless: Aristotle does not explain it directly, but some of its elements can be deduced from his image of the ideal *polis*. The first point is de-fense. Whether he is talking about the city's geographical position (*Pol.* VII 5, 1326b39–1327a7), including its access to the sea (VII 6, 1327a18–25), the expan-sion of the state (VII 10, 1330a16–23), or the building of roads (VII 11, 1330b17–31), Aristotle is always aware of problems of military security. A second element is commercial relations (VII 5, 1327a7–10), or general questions of eco-nomical politics. A third element consists in the apportioning of arable land. Aris-totle suggests a division into four (not explicitly equal) parts: (1) commonly owned (state) land, the produce of which covered (1.1) the costs of cultic functions and (1.2) those of communal meals; and (2) private property. Presumably for reasons of justice as well as in order to achieve harmony among mutually hostile neighbors, each citizen is allotted two plots of land: (2.1) one near the state borders and (2.2) one in the interior of the country, near the city (VII 10, 1330a9–23). This mixed system of communal and private property is directed against both extremes—com-plete "socialization" or nationalization of the land as well as exclusively private land ownership. Two things are to be secured through communal property: the funding of public activities (in Aristotle this is related to cultic functions only) and a suffi-cient livelihood ("communal meals") for every citizen.

Considering the social purposes of communal property, one could say that Aristotle shows the beginnings of a tendency toward welfarism and fair distribu-tion. There are communal meals funded with public moneys (II 10, 1272a12 ff.)—following the example of Crete (II 10, 1272a19–21) but unlike, for example, Sparta. Because of its fundamental importance, the ideal state is even concerned with water, decreeing which water may be used for drinking only and is not available for any other uses (VII 11, 1330b11 ff.). *Pace* Nussbaum (in: Patzig 1990), one must not overrate the scope of Aristotle's welfarism, since Aristotle objects to democratic institutions such as attendance fees, which would allow even poorer citizens to participate in the people's assembly. Another element can be interpreted as welfarist at first glance but not on closer inspection: in the context of his critique of the *Politeia,* Aristotle advocates a mixed form of property: ownership *(ktê-sis)* should remain private, while its use *(chrêsis)* should be communal. This communal use could be understood as welfarism only if it was directed by the state. However, Aristotle is not in favour of a state-controlled, that is, anonymous as well as enforced, form of collective use, but advocates its personal and voluntary form within the framework of friendship distinguished by generosity (despite VII 10, 1329b39 ff.). The strongly aristocratic traits of Aristotle's ideal *polis* also constitute an argument against welfarism: while the land is divided between all citizens, it is cultivated by slaves (VII 10, 1330a25–33). Along with slaves and metics, craftsmen, merchants, and ordinary farmers are also excluded from citizenship. Thus, those who remain eligible for the good life that is to be promoted are the members of the small group of men not working for a living, who devote themselves to military service in their youth, the administration of the state and of justice in their prime, and to priestly tasks in their old age (*Pol.* VII 9).

If one combines the two prerequisites of prime importance, that is, disassociation from despotism and commitment to the common good, legitimate rule—always with the restriction that this is valid only within the framework of the citizenry as such—excludes political oppression ("rule over those who are not free") as well as exploitation ("government for the benefit of the ruler"). Nevertheless, Aristotle does not have the ambitious principle of equality for all humans; neither women nor slaves have full rights as humans, nor do, in the ideal *polis,* farmers, craftsmen, and merchants.

Finally, among the forms of government oriented toward the common good, Aristotle prefers the rule of the many, the polity, to the constitutions ruled by one man, the king, or a small group, the aristocrats. (Strangely enough, in *EN* VIII 12, 1160a32–36 the polity or timocracy is considered inferior to monarchy and aristocracy.) The polity is the political constitution *tout court,* the "political *polis*" or the "citizens' state," in which the citizenry—which is, however, constituted by only a part of the population—is defined by its political participation in an emphatic sense, by taking part in the government. Transmitted via the Latin translation *res publica,* republic, the polity survives in all European languages as an ideal that excludes any constitution that limits power and official authority to an individual or to a small group. Nowadays "republic" as well as its translation "free state" is a concept belonging to constitutional theory, designating a state in which the king and the aristocracy have lost their priviledge to rule. The Greek model contains two further elements: the commitment of governance to the common weal and a degree of direct democracy that goes beyond even the Swiss cantons and citizens' assemblies. Citizens in the full sense of the word take part in all leading offices (*Pol.* III 5, 1278a36) and take turns in ruling themselves (I 1, 1252a15 f.). The majority of offices is even decided by lot. (Cf. *State of the Athenians* chs. 42–69, where the plethora of offices and office-like functions is listed in the greatest detail, including modes of appointment, terms of office, and remunerations; on this topic, see Chambers 1990.) This rejects any consolidation of power as it is preponderant in modern democracies, in particular because of their system of representation and the professionalization of the representatives. According to Aristotle, fully legitimate rule needs to contain a relation of mutuality and symmetry, corresponding to the relationship between orphaned siblings who, in the absence of a father, rule themselves alternately. In the *polis,* for which Aristotle sees humans as destined by nature, the citizens are equal in the true sense of the word, peers who are of the same status like the members of the British House of Lords, the *confrères* of the Académie Française, or the *Ordinarien* at the classical German university.

16.3 DEMOCRACY OR POLITY?

From the viewpoint of the theory of legitimation, the modern state rests on two pillars, democracy ("All power emanates from the people"), which is a concept of constitutional theory, and the strict human rights concept of equality. Given that Aristotle does not know human rights equality and explicitly rejects democracy, his political ideal appears to be premodern. However, his critique of democracy does not support the constitution that has been replaced by modern democracy, namely, monarchy. Rather, on the one hand, he introduces a differentiation into the concept of democracy and on the other he considers as ideal the constitution that is a combination of democracy and oligarchy (*Pol.* IV 8–9 and 11 ff.), that is, the citizens' state ("polity"), which is unknown in this definition as mixed constitution today, but survives in substance under the name "republic."

1. In his discussion of democracies, Aristotle combines a question concerning the theory of constitutions—"Who is the sovereign *(kyrios)?"*—with another, pertaining to social economics, about the group within the population that possesses sovereignty. In an oligarchy, the most important alternative to democracy, it is the rich who are sovereign, while in a democracy it is not the entire people but the group of the poor (*Pol.* IV 4, 1290b1 f.). By this Aristotle does not mean beggars, but—revealing his aristocratic background—farmers, paid laborers, craftsmen, and merchants.

According to the group of citizens capable of governing (admitted to rule) and the range of their competence for ruling, Aristotle distinguishes between four forms, thus introducing a comparative concept of democracy (IV 4). What the first three forms have in common is a connection with the law. Within the framework of this constitutionality, the first and weakest form of democracy is based on a census or property qualification. In the second, stronger, form incontestable lineage is sufficient: both parents need to be citizens. In the third, even stronger, form, the criterion of descent is relaxed and all citizens are capable of governing. Only in the fourth form, when all citizens have access to the offices and furthermore the link with the law is severed, does democracy achieve its radical or complete form. In this last case all citizens are capable of governing, and just as the leaders of the people *(dêmagogoi)* want, the people, unfettered by any statutory limitations, can decide on everything in the assemblies—and therefore allow itself flagrant violations of the law. Given that it tends to have in mind its own advantage rather than the common good, the people rules despotically over its "betters"; radical democracy results in a tyranny of the majority (IV 4, 1292a15 ff.; cf. IV 14, 1298a31–33 and *passim*).

In a second description of the four forms of democracy (IV 6), Aristotle names the reason for the acceptance or nonacceptance of laws. Surprisingly, it does not consist in the insight—which belongs to the theory of legitimation—that laws are impartial, although this insight features elsewhere in Aristotle (e.g., *Pol.* III 15, 1286a17–21: freedom from passions). Instead, he cites the social and economical reason that one should leave the laws to rule where the sovereign, for example the farmers, lacks the leisure *(scholê)* for permanent politics. When the cities become larger and in particular richer, so that the poor, especially craftsmen and paid laborers (cf. IV 12, 1296b29 f.), have the necessary leisure for politics because of adequate pay, the laws are abolished and the people takes over the entire rule (IV 6, 1292b41–1293a10). Aristotle has two concepts of freedom, the foundation of democracy: positive political freedom, according to which one alternately rules and is ruled (VI 2, 1317b2 f.) and negative political freedom, the remarkably liberal concept that one is free to live according to one's wishes (b12; see VII 12, 1316b24; VIII 4, 1319b30). The first concept results in the democratic institutions (b27 ff.): all offices are filled with all (citizens); all, or at least the most important, decisions lie with the people's assembly, etc.

Aristotle criticizes mainly radical democracy. For example, he objects to attendance fees (for taking part in the people's assembly), which are financed through a property tax and the confiscation of property (*Pol.* VI 5, 1320a17–24). A more fundamental accusation is that of technical incompetence: the people's assembly is morally and intellectually overtaxed (*Pol.* III 11, 1281b25 ff.). Looking at the Peloponnesian War, which was objected to by the rich—who were to pay for the fleet—but supported vehemently by the majority, that is, the poor, one could say that he may have been right; as is well known, the war ended with the defeat of Athens. On the other hand, Aristotle also advances arguments in the favor of democracy; for example, he considers the majority more competent than a small élite (III 11, 1281a39 ff.).

This argumentation is startlingly nonchalant and contradicts the charge of incompetence—as if the virtue and intelligence of different people could simply be added so that it results in a superior collective competence both in character and intellectually. I am not discussing the validity of the argument but its pro-democratic content. Another pro-democratic remark is that the good citizen needs to be capable both of being ruled and of ruling (III 4, 1277b14 f.). What Aristotle means is the ability to obey and command in turn, as well as the readiness to work "selflessly" for the common good in both functions.

2. The citizens' state. Aristotle's political ideal consists in a mixture of democracy and oligarchy. This ideal is not reached "deductively," but, rather, puts into practice a reality that had been emerging since Solon's reforms. Again Aristotle combines elements of constitutional theory with viewpoints of a political sociology. In order to achieve a political as well as social balance between the (rich) leading élite and the (not so rich) masses, he advocates the cultivation of a broad middle class. The reasons he lists are that those with a medium amount of property will most easily obey reason, friendship develops more easily, sedition and strife are least likely, and, not least, the best lawgivers (Solon, Lycurgus, Charondas) came from the middle classes (*Pol.* IV 11).

The idea of a mixed constitution is hinted at already in Thucydides' *History of the Peloponnesian War,* where the author describes the constitutional development of the year 411 B.C.E. (VIII 47 f., 63 ff. and 89 ff.). Rudiments of a theory do not appear until the late Platonic *Laws* (III 693d ff.) and the *Eighth Letter* (*Ep.* VIII 354a ff.); however, Plato's model is not Athens but its archrival Sparta.

The concept of democracy decides the question to what extent the citizens' state, or the mixed constitution is compatible with democracy in the present-day sense. While Aristotle does not ask himself the question that is the foundation of modern democracy, namely, that about the legitimation of rule, he rejects—partly explicitly, partly implicitly—the forms of legitimation that are the alternatives to modern democracy: that all power originates with God or a superior power or the appropriate lineage. Given, furthermore, that the mixed constitution is committed to the welfare of all those involved, the common good, and that in this constitution the most important decisions are made by the *ekklêsia,* the people's assembly, it can be considered largely democratic even in the modern sense as far as the basis for its legitimization is considered. In addition, Aristotle concedes that "what we call polity (or republic) today, used to be called democracy" (*Pol.* IV 13, 1297b24 f.). Therefore—and we must not forget that—republican thinking has its origin in neither the American nor the French revolution, nor in Republican Rome, but in Athens, and its most important theoretician there is Aristotle.

A further point that Aristotle's political ideal has in common with modern times is that the magistrates are chosen by the people—directly at the time, while it is done indirectly now—and are responsible to it. Governmental offices, on the other hand, are assigned to individuals who as a rule belong to the upper class in order to avoid a degeneration of democracy (cf. *Pol.* II 12, 1274a18 ff.). Only at this point one can discern a nondemocratic, that is, aristocratic or oligarchic element. On the other hand, there are also decisive differences between the mixed constitution and modern democracy. While in modern, representative, democracies the element of direct democracy is either lacking or only weakly developed, the ancient citizens' state lacks institutions such as basic or human rights, parties and syndicates, the press, or a constitutional court. A legislator in the modern sense is also still absent.

PART V

THE RECEPTION

The history of Aristotle's influence is almost unique. For two millennia, up to the threshold between the seventeenth and the eighteenth centuries, philosophy and the sciences were shaped partly by the reception and development, and partly by the critique of Aristotle's thought. Many of the philosopher's concepts—some directly, but the majority via Latin translation—have become a definite component of the languages of the sciences and even of colloqial speech in Europe and adjacent countries. Equally, the names of numerous disciplines and in particular their basic concepts and many patterns of argumentation go back to Aristotle. Even after the wane of his influence in the course of early modern times, Aristotle time and again became an important starting point for systematic philosophizing. It goes without saying that in the following these tangled—and not yet fully investigated—paths can be discussed only summarily.

17

ANTIQUITY AND THE MIDDLE AGES

17.1 ANTIQUITY

Aristotle was esteemed by his immediate contemporaries in particular for his contributions to logics and ethics, but hardly at all for his learned as well as astute research into nature. After his death, his influence increased, emanating from the school of Athens, which stood its ground with varying success until the third century C.E. Under its first head, Theophrastus (372–287 B.C.E.), it attracted an unusually large number of students—no fewer than 2,000 according to Diogenes Laertius (V 2, 37). While Theophrastus preserved Aristotle's broad intellectual horizon—he became famous for his *Metaphysics* as well as his botanical writings and his book about *Characters*—his successor Strato brought empirical research into the natural sciences to the fore. After him, with Lycon, the "death-like sleep of Aristotelian philosophy" (U. v. Wilamowitz) set in. There were still a few outstanding achievements in some specialized disciplines, but no more philosophical impulses. At the best, Aristotle's philosophical tradition was continued in Rhodes in some way or the other by his pupil Eudemus who, mediated by the Stoics Panaetius and Poseidonius, was to influence Cicero.

One of the causes responsible for the decline of the Peripatetic school was the loss of the official school library. Because of this loss, Aristotle was known in Hellenistic times for his dialogues and some exoteric texts, but rarely for his didactic writings. Although copies appear to have existed in Athens and Rhodes, these had no influence. Another decisive factor was a high degree of specialization. On the one hand, this makes it possible to attribute to the Aristotelian school the great researchers and scholars of the Hellenistic age, such as: the geographer and polyhistor Dicaearchus of Messene (born before 340 B.C.E.); Aristarchus of Samos (*c.* 310–230 B.C.E.), who was the founder of a heliocentric model of the planets; the mathematician, geographer, and astronomer Ptolemy (*c.* C.E. 86–160); the creators of grammar and syntax, Apollonius Dyscolus and his son Herodianus (both second century C.E.; the latter systematized metrics and prosody), and not least the physician, polymath, and commentator of Aristotle, Galen. On the other hand, specialization also made it more difficult to continue Aristotle's combination of empirical research with (fundamental) philosophical interests. Not least, an advantage according to the theory of science, that is, the absence of a homogeneous system, contributed to the decay of the Aristotelian school.

Only Andronicus of Rhodes, the eleventh head of the school, emphasized the teaching of philosophy again, organizing an edition of the hitherto forgotten treatises in Rome for that purpose (second half of the first century B.C.E.). According to ancient tradition, it was based on original manuscripts, which through fortunate and almost unbelievable circumstances reached Rome, the political and cultural center of the time: Neleus who, being the last member of the school of Aristotle, had inherited the manuscripts from Theophrastus, took them to his home town, Scepsis in Asia Minor, near the ancient city of Troy. Two hundred years later they were bought there by a bibliophile called Apellicon and made accessible to those interested in an, albeit not very reliable, "edition" in Athens. In 86 B.C.E., when Athens was captured by the consul Sulla, who was well disposed toward the Peripatos, he took back Apellicon's library as part of his loot of books and works of art.

The edition organized by Andronicus was the impulse for an Aristotle renaissance, which had more than just intellectual impact. Influential Romans such as the young Octavianus (Augustus) studied with Aristotelians, and later Marcus Aurelius established a chair for Aristotelian studies in Athens. In this period, Aristotle's teaching was partly unified, for example in the *Epitome of Aristotelian Ethics*. Partly it was amalgamated with Platonic thought, for example, in the short work *Peri kosmou (De mundo), About the World* (cf. Strohm 1984³), which for a long time, despite the doubts voiced by Proclus, was considered as Aristotle's own synopsis of his cosmology. The aforementioned Galen based himself partly on Plato, but relied on Aristotle for questions pertaining to the natural sciences. His attempt to establish medicine as a science by using Aristotelian methodology gave philosophy the status of medical propaedeutics. As a result, as late as the thirteenth century, according to a regulation by the emperor Frederick II (*Liber augustalis,* III, 46), the future doctor would study philosophy—mainly logic and theory of science—for three years and then medicine for five.

Andronicus's was the first of numerous commentaries to appear in the course of the first Aristotle renaissance (cf. Moraux 1973 and 1984, as well as Sorabji 1990). Written not only by Aristotelians but also by Stoics and Platonists, these were initially concerned mainly with the *Categories,* that is, Aristotle's early ontology, and later, for example, in Aspasius (first half of the second century C.E.), with the *Ethics* as well. The climax of commentaries on Aristotle in antiquity was reached with Alexander of Aphrodisias (*c.* 200 C.E.) who was active in Athens. Because of the clarity and reliability of his commentaries, he is called the "second Aristotle," ignoring the fact that interpretation has taken the place of autonomous philosophizing. Nevertheless, Alexander is not a mere commentator; he attempts to prove the existence of free will in the sense of freedom of choice on the basis of the human ability for deliberation. He is also the originator of a logical diagram, the *pons asinorum.* By equating the Unmoved Mover with the active intellect *(nous poiêtikos)* he becomes a key figure in the history of metaphysics of the mind; by way of Neoplatonism he influences Averroes and the Germans Mystics (see Merlan 1955, also Krämer 1967²).

In the period following Alexander of Aphrodisias, Aristotle was initially pushed into the background, until he attracted the attention of the Neoplatonists, who in general aimed at a synthesis of Platonist and Aristotelian thought. While the great Neoplatonists—Plotinus (204–270) and in particular his pupil Porphyry (240–325)—were aware of the differences in teaching, they nevertheless did not abandon the intention of achieving a synthesis. In Neoplatonism, Aristotle's works were commentated upon meticulously, for example, in Constantinople, the *De anima* by Themistius (fourth century), as well as the *Metaphysics* by Proclus's teacher Syrianus and, in Alexandria, first the *Categories,* the *Hermeneutics,* and the *Prior Analytics* by Ammonius, and later the *Categories,* the *De anima, De caelo,* and *Physics* by Ammonius's pupil Simplicius. It can be said generally that in the intellectual centers of the time—Athens, Constantinople, and Alexandria—philosophy was taught by using commentaries on Aristotle. However, the most famous text written about Aristotle's works by a Neoplatonist is Porphyry's introduction *(Isagôgê)* to Aristotle's *Categories.* Boethius was to translate it into Latin together with Aristotle's work, and even today it is customary to preface Aristotle's *Categories* with Porphyry's work.

17.2 CHRISTIANITY, ISLAM, AND JUDAISM

The three religions based on revelation all grappled—first Christianity, then Islam, and then Judaism—with Aristotle, since they needed to adjust to the intellectual level of "pagan" philosophy for apologetic purposes. In order to do so they adopted the propositions of the *Organon* on logic and the theory of science, and with their help committed theology to conceptual clarity and argumentative stringency. Furthermore, they used *Physics* VIII 5 and *Metaphysics* XII 6 as an orientation for the conception of a "proof" of the existence of God. In doing so, they approached the philosophical works almost as though they were religious texts: they cited them and commented on them, but hardly ever attempted a critical analysis. Aristotle was considered *the* philosopher, even the "praecursor Christi in naturalibus," the precursor of Christ in what concerns the natural, that is, worldly, things.

With respect to some important questions, however, the theologians found Aristotle problematic: (1) the concept of the Unmoved Mover can hardly be made to agree with the idea of a personal God; (2) the cosmological concept of a self-sufficient God leaves no room for divine providence or God's care for the world; (3) in contradiction of the idea of Creation, Aristotle considers the world eternal; (4) he rejects the immortality of the soul; (5) not least, appeals to divine commandments are alien to Aristotle's ethics.

The reactions of early Christian theology to difficulties of this kind varied. The Latin patristic writers, Christian Platonists such as Tertullian (*c.* 160–220) and Jerome (347–419), were unable to forgive Aristotle's critique of the theory of ideas or the aforementioned views that contradict Christianity. With the exception of Johannes Scotus Eriugena (810–877), before the twelfth century the Latin world knew only one mediator of Aristotle of the first order: Boethius (about 480–524/5), the "teacher of the West." Given that his project to translate all of

Aristotle's works was put into practice for the *Organon* only, without the *Posterior Analytics* (*c.* 510–522), and only two translations remain known, these—the *Categories* and the *Hermeneutics*—became the Aristotelian writings most discussed in the Middle Ages. The only philosophical discipline contained in the curriculum for monastic and cathedral schools that Charlemagne had sanctioned and that remained valid for more than four centuries, the *septem artes liberales* or seven liberal arts, was logic, based on the *Categories* and the *Hermeneutics*. Greek patristic writing, on the other hand—from Origen (*c.* 185–250), through Gregory of Nyssa (*c.* 330–395) and Nemesius to Pseudo-Dionysius the Areopagite (fifth/sixth century), was strongly influenced by Aristotle. Beginning with Leontius of Byzantium (sixth century), it even made more use of Aristotle than of Plato. Only Michael Psellus reversed the situation, but his pupil John Italus again gave preference to Aristotle.

Because of the absence of religious or speculative tendencies, the model for an exegesis of Aristotle that is faithful to the text, namely the philosophical school of Alexandria, had no problems with Christianity, the new power. Thus, for example, Ammonius, head of the school since 485, converted to Christianity without, however, renouncing all the theses of Aristotle that contradict it. The Athenian Academy, on the other hand, did not find a compromise with Christianity, and therefore in 529 Justinian prohibited the study of philosophy and jurisprudence there, an injunction amounting to the closure of the Academy. A hundred years later Stephanus was called from Alexandria to Constantinople (Byzantium), the capital of the Eastern Roman Empire, which rose to become a center of Aristotelian studies for five hundred years (cf. Oehler 1968). While Latin Europe dealt only with the *Hermeneutics* and the *Categories,* in the East the *Physics* and *Metaphysics,* as well as the *De partibus animalium* and *De generatione animalium,* and not least the *Ethics* and *Politics,* were also studied.

Aristotle gained even greater influence among the Syrian Christians, the Nestorians. In the fifth century they founded a school in Edessa, which succeeded that of Antioch and was run by an outstanding translator of Aristotle, Ibas (d. 475). The treatise *Theology of Aristotle,* too, was written in Syria; in reality it contains a paraphrase from Plotinus's metaphysics, the *Enneads* IV–VI, and shapes the future reception of the *Metaphysics,* influenced by Neoplatonism. The situation is similar for the *Liber de causis:* while Albert the Great still considered it the completion of Aristotelian metaphysics, it is in fact a collection of excerpts from the *Elementatio theologica* of Proclus.

From Syria, Aristotle was transmitted to the Islamic-Arabic cultural area, which was to become the center of philosophy and science. The Arab rulers, well familiar with Aristotle in their turn, employed Syrian doctors who, together with the works of Ptolemy and Euclid, brought along Aristotle's works, and not merely a selection of them. The only exception was the *Politics,* because Plato's *Politeia* was preferred. In 830, an academy was founded in Baghdad, the capital of the Arab world: the Bait-al-Hikma or house of wisdom, which was intended for making all sciences available in Arabic by way of translations from the Greek, Syriac, and Pahlavi (Middle Persian). The most important translator, Hunain (Johannitius;

ninth century), a Syrian and a Christian, was called the "Cicero of Arab culture" because of his achievements (Düring 1954, 280).

The most important early philosopher writing in Arabic, Al-Kindi (d. 873), the translator of the *Metaphysics,* read Aristotle in the spirit of Neoplatonism. Similarly, the mathematician, theoretician of music, philosopher, and theologian al-Farabi (*ca.* 870-950), praised by his contemporaries as the "second teacher" (after Aristotle). His countless writings, as well as the pseudo-Aristotelian *Theology of Aristotle* and Aristotle's own works were a strong influence on the Persian philosopher and physician Ibn Sina (Avicenna; 980–1037), the first great thinker of Islam.

From the eighth century, the study of Aristotle—his logic, theory of science, physics, metaphysics, and psychology, and not least his poetics and rhetoric—became part of the canon of Arab education. With the conquest of Baghdad by the Turks (1055) this era of Islamic-Arabic Aristotlelian tradition came to an end. Nevertheless, Aristotle was not entirely lost to Islam, because Graeco-Arab scholars had settled in Sicily and in particular in the Spanish city of Cordoba before that date. The latter, the "Baghdad of the West," was the background for the works of Ibn Rushd (Averroes; 1126–98) who through his commentaries on Aristotle became an important mediator of Aristotle to European Scholasticism. Averroes refuted al-Ghazali's (1058–1111) religiously motivated skepticism against philosophy, claiming instead that rational metaphysics is superior to theology. More faithful to Aristotle than Avicenna, he rejected the ideas of Creation, divine providence, and individual immortality of humans, thus founding Averroism which was to have great influence in the thirteenth and fourteenth centuries.

Jewish philosophy received its first Aristotelian impulses from Syria and Persia in the seventh and eighth centuries. Saadja (882–942) had already made the attempt to prove truths of faith by means of reason, but it was only after the reception of the teachings of al-Farabi and Avicenna that one can speak of a Jewish Aristotelianism that developed on the territory of Islamic culture and in Arabic language. The earliest writing that is entirely pervaded by an Aristotelian spirit is Abraham Ibn David's *The Sublime Faith* (1161). Abraham declares the study of Aristotle an unrenouncable prerequisite for the cognition of faith, but unlike Aristotle he holds fast to the idea of Creation. The same is true for a contemporary of Averroes, the eminent scholar Moses Maimonides (1135–1204). He is the author of the most important work of Jewish enlightenment in the Middle Ages, the *Dalalat al-Ha'irin (Guide of the Perplexed),* written in Arabic. It combines Aristotelian thought with Neoplatonic elements such as the theory of emanation, and was received by Albert the Great, Thomas Aquinas, and Duns Scotus. After the time of Maimonides, however, Averroes prevailed in Jewish Aristotelianism; Levi ben Gerson (1288–1340), for example, rejected the idea of a creation *ex nihilo.*

17.3 THE GREAT ARISTOTELIAN RENAISSANCE

As far as Aristotle was concerned, the learned world of the Middle Ages was content with the *logica vetus,* the "old logic," which consists in the Latin translations of the *Categories,* the *Hermeneutics,* and the *Isagôgê* of Porphyry, as well as the logical treatises of Boethius. The first translation into the vernacular, German by the way, made by the monk Notger (950–1022) of St. Gall, was of the *Categories* and the *Hermeneutics*. Around 1120 a second, richer, reception of Aristotle set in, which by the middle of the thirteenth century developed into the most powerful Aristotelian renaissance (cf. Kretzmann et al. 1982). It was spread by a new type of scientist—professional rather than monastic, as well as with an international orientation. First, Boethius's other translations of the *Organon* reappeared. This opened the second period of medieval logic, the *logica nova* ("new logic"), which included both *Analytics* and the *Topics*, achieving the status of logical and methodological propaedeutics for the whole of Europe.

This richer version of Aristotle (and with it, Euclid, Ptolemy, Hippocrates, and Galen), not restricted to the *Organon*, reached the West not because his works had been studied continually in Athens or Rome, the place of their first edition, but via Syrian-Arab and Byzantine Aristotelianism. The necessary activity of translation began in Byzantium (Jacob of Venice), Sicily, and Spain (e.g., Gerard of

ARISTOTLE (Portal Royal of Chartres Cathedral, twelfth century)

Cremona in Toledo). It continued at Oxford (Robert Grosseteste; esp. the *Nico-machean Ethics*), reaching its high point with the Dominican William of Moer-beke; his translations served as the foundation of the work of Thomas Aquinas, who himself did not read Greek.

Along with the *Poetics,* which was translated but remained unknown all the same, Aristotle's *Politics* also surfaced at this time. It is commentated upon by, for example, Albert the Great, Thomas Aquinas, and Nicholas of Oresme (fourteenth century), but notably not by jurists. If one goes by the number of commentaries, Aristotle was nevertheless dealt with mainly as a logician, then as a metaphysician, and only in third place as a philosopher dealing with morals and politics. All the same, political philosophy as a university discipline took Aristotle as its point of departure. Through two writings directed against claims to power made by the pa-pacy, his *Politics* even achieved an influence that went beyond mere learned stud-ies. Dante's work about empire, *De Monarchia* (about 1310), and the treatise by Marsilius of Padua about peace (*Defensor Pacis,* 1324) breathe the spirit of Aris-totle; while Dante makes political power originate in God, according to Marsilius it emanates from the people.

The large-scale reception of Aristotle was not uncontested. However, the nu-merous prohibitions of Aristotelian works issued by the Church or the universities (e.g., 1196 in Cordoba, 1210 at a Paris synod, 1215 at the Lateran Council) were directed not so much against Aristotelianism on the whole as against those aspects of it that are contradictory to Christianity. At any rate the prohibitions against Aristotle were unable to check the philosopher's steadily increasing influence. On 19 March 1255 the most influential faculty of arts of Paris stipulated the study of all the writings of Aristotle that were known at the time, that is, not only the *log-ica nova* but for example also the *Physics, De anima, Metaphysics,* and *Ethics.* One could say that this acknowledgment of Aristotle's philosophy constituted the birth of the faculty of arts, namely of its independence vis-à-vis theology. Soon it be-came the norm everywhere, and in many places remained so until the end of the Middle Ages, that Aristotle was the core, and often the exclusive content, of the study of philosophy.

The first to break with the initially selective transmission of Aristotle was the "doctor universalis," the natural scientist, philosopher, and theologian Albert the Great (1193–1280). Being the first to make all of Aristotle's works (including his research into nature) fruitful for theology, he became the pioneer of a system of Christian Aristotelianism permeated by Augustinian elements, which Albert's pupil—the "prince of Scholasticism" and "doctor communis," Thomas Aquinas (1224/5–74)—would lead to the apogee of medieval thought. In the middle of the thirteenth century Aristotle was the towering intellectual authority for the Occi-dent: the "master of those who know," as the great lay philosopher Dante praises him in the *Divine Comedy* ("Inferno," IV 131). And in Syria the Jacobite bishop and scholar Bar Hebraeus published an encyclopaedia of Aristotelian philosophy with the title *Butyrum Sapientiae (Cream of Wisdom).*

Albert and Thomas have three characteristics in common. Both make a clear systematic division between philosophy and theology, with the effect that philosophy, previously defined as the "ancilla theologiae," the handmaid of theology, can pursue its own questions. Furthermore, both tend to regard Aristotle's philosophy as a coherent set of dogmas and therefore as something that is finished and completed; thus, philosophy is only a small step away from dogmatism, the mortal enemy of living thought. And finally, both believe in a harmonic union between philosophy and Christianity.

To cite just a few elements: in contrast with Averroes and Aristotle himself, Thomas considers the world as God's creation and sees this fact as the foundation of its dignity. However, the perfection of created things relies on their independence and autonomous activity and, in the case of humans, the ability to recognize truth on their own initiative. In this way the world and human reason are freed from any patronizing by faith; although it is oriented toward God, it is, so to speak, left to its own devices. Thomas's doctrine of the five ways ("quinque viae") for proving the existence of God (for the world he is the first cause, the prime mover, the necessary being, etc.) closely follows Aristotelian models (cf. Seidl 1986[2])—as well as John of Damascus, Avicenna, Averroes, and Maimonides. Beginning with his early work *De ente et essentia,* which soon attracted many commentaries, Thomas brings Aristotle's ontology to bear again, for example the pairs of concepts actuality-potentiality and form-matter as well as matter as the principle of individuation. At the same time he develops a doctrine that is only hinted at in Aristotle: the definitions that belong to every being as such, the *transcendentalia: ens* (being), *unum* (one), *verum* (true in the sense of cognizable), and *bonum* (in the sense of appraisable) (*De veritate* I 1). In his ontology and epistemology, Thomas advocates realism to the extent that he attributes a real existence to the universals. As far as action is concerned, he assumes, more optimistically than Aristotle, that by nature every human has the propensity toward reason. In his ethics he adopts Aristotle's concept of happiness. However, the political life is given far less weight than it is in Aristotle; he also postpones perfect happiness to the beyond (*Summa theologiae* I–II, quaestio 1–5); to Aristotle's "natural" virtues he adds supernatural ones (I–II, quaestio 55–67).

In his political philosophy, Thomas follows Aristotle, as can be seen in the relevant parts of the *Summa theologiae* (I–II, quaestio 30–105, about law; II–II, 57–79, about right and justice) as well as those of the *Summa contra gentiles* and the two short treatises *De regimine principum (On the Rule of Princes)* and *De regno (On Rule).* Thomas, too, assumes that man exists for his own sake, but nevertheless he does not reject slavery *(servitus),* which he interprets as a consequence of the Fall. He considers man a social, or rather political, being, sees the state as the perfect form of community and commits the state's laws to the common good. The idea of peace as the mean of the common good is new, but peace is considered a work of justice ("opus iustitiae pax"), again a thought that is close to Aristotle. By rejecting theocratic tendencies, Thomas emphasizes the proper right of the political. Concerning natural law, he says more distinctly than Aristotle that the *lex naturalis,* natural law, must not be infringed, but that otherwise the *lex humana,* human law, is free to make the more detailed stipulations. However, by positing that with the Fall human reason lost the ability to recognize original justice (*Summa theologiae* I–II, quaestio 91, art. 6), Thomas follows Augustine. Not least, he deviates from Aristotle insofar as—unlike his teacher Albert—he does not consider empirical research into nature important.

The synthesis of Christian, Aristotelian, and other philosophical thought that Thomas Aquinas constructs—Thomism—was by no means universally successful, although Aristotle was given great authority even by the opponents of Thomism. In general it can be said that from the second half of the thirteenth century philosophical and theological schools differed mainly in their position vis-à-vis Aristotle. The Aristotelianism of Bonaventura (1217–74), who returned to subordinating philosophy to theology, was influenced more strongly by Augustine and, through him, by Plato. The opposite position, represented by Siger of Brabant (1235–82), followed Averroes inasmuch as it acknowledges also elements that are contrary to Christian doctrines; this led to the doctrine of double truth and finally to the complete emancipation of philosophy from theology. The champion of lay reason in the dispute about universals, William of Ockham (1285–1347/49), following Aristotle's critique of the doctrine of ideas, denied that the general concepts (universals) have

ARISTOTLE AT HIS LECTERN;
MS of the writings on natural sciences, Rome 1457 (Vienna,
Österreichische Nationalbibliothek, Cod. phil. gr. 64)

an existence outside the spirit; so, in contrast with Thomas, he advocated nominal-ism. He also developed his famous principle of economy in his commentary on the *Physics,* which, however, is not truly Aristotelian (see ch. 7.2).

In the fourteenth century Aristotle's authority was still uncontested in many places, and the newly founded universities in Prague, Vienna, Cologne, and Hei-delberg revolve around Aristotelianism. Needless to say, countermovements formed at the same time, namely, in Oxford and Paris (Buridan, Oresme, Albert of Saxony), which were directed no longer against Aristotle's anti-Christian ele-ments, but against certain theorems of his ontology, epistemology, and natural philosophy: for example, the so-called impetus theory, which was to become an important step away from Aristotelian theory of motion toward (early) modern physics (see Clagett 1961).

Given the belief in authority in which Western Aristotelianism soon ossified, what had begun as intellectual avant-garde in the eleventh century turned more and more into scientific and philosophical reactionism. During Humanism and the Renaissance, it often met with sharp rejection, from a scientific as well as a philosophical and theological point of view. Nicholas of cues wanted to refute the law of contradicition, a foundation of scholastic Aristotelianism, even for specula-tive thought (cf. the concept of a *coincidentia oppositorum* or *coincidentia contra-dictorium*). Whether he succeeded and truly did not want to designate anything, is a different question. On the other hand, the third reception of Aristotle in the West began at the end of the fifteenth century, initially with a philological orien-tation. Like many other ancient writers, the philosopher was edited in the origi-nal and translated both into Latin and into the vernaculars. The model for all later complete editions, the five-volume *Aldina* (1495–98), was created in this period.

18

THE MODERN AGE AND THE PRESENT

18.1 DETACHMENT AND RENEWED INTEREST

At the end of the Middle Ages, Aristotle's potential for innovation appeared to be exhausted. Be it the rise of mathematical and experimental natural sciences, the Reformation, the philosophy of subjectivity (Descartes) and political contract theories since Hobbes, British empiricism, or Kant's transcendental philosophy—the great innovations were no longer essentially influenced by Aristotle. It is a fact that the third reception of Aristotle is distinguished by a variety that by its very diversity contributed to the breakup of the harmonic world view of the Middle Ages and its commitment to authorities, and instead made room for the Aristotelian spirit of free investigation. In Italian Humanism the *Nicomachean Ethics* was studied intensively and integrated into the new way of thinking.

Let us begin with the Reformation: while Cajetan, the theologian appointed by the Pope to negotiate with Luther at the Diet of Augsburg, brought Aristotelian-Thomist philosophy to a new heyday, Luther's relationship to Aristotle was ambiguous. Given that he was influenced by Augustinianism, but principally because he saw Aristotle as an intellectual power that threatened to displace the scriptural viewpoint, in particular the doctrines of original sin and of the crucifixion of Jesus, he leveled, at times very sharp, criticism against Aristotle (e.g., Weimar edn., I 365, VI 186, VII 282, VIII 127). He countered the opinion of many scholastics that no one could become a theologian without Aristotle with the exact opposite: "No one becomes a theologian unless he becomes one without Aristotle" (I 226). On the other hand he gave lectures about the *Ethics,* praised its book on justice as Aristotle's best work (VI 345) and recommended reading the *Logic, Rhetoric,* and *Poetics* (VI 458; cf. Kohls 1975; cf. Joest 1967, 80ff.). Incidentally, as soon as Protestant theology saw its scientific foundations endangered by mysticism and zealotism, it fell back on Aristotle in order to form a clear system. Beginning with Melanchthon, Protestant scholastic philosophy built on the *Topics, Physics, On the Soul,* and the *Ethics.* Authors such as Taurellus (1546–1606), C. Timpler (1567/8–1624), and J. Thomasius (1622–84) even called upon the *Metaphysics.* The struggle against Protestant Aristotelianism, beginning at the end of the sixteenth century with D. Hofmann, was directed not against Aristotle himself but against the intellectualization of the faith.

The actual attack against Aristotle came from the side of empirical natural sciences, in particular physics, astronomy, and technology, all of which have an interest in the domination of nature. While this attack is justified, for example, against Aristotle's dynamics (see ch. 7.2), one must not ignore the methodological impulses that even research in the natural sciences derived from commentating Aristotle. In the course of a new interpretation of Aristotelian logic and theory of science, the school of Padua (Pietro d'Abano, Hugo of Siena, G. Zabarella)—influenced by Aristotle—distinguished between an "inductive" ("metodo risolutivo") and a "deductive" method ("metodo compositivo"). Galileo took it up, but he replaced the still-qualitative procedure with a quantitative method. The Aristotle-critic Hobbes, too, took the resolutive-compositive method of Padua as a guideline. Even his theory of action (*Leviathan,* ch. 6) gives the impression of being influenced by Aristotle, for example by *MA* 6–7.

It is also true, however, that the new kind of research into nature had to contend with an Aristotelianism hostile to empiricism. Therefore, Giordano Bruno was able to say that two chapters of Copernicus contribute more to knowledge than Aristotle and all the Peripatetics put together. On the other hand, Galileo criticizes the attitude that gives authority to Aristotle's words rather than to his spirit of investigation; if, he says, Aristotle had had a telescope, he would have supported the new opinions (*Dialogo sopra i due massimi sistemi del mondo,* 1632, Florence 1968, 76). Nor is Copernicus a mere anti-Aristotelian; on the contrary, he considers his heliocentric cosmology as an actual prototype constructed on the (modified) basis of the Aristotelian *Physics* (*De revolutionibus orbium coelestium,* 1543, Preface).

As is well known, Galileo was forced by the Inquisition to abjure his heliocentric "error" on his knees. However, a few years after his death (1642) a new institution opposing Aristotelianism and its support, churches and universities, was created: the scientific societies that were founded in quick succession in Germany (Leopoldina, Halle, 1652), Italy (Accademia del Cimento, 1657), Britain (Royal Society, Oxford, 1660), and France (Académie des Sciences, 1666). Shortly after the foundation of the Royal Society, the English philosopher and theologian Glanvill says of it that in that short time it had achieved more successes than any conceptual philosophy since Aristotle (*The Vanity of Dogmatizing . . . with some Reflections on Peripateticism . . .* , 1661). Nevertheless, as late as 1674 Malebranche had to acknowledge, concerning Paris, what Petrarca had noticed more than three centuries earlier (*Epist.* 1, IX 14): "Whoever recognises any kind of truth, must to this day still demonstrate that Aristotle saw it, and if Aristotle is opposed to it, the discovery will be false" (*De la recherche de la vérité,* book IV, ch. 3, section III). In many universities and Church institutions—in particular in the schools of the Dominicans and Jesuits, but also those of the Protestants—Aristotelian-Thomist philosophy remained the mandatory doctrine up to the end of the *ancien régime,* and in some places beyond that.

Although early modern philosophy and history of science reads like a demolition of Aristotle in many areas, the philosopher's authority remained intact in others. To present just a few examples: the *Poetics,* for instance, developed a particular influence of its own. Furthermore, Locke, despite his harsh criticism of Aristotelian theory of science, recommends reading book II of the *Rhetoric* as a means to come to know the human mind (*Some thoughts concerning reading and studying for a gentleman,* 1703/1720). Kant contributes to the further undermining of Aristotle's authority, but in long passages, especially in the *Critique of Pure Reason,* he makes use of Aristotelian and Aristotelist concepts transmitted to him via the German Aristotelian tradition, in particular Christian Wolff. Among Kant's successors, especially Neo-Kantianism, the rejection of Aristotle was to prevail.

The first great philosopher to study Aristotle's work again after a long time, and even in the original Greek, was Hegel. The chapter on Aristotle in his *Vorlesungen über die Geschichte der Philosophie* (*Werke,* 19, 132–249) remains worth reading to this day. In addition, Hegel is influenced by Aristotle especially in his philosophy of law. While modern contract theories take ready-made individuals as their starting point, in Aristotle the *polis* originates from elementary social relationships. More distinctly and in a far more sophisticated way as well as starting from the early modern theory of subjectivity, Hegel demonstrates that individuality requires a consciousness of one's own self; this is shaped only in processes of interaction and communication and allows a universally successful life only within its institutional forms—the family, civic society, and the state. In the *Enzyklopädie,* Hegel makes the height of absolute spirit, (his own) philosophy, culminate in Aristotle's idea of *theôria,* of the (divine) spirit thinking itself (vol. 10, 395).

For Fichte on the other hand, another representative of German Idealism, Aristotle was of no relevance, whereas he was esteemed by Schelling after the latter was called to Berlin, where Hegel was active. However, Schelling's reflections left no mark. The situation is not that different when it comes to Marx's and Engel's appreciation for Aristotle. While, for example, *Das Kapital* speaks of a "great investigator" or even the "greatest thinker of the Occident," "the first to analyze the form of value as well as many forms of thought, society and nature" (vol. I, I, 1: MEW 23, 73, 430), there is practically no positive response to Aristotle in more recent critical theory.

18.2 ARISTOTLE RESEARCH AND NEO-ARISTOTELIANISMS

The nineteenth and twentieth centuries abound in historical and philological studies. These are based on the text of the edition of *Aristotelis Opera* produced by the Prussian Academy of Sciences on the incentive of F. Schleiermacher. The Greek text, edited by Immanuel Bekker, appeared in two volumes in the year of Hegel's death (1831), and these have been the standard complete edition ever since. Although improved texts are now available for some of the works, citations still follow Bekker's references by page, column, and line. Volume III of the *Opera* (1831) contains Latin translations dating from the third wave of reception in the Renaissance; volume IV provides the scholia (edited by Chr. A. Brandis, 1836), that is, ancient notes, and volume V (1870), along with the—by now controversial—collection of fragments (V. Rose) contains the *Index Aristotelicus* edited by Hermann Bonitz, which is still considered exemplary. The same Academy edited the 15,000 pages of *Commentaria in Aristotelem Graeca* (23 vols., 1882–1909; an English translation is in process under the direction of R. Sorabji; London 1987 ff.).

Let us mention only a few of the plethora of philologists dealing with Aristotle: for the nineteenth century, apart from Bekker and Bonitz, H. Maier and A. Schwegler, and for the first third of the twentieth century, H. von Arnim, W. Jaeger, A. Jourdain, L. Robin, and W. D. Ross. As far as translation and commentary are concerned, important publications are the series Aristoteles' "Werke in deutscher Übersetzung,"founded by E. Grumach and edited by H. Flashar, as well as the Clarendon Aristotle Series initiated by Austin, with J. L. Ackrill as its chief editor. Moreover, Aristotle is one of the philosophers studied worldwide: even a complete Chinese translation of his works is under way. Let us point out, by way of example, the Louvain school (A. and S. Mansion, E. de Strycker, G. Verbeke), the Berlin Aristotle Archive (P. Moraux), and the Symposium Aristotelicum, which has been organized triennially since 1957.

After Hegel, Aristotle achieves more than merely historical and philological importance with A. Trendelenburg and his pupil Franz Brentano who, in his own words, "born in a time of the most lamentable decline of philosophy, [could] find no better [master] than Aristotle" (letter of 21 March 1916). Furthermore, Lukasiewicz owes his development of a polyvalent logic to an intensive study of Aristotle. One could also say that twentieth-century physics is closer to Aristotle than it is to Newton, since it abandons the idea of mass particles resembling billiard balls in favor of complex functional systems. In his *Process and Reality* (1929; German translation 1979), the only philosophical "outline of a cosmology" of any importance produced in the twentieth century, Whitehead praises Aristotle's "masterful analysis of the concept of 'generation'" (ch. X, 1).

Aristotle had a lasting influence upon the early Martin Heidegger, who was prompted in this case by Brentano's first work *Von der mannigfachen Bedeutung des Seienden nach Aristoteles* (1862). It is visible even on the surface that *Sein und Zeit* (1927) is the result of an intensive involvement with Aristotle: Aristotle is the author most frequently cited in it, exceeding even Kant. Also, according to § 8, the second part of *Sein und Zeit* (which, however, was never published)—"Grundzüge einer phänomenologischen Destruktion der Geschichte der Ontologie" ("Outlines of a phenomenological destruction of the history of ontology")—was to interpret, among other works, Aristotle's discussion of time in *Physics* IV 10. As his lectures given in the twenties suggest (e.g., Gesamtausgabe [= GA], vols. 18,19,21–22), when Heidegger finds in Aristotle thought akin to his own, such as a "radical phenomenological anthropology," he carries out an original as well as productive combination of the analysis of time according to natural philosophy (*Physics* IV 10) with the theory of forms of knowledge in the *Ethics* (*EN* VI and X 6–7; also *Metaph.* I 1–2) and with the discussion of truth in the *Metaphysics* (IV 7; VI 4; IX 10; on *Metaph.* IX, see GA, vol. 31). However, Aristotle is reinterpreted: in *Sein und Zeit* the relatively autonomous analyses of philosophical and moral-political existence, as well as the incisive division between ontology and ethics are replaced by an analysis of pre-political existence elevated to the level of ontology and fundamental philosophy.

While Heidegger's interest in Aristotle was reflected in lectures but rarely in publications, a number of major monographs on Aristotle originated in his vicinity. The studies by W. Bröcker, K. Ulmer, and E. Tugendhat are influenced by Heidegger, as is the section on the "hermeneutic actuality of Aristotle" in Gadamer's *Wahrheit und Methode* (1960, 295 ff.).

The wide-ranging rehabilitation of practical philosophy that commenced in the middle of the twentieth century demonstrates that Aristotle's works contain further potential for innovation. While later philosophers are to fall back on Kant as a counterbalance, initially Aristotle is of greater importance. For example, J. Ritter's renewal of political philosophy is undertaken in the name of Aristotle and Hegel. Furthermore, in their attempt to determine the characteristic method of jurisprudence and political sciences as distinct from that of natural sciences, Ch. Perelman, Th. Viehweg, and W. Hennis fall back on the tradition of topics and rhetoric and, in doing so, on Aristotle. Aristotle is important also in analytical ethics, for example in its discussion about the basic concepts of the theory of action and in its renewed debate about the virtues (e.g., E. Anscombe, Ph. Foot, A. Kenny). And recently Aristotle's ethics and politics have been cited in order to counterbalance the oblivion of tradition in critical theory (O. Marquard) and the political philosophy of liberalism (communitarianism).

Considering his outstanding importance for practical philosophy, it may look as though Aristotle carried systematic weight only here, but the philosophy of linguistic analysis shows this to be different. The Oxford school in particular presents a multilayered affinity with Aristotle: with his investigations of elementary equivocations *(pollachôs legomena),* his theory (e.g., *SE*) and practice of the critique of language, as well as with his discussion of aporias. Nevertheless, the tendency to resolve all philosophical speculation into therapy of language diverges from Aristotle.

In its first phase, that is, in J. L. Austin's discussion of philosophical questions, which focuses on everyday language, analytical philosophy makes use of only some of Aristotle's methodical maxims, while at the same time violently attacking some of his theories, in particular his ontology. Quine—with his variant of "anti-essentialism"—is the most consistent in rejecting any kind of metaphysics of substance. However, Ryle already distances himself from this by falling back on Aristotle's ability to make fundamental distinctions between concepts (*The Concept of Mind,* 1949, 112 and 149). Even more important is Strawson's "essay about descriptive metaphysics," *Individuals* (1959). His idea of a nonrevisionary metaphysics neutralizes the analytical anathema against ontology of substance, making room for a disposition toward a "good old-fashioned Aristotelian essentialism" (Brody, in: *Synthese* 1975). Nonrevisionary metaphysics limits itself to a description of the actual structure of our thinking about the world. The so-called sortal predicates (cf. for example D. Wiggins, *Sameness and Substance,* 1980), that is, substantival terms saying *what* a certain object is, appear to amount to a rediscovery of the Aristotelian concept of the predicate of substance. The concept of "natural kinds" as an elementary class of sortal concept, too, is reminiscent of Aristotle.

A few general words as a conclusion to this "brief history" of Aristotle's influence: the aim of a philosophical dialogue with a work is not to save it or produce an apologia for it, but rather to achieve a better understanding of nature and man. Consequently, what is important is not so much the rediscovery of Aristotle but the ability to advance thought by means of a productive reception. Therefore, the question whether Aristotle still has the potential for innovation today is decided not only by his work but also by his readers' capacity for innovation.

Chronology

384 B.C.E.	Aristotle born in Stagira (Chalcidice); his father Nicomachus is court physician at the Macedonian court.
367–347	First sojourn in Athens: Aristotle studies at Plato's Academy, where he becomes familiar with Plato's late philosophy, including the lecture "On the Good," and produces the logical works *(Organon)* as well as the first drafts for the *Physics, Metaphysics, Ethics,* and *Rhetoric.*
c. 350	Political tension between Macedonia and Athens; Aristotle's pro-Macedonian persuasion gives rise to problems during his stay in Athens.
347	Death of Plato; Aristotle goes to Assus (Asia Minor) upon the invitation of Hermias of Atarneus.
345–344	Collaboration with Theophrastus (especially in zoology and botany) in Mytilene (Lesbos).
342–341	Upon the request of Philip II of Macedon, Aristotle becomes tutor to the king's son Alexander, who is put in charge of state affairs soon thereafter (340–339).
341–340	Aristotle marries Pythias, the sister (or niece) of Hermias (who has been murdered in the meantime).
338	Battle of Chaeronea; Macedon becomes the leading power in Greece.
335–334	Aristotle returns to Athens and teaches at the Lyceum ("Peripatos"), situated near the Lycabettos.

323	Death of Alexander; the renewed anti-Macedonian sentiment in Athens turns against Aristotle as well.
323–322	Aristotle moves to his mother's house in Chalcis (Euboea).
322	He dies there aged 62.
Third century B.C.E.	Decline of the Aristotelian school, the Peripatos.
c. 50 B.C.E.	First complete edition of Aristotle's esoteric writings produced by Andronicus of Rhodes in Rome; the works are subdivided into four groups (the *Organon;* ethical/political/rhetorical writings; scientific/biological/psychological writings; the *Metaphysics*). Beginning of the activity of commentators, but also loss of the Aristotelian dialogues, which still had a strong influence on Cicero.
c. 200 C.E.	Zenith of ancient commentaries on Aristotle with Alexander of Aphrodisias. Subsequent neo-Platonist commentators (Porphyry, Iamblichus, Simplicius) attempt a synthesis of Platonist and Aristotelian elements; Christian neo-Platonists (John Philoponus, Elias, Olympiodorus) mediate between Aristotelianism and Christianity.
Sixth century	Boethius translates and commentates *Cat.* and *Int.*; in the early Western Middle Ages, Aristotle is represented only by this *logica vetus*.
Seventh century	Growing influence of Aristotle in the Syrian and Arab world—at first as an authority on natural sciences.
830–1055	Development of a comprehensive Arab Aristotelianism—with Hunain ibn Ishaq, al-Farabi, and Ibn Sina (Avicenna)—which influences Islamic theology.
Ninth century	Start of the reception of Aristotle in the West with Johannes Scotus Eriugena.
Twelfth century	Ibn Rushd (Averroes) and other Arab and Jewish commentators impart the knowledge of Aristotle to the Latin world.

Eleventh–Thirteenth century	Translation of almost the complete Corpus Aristotelicum into Latin; as a consequence the natural sciences become emancipated from theology, deriving a strong impetus.
Thirteenth century	Western reception of Aristotle through Siger of Brabant (Averroism), Albert the Great, and Thomas Aquinas leads to the thesis of the independence of philosophy from theology.
1210, 1231, etc.	The Church prohibits the teaching of Aristotelian writings, especially of the *Physics* and *Metaphysics*.
1255	The University of Paris officially adopts Aristotle's writings into its curriculum.
1500–1650	Rise of disparate Aristotelianisms, such as Italian Renaissance Aristotelianism (P. Pomponazzi), Protestant Aristotelianism with Melanchthon, and Jesuit Thomism.
Sixteenth–Seventeenth centuries	The Church takes measures against anti-Aristotelian natural sciences in Copernicus and Galileo. Anti-Aristotelianism in the natural philosophy of F. Bacon and P. Gassendi.
1831–37	Definitive edition of Aristotle made by I. Bekker upon the request of the Prussian Academy of Science.

BIBLIOGRAPHY

I. PRIMARY SOURCES AND WORKS OF REFERENCE

1. EDITIONS OF COMPLETE AND INDIVIDUAL WORKS IN GREEK

Page and line numbers are still cited according to the classical edition of the complete works made on behalf of the Königliche Preußische Akademie der Wissenschaften:

Bekker, I. (ed.) *Aristotelis Opera,* 5 vols. Berlin 1831–70 (I–II: Greek text; III: Renaissance Latin translations; IV: scholia; V: fragments).

Bonitz, H. *Index Aristotelicus,* revised edition by O. Gigon. Berlin 1960; Separate edn. of the *Index Aristotelicus:* Graz 1955² (an indispensable word index).

A collection of the extant fragments that is outdated but has yet not been replaced by another:

Rose, V. *Aristotelis qui ferebantur librorum fragmenta.* Leipzig 1886³ (cf. Ross, W. D. *Aristotelis fragmenta selecta.* Oxford 1955).

Reliable and reasonably priced editions of individual works can be found in the series "Scriptorum Classicorum Bibliotheca Oxoniensis" (Oxford Classical Texts), 1894 ff.

Texts with introductions and commentaries that are still excellent (with numerous, partly improved, re-editions):

Ross, W. D., Oxford, Clarendon Press:

> *Metaphysics,* 2 vols., 1924.
>
> *Physics,* 1936.
>
> *Prior and Posterior Analytics,* 1949.
>
> *Parva Naturalia,* 1955.
>
> *De Anima,* 1961.

Important editions of single works with commentaries:

Bonitz, H. *Aristotelis Metaphysica,* 2 vols. Bonn 1849 (reprint Hildesheim 1960).

Brunschwig, J. *Topiques.* I: *Livres I–IV.* Paris 1967.

Burnet, J. *The Ethics of Aristotle.* London 1900.

Cope, E. M. *The Rhetoric of Aristotle with a Commentary.* Cambridge 1877.

209

Düring, J. *Aristotle's Chemical Treatise. Meteorologica IV.* Göteborg 1944.

Grant, A. *The Ethics of Aristotle.* 2 vols. London 1857.

Hicks, R. D. *De Anima.* Cambridge 1907.

Joachim, H. H. *De Generatione et Corruptione.* Oxford 1922.

Lucas, D. W. *Aristotle. Poetics.* Oxford 1968.

Newman, W. D. *The Politics of Aristotle,* 4 vols. Oxford 1887–1902, repr. 1950.

Schwegler, A. *Die Metaphysik des Aristoteles. Grundtext, Übersetzung und Commentar nebst erläuternden Abhandlungen.* Tübingen 1847–48.

2. TRANSLATIONS AND COMMENTARIES

The Complete Works of Aristotle. The Revised Oxford Edition, ed. J. Barnes, 2 vols. Princeton 1984.

Aristoteles: Werke in deutscher Übersetzung (German translations with introduction and commentaries), founded by E. Grumach, ed. H. Flashar. Berlin. The volumes published to date are:

Analytica Posteriora, 2 vols. (W. Detel), 1933.

Eudemische Ethik (F. Dirlmeier), 1984[4].

Kategorien (K. Oehler), 1986[2].

Magna Moralia (F. Dirlmeier), 1983[5].

Meteorologie, Über die Welt (H. Strohm), 1984[3].

Nikomachische Ethik (F. Dirlmeier), 1986[9].

Opuscula I: Über die Tugend (E. A. Schmidt), 1986[3].

Opuscula II und III: Mirabilia (H. Flashar) *und De Audibilibus* (U. Klein), 1990[3].

Parva Naturalia III (Ph. J. van der Eijk), 1994.

Peri hermeneias (H. Weidemann), 1994.

Physikvorlesung (H. Wagner), 1989[5].

Politik, Buch I, II und III (E. Schütrumpf), 1991; *Buch IV–VI* (E. Schütrumpf, H. J. Gehrke), 1996.

Problemata Physica (H. Flashar), 1991[4].

Der Staat der Athener (M. Chambers), 1990.

Über die Seele (W. Theiler), 1986[7].

Zoologische Schriften II (J. Kollesch), 1985.

Some translations of individual works with commentaries:

De motu animalium, translated with commentary by M. C. Nussbaum. Princeton 1978.

De anima, translated with commentary by R. D. Hicks. London 1907, Amsterdam 1965².

Metaphysik, translated by F. Bassenge. Berlin 1960.

La Metafisica, translated with commentary by G. Reale, 2 vols. Naples 1968.

La décision du sens. Le livre Gamma *de la* Métaphysique, introduction, text, translation, and commentary by B. Cassin and M. Narcy. Paris 1989.

Metaphysik Z, translated with commentary by M. Frede and G. Patzig. Munich 1988.

On Rhetoric. A Theory of Civic Discourse, newly translated with introductions, notes, and appendices by G. A. Kennedy. New York/Oxford 1991.

Protreptikos, edited by I. Düring. Frankfurt/Main 1969.

Prior Analytics, translated with commentary by R. Smith. Indianapolis 1991.

L' Éthique à Nicomaque, translated with commentary by R. A. Gauthier and J. Y. Jolif, 4 vols. Louvain 1970².

The "Clarendon Aristotle Series," edited by J. L. Ackrill, Oxford, provides translations that follow the text closely, with systematic and critical notes:

Ackrill, J. L. *Categories and De Interpretatione,* 1963.

Annas, J. *Metaphysics Book M and N,* 1976.

Balme, D. M. *De Partibus Animalium I—De Generatione Animalium I,* 1972.

Barnes, J. *Posterior Analytics,* 1975, 1994³.

Bostock, D. *Metaphysics Book Z and H,* 1994.

Charlton, W. *Physics I–III,* 1970.

Hamlyn, D. W. *De Anima,* 1975.

Hussey, E. *Physics III–IV,* 1983.

Keyt, D. *Politics IV–VI,* 1999

Kirwan, C. *Metaphysics IV–VI,* 1971.

Kraut, R. *Politics VII and VIII,* 1997.

Robinson, R. *Politics III–IV,* 1973, 1995².

Saunders, T. J. *Politics I–II,* 1995.

Smith, R. *Topics I and VIII,* 1997.

Williams, C. J. F. *De Generatione et Corruptione,* 1982.

Woods, M. *Eudemian Ethics, Books I, II and VIII,* 1982.

Further important commentaries on individual works can be found under the respective headings.

II. SECONDARY LITERATURE

1. General Introductions and Multi-author Volumes

Ackrill, J. L. 1981. *Aristotle— The Philosopher* Oxford.

Allan, D. J. 1922, 1970². *The Philosophy of Aristotle.* Oxford.

Anscombe, G. E./Geach, P. T. 1973. *Three Philosophers: Aristotle. Aquinas. Frege.* Oxford.

Barnes, J. 1991. *Aristotle.* Oxford.

———. (ed.) 1994. *The Cambridge Companion to Aristotle.* Cambridge.

Cherniss, H. 1964². *Aristotle's Criticism of Plato and the Academy.* (1st edn., Baltimore 1944).

Chroust, A.-H. 1973. *Aristotle.* London.

Düring, I. 1957. *Aristotle in the Ancient Biographical Tradition.* Göteborg, Acta Universitatis.

———. 1966. *Aristoteles, Darstellung und Interpretation seines Denkens.* Heidelberg.

Düring, I./Owen, G. E. L. (eds.) 1960. *Aristotle and Plato in the Mid-fourth Century.* Göteborg.

Flashar, H. 1983. "Aristoteles." In *Grundriß der Geschichte der Philosophie, Die Philosophie der Antike* (Ueberweg), vol. 3, ed. H. Flashar. Basel/Stuttgart, 175–457.

Guthrie, W. K. C. 1981. "Aristotle: An Encounter." In *A History of Greek Philosophy VI.* Cambridge.

Jackson, H. 1920. "Aristotle's Lecture Room." *Journal of Philosophy* 35: 191–200.

Jaeger, W. 1955². *Aristoteles. Grundlegung einer Geschichte seiner Entwicklung.* Berlin.

Kiernan, Th. P. 1961. *Aristotle Dictionary.* New York.

Lear, J. 1988. *Aristotle. The Desire to Understand.* Cambridge.

Lloyd, G. E. R. 1968. *Aristotle. The Growth and Structure of His Thought.* Cambridge.

Merlan, Ph. 1946. "The Successor of Speusippus." *Transactions of the American Philological Association* 77 (2nd edn. *Kleine philosophische Schriften.* Hildesheim/New York, 1976, 144–52).

Moraux, P. 1962. *Aristote et son école.* Paris.

———. (ed.) 1968. *Aristoteles in der neueren Forschung.* Darmstadt.

———. (ed.) 1975. *Die Frühschriften des Aristoteles.* Darmstadt.

Moraux, P./Wiesner, J. (eds.) 1983. "Zweifelhaftes im Corpus Aristotelicum." *Akten des 9. Symposium Aristotelicum.* Berlin/New York.

Moravcsik, J. M. E. (ed.) 1968. *Aristotle. A Collection of Critical Essays.* London.

Reale, G. 1988⁶. *Storia della filosofia antica*, vol. II: *Platone e Aristotele.* Milan.

Ross, W. D. 1949⁵. *Aristotle.* London.

Russell, B. 1975⁸. *History of Western Philosophy.* London, 173–217.

Zeller, E. 1921[4]. *Die Philosophie der Griechen, in ihrer geschichtlichen Entwicklung dargestellt. Zweiter Teil, Zweite Abteilung: Aristoteles und die alten Peripatetiker.* Leipzig.

2. KNOWLEDGE AND SCIENCE

Barnes, J. 1969. "Aristotle's Theory of Demonstration." *Phronesis* 14: 123–52.

―――. 1993. "Aristotle's Theory of Sciences." *Oxford Studies in Ancient Philosophy* XI, 225–41.

Barnes, J./Schofield, M./Sorabji, R. (eds.) 1975. *Articles on Aristotle*, vol. I: *Science.* London.

Beriger, A. 1989. *Die aristotelische Dialektik. Ihre Darstellung in der Topik und in den Sophistischen Widerlegungen und ihre Anwendung in der Metaphysik M 1–3.* Heidelberg.

Berti, E. (ed.) 1981. *Aristotle on Science. The "Posterior Analytics," Proceedings of the Eighth Symposium Aristotelicum.* Padua.

Brandis, Ch. A. 1835. "Über die Reihenfolge der Bücher des Aristotelischen Organons und ihre griechischen Ausleger." *Historisch-philologische Abhandlungen der Königl. Akad. d. Wiss. zu Berlin 1833.* Berlin, 249–91.

Chen, C.-H. 1976. *Sophia. The Science Aristotle Sought.* Hildesheim/New York.

Cole, T. 1991. *The Origins of Rhetoric in Ancient Greece.* Baltimore.

Devereux, D./Pellegrin, P. (eds.) 1990. *Biologie, logique et métaphysique chez Aristote. Actes du séminaire CNRS-NSF.* Paris.

Ebbinghaus, K. 1964. *Ein formales Modell der Syllogistik des Aristoteles.* Göttingen.

Ebert, Th. 1995. "Was ist ein vollkommener Syllogismus des Aristoteles?" *Archiv für Geschichte der Philosophie* 77: 221–47.

Else, G. 1957. *Aristotle's Poetics. The Argument.* Cambridge, Mass.

Evans, J. D. G. 1977. *Aristotle's Concept of Dialectic.* Cambridge.

Flashar, H. 1974. "Aristoteles und Brecht." *Poetica* 6: 17–37.

v. Fritz, K. 1971. *Grundprobleme der antiken Wissenschaft.* Berlin/New York.

―――. 1978. *Schriften zur griechischen Logik,* 2 vols. Stuttgart.

Fuhrmann, M. 1992[2]. *Einführung in die antike Dichtungstheorie.* Darmstadt.

Furley, D. J./Nehamas, A. (eds.) 1994. *Aristotle's Rhetoric. Philosophical Essays. Proceedings of the 12th Symposium Aristotelicum.* Princeton.

Garver, E. 1994. *Aristotle's Rhetoric. An Art of Character.* Chicago/London.

Granger, G. G. 1976. *La théorie aristotélicienne de la science.* Paris.

Grimaldi, W. M. A. 1980/88. *Aristotle. Rhetoric I/II. A Commentary.* New York.

Hager, F. P. (ed.) 1972. *Logik und Erkenntnislehre des Aristoteles.* Darmstadt.

Halliwell, S. 1986. *Aristotle's Poetics.* London.

Hartmann, N. 1957[2]. "Aristoteles und Hegel." In *Kleinere Schriften*, vol. II. Berlin, 214–52.

Hellwig, A. 1973. *Untersuchungen zur Theorie der Rhetorik bei Platon und Aristoteles.* Göttingen.

Hintikka, J. 1972. "On the Ingredients of an Aristotelian Science." *Noûs* 6: 55–69.

———. 1973. *Time and Necessity. Studies in Aristotle's Theory of Modality.* Oxford.

———. 1980. "Aristotelian induction." *Revue internationale de la philosophie* 34.

Irwin, T. 1989. *Aristotle's First Principles.* Oxford.

Jones, J. 1986. *Aristotle on Tragedy.* London.

Kahn, Ch. 1978. "Questions and Categories. Aristotle's Doctrine of Categories in the Light of Modern Research." In *Questions,* ed. H. Hiz. Dordrecht, 227–78.

Kapp, E. 1920. "Die Kategorienlehre in der aristotelischen Topik." In *Ausgewählte Schriften,* ed. H. and I. Diller. Berlin 1968, 215–53.

———. 1942. *Greek Foundations of Traditional Logic.* New York.

Kennedy, G. A. 1963. *The Art of Persuasion in Greece.* Princeton.

Kneale, W./Kneale, M. 1962. *The Development of Logic.* Oxford.

Kretzmann, N. 1974. "Aristotle on Spoken Sound Significant by Convention." In *Ancient Logic and its Modern Interpretations,* ed. J. Corcoran. Dordrecht, 3–21.

Larkin, T. 1971. *Language in the Philosophy of Aristotle.* The Hague.

Lear, J. 1980. *Aristotle and Logical Theory.* Cambridge.

Lesher, J. H. 1973. "The Meaning of Nous in the Posterior Analytics." *Phronesis* 18: 44–68.

Leszl, W. 1970. *Logic and Metaphysics in Aristotle. Aristotle's Treatment of Types of Equivocity and its Relevance to his Metaphysical Theories.* Padua.

Lukasiewicz, J. 1958[3]. *Aristotle's Syllogistic from the Standpoint of Modern Formal Logic.* Oxford.

Maier, H. 1896–1900. *Die Syllogistik des Aristoteles,* 3 vols. Tübingen.

Mansion, S. (ed.) 1961. *Aristote et les problèmes de méthode. Communications présentées au Symposium Aristotelicum à Louvain.* Louvain/Paris.

Marx, Fr. 1900. Aristoteles' Rhetorik. In *Rhetorica. Schriften zur aristotelischen und hellenistischen Rhetorik,* ed. R. Stark. Hildesheim, 1968, 36–123.

McKirahan, R. D. 1992. *Principles and Proofs. Aristotle's Theory of Demonstrative Science.* Princeton.

Menne, A./Öffenberger, N. (eds.) 1983, 1985, and 1988. *Zur modernen Deutung der aristotelischen Logik.* Hildesheim/New York. Vol. I. *Über den Folgerungsbegriff in der aristotelischen Logik*; vol. II. *Formale und nicht-formale Logik bei Aristoteles*; vol. III. *Modallogik und Mehrwertigkeit.*

Miller, J. W. 1938. *The Structure of Aristotle's Logic.* London.

Nortmann, U. 1996. *Modale Syllogismen, mögliche Welten, Essentialismus. Eine Analyse der aristotelischen Modallogik.* Berlin/New York.

Oehler, K. 1962. *Die Lehre vom noetischen und dianoetischen Denken bei Platon und Aristoteles. Ein Beitrag zur Erforschung des Bewußtseinproblems in der Antike.* Munich.

Owen, G. E. L. 1961. "Tithenai ta phainomena." In *Aristote et les problèmes de méthode,* ed. S. Mansion. Louvain, 83–103.

———. (ed.) 1968. *Aristotle on Dialectic. The Topics. Proceedings of the Third Symposium Aristotelicum.* Oxford.

de Pater, W. A. 1965. *Les Topiques d'Aristote et la dialectique platonicienne.* Fribourg.

Patterson, R. 1995. *Aristotle's Modal Logic. Essence and Entailment in the Organon.* Cambridge.

Patzig, G. 1969³. *Die aristotelische Syllogistik. Logisch-philosophische Untersuchungen über das Buch A der "Ersten Analytiken."* Göttingen.

Prantl, K. 1955³. *Geschichte der Logik im Abendlande,* vol. I (1st edn. Leipzig 1855). Graz/Berlin.

Primavesi, O. 1996. *Die Aristotelische Topik. Ein Interpretationsmodell und seine Erprobung am Beispiel von Topik B,* München.

Rapp, Ch. 1993. "Aristoteles über die Rechtfertigung des Satzes vom Widerspruch." *Zeitschrift für philosophische Forschung* 47: 521–41.

Rorty, A. O. (ed.) 1992. *Essays on Aristotle's Poetics.* Princeton.

———. (ed.) 1996. *Essays on Aristotle's Rhetoric.* Berkeley.

Schadewaldt, W. 1955. "Furcht und Mitleid? Zur Deutung des Aristotelischen Tragödiensatzes." In *Die Aristotelische Katharsis. Dokumente ihrer Deutung im 19. und 20. Jahrhundert,* ed. M. Luserke. Hildesheim/Zurich/New York, 1991, 246–88.

Seel, G. 1982. *Die Aristotelische Modaltheorie.* Berlin/New York.

Solmsen, F. 1975². *Die Entwicklung der Aristotelischen Logik und Rhetorik.* Berlin.

Spengel, L. 1851. *Über die Rhetorik des Aristoteles.* Abhandlung der bayrischen Akademie der Wissenschaften, philosophisch-philologische Klasse 6,2. Munich.

Sprute, J. 1982. *Die Enthymemtheorie der aristotelischen Rhetorik.* Göttingen.

Welsch, W. 1987. *Aisthesis.* Stuttgart.

Whitaker, C. W. A. 1996. *Aristotle's De Interpretatione. Contradiction and Dialectic.* Oxford.

Wörner, M. H. 1990. *Das Ethische in der Rhetorik.* Freiburg/Munich.

Wolf, U. 1979. *Möglichkeit und Notwendigkeit bei Aristoteles und heute.* Munich.

3. NATURAL SCIENCES, NATURAL PHILOSOPHY, AND PSYCHOLOGY

Cassirer, H. 1932. *Aristoteles Schrift "Von der Seele" und ihre Stellung innerhalb der aristotelischen Philosophie.* Tübingen.

Cooper, J. 1982. "Aristotle on natural teleology." In *Language and Logos,* ed. M. Schofield and M. Nussbaum. Cambridge, 197–222.

Craemer-Ruegenberg, I. 1980. *Die Naturphilosophie des Aristoteles.* Freiburg/Munich.

Devereux, D./Pellegrin, P. (eds.) 1990. *Biologie, logique et métaphysique chez Aristote.* Paris.

Dierauer, U. 1977. *Mensch und Tier im Denken der Antike.* Amsterdam.

Düring, I. (ed.) 1969. *Naturphilosophie bei Aristoteles und Theophrast.* Heidelberg.

―――. 1961. "Aristotle's Method in Biology." In *Aristote et des problèmes de méthode. Communications présentées au Symposium Aristotelicum tenu à Louvain,* ed. S. Mansion. Louvain, 213–21 (German tr. in. G. A. Seeck, ed. *Die Naturphilosophie des Aristoteles.* Darmstadt 1975, 49–58).

Fortenbaugh, W. W. 1975. *Aristotle on Emotion.* London.

Furley, D. J. 1967. *Two Studies in the Greek Atomists.* Princeton.

Furth, M. 1988. *Substance, Form, and Psyche. An Aristotelian Metaphysics.* Cambridge.

Freudenthal, G. 1995. *Aristotle's Theory of Material Substance, Heat and Pneuma, Form and Soul.* Oxford.

Gill, M. L. 1989. *Aristotle on Substance. The Paradox of Unity.* Princeton.

Gill, M. L./Lennox, J. G. 1994. *Self-Motion. From Aristotle to Newton.* Princeton.

Gotthelf, A. (ed.) 1985. *Aristotle on Nature and Living Things.* Pittsburgh/Bristol.

Gotthelf, A./Lennox, J. (eds.) 1987. *Philosophical Issues in Aristotle's Biology.* Cambridge.

Granger, G. G. 1976. *La théorie aristotélicienne de la science.* Paris.

Heath, T. 1949. *Mathematics in Aristotle.* Oxford.

Horn, H. J. 1994. *Studien zum dritten Buch der aristotelischen Schrift* De Anima. Göttingen.

Horstschäfer, T. M. 1998. *Über Prinzipien. Eine Untersuchung zur methodischen und inhaltlichen Geschlossenheit des ersten Buches der* Physik *des Aristoteles.* Berlin/New York.

Judson, L. (ed.) 1991. *Aristotle's Physics. A Collection of Essays.* Oxford.

Kosman, L. A. 1969. "Aristotle's Definition of Motion." *Phronesis* 14: 40–62.

Krämer, H. J. 1968. "Grundbegriffe akademischer Dialektik in den biologischen Schriften von Aristoteles und Theophrast." *Rheinisches Museum* 111: 293–333.

Kullmann, W. 1979[2]. *Wissenschaft und Methode. Interpretationen zur aristotelischen Theorie der Naturwissenschaft.* Berlin/New York.

―――. 1998. *Aristoteles und die moderne Wissenschaft.* Stuttgart.

Kullmann, W./Föllinger, S. (eds.) 1997. *Aristotelische Biologie. Intentionen, Methoden. Ergebnisse.* Akten des Symposiums über Aristoteles' Biologie von 24.―28. Juli 1995. Stuttgart.

Le Blond, J.-M. 1939 (1973[3]). *Logique et méthode chez Aristote. Étude sur la recherche des principes dans la "Physique" aristotélicienne.* Paris.

Lesky, E. 1951. *Die Zeugungs- und Vererbungslehre in der Antike und ihr Nachwirken.* Mainz.

Lewis, F. A./Bolton, R. (eds.) 1996. *Form, Matter, and Mixture in Aristotle.* Oxford.

Lloyd, G. E. R. 1961. "The Development of Aristotle's Theory of the Classification of Animals." *Phronesis* 6: 59–81.

———. 1996. *Aristotelian Explorations.* Cambridge.

Lloyd, G. E. R./ Owen, G. E. R. (eds.) 1978. *Aristotle on Mind and Senses.* Cambridge.

Meyer, J. B. 1855. *Aristoteles Thierkunde. ein Beitrag zur Geschichte der Zoologie, Physiologie und alten Philosophie.* Berlin.

Modrak, D. K. W. 1987. *Aristotle. The Power of Perception.* Chicago.

Nussbaum, M. C./Rorty, A. O. (eds.) 1992. *Essays on Aristole's* De anima. Oxford.

Nuyens, F. 1948. *L'évolution de la psychologie d'Aristote.* Paris.

Pellegrin, P. 1982. *La classification des animaux chez Aristote. statut de la biologie et unité de l'aristotélisme.* Paris.

Preus, A. 1975. *Science and Philosophy in Aristotle's Biological Works.* Hildesheim/New York.

Robinson, H. M. 1974. "Prime Matter in Aristotle." *Phronesis* 19: 168–88.

Seeck, G. A., ed. 1975. *Die Naturphilosophie des Aristoteles.* Darmstadt.

Solmsen, F. 1960. *Aristotle's System of the Physical World.* Ithaca/New York.

Sorabji, R. 1980. *Necessity, Cause, and Blame. Perspectives on Aristotle's Theory.* Ithaca/New York.

———. 1983. *Time, Creation and Continuum. Theories in Antiquity and the Early Middle Ages.* London.

Theiler, W. 1924. *Zur Geschichte der teleologischen Naturbetrachtung bis auf Aristoteles.* Berlin (seond edn. 1965).

Waterlow, S. 1982. *Nature, Change, and Agency in Aristotle's Physics.* Oxford.

———. 1982. *Passage and Possibility.* Oxford.

Wieland, W. 1992³. *Die aristotelische Physik. Untersuchungen über die Grundlagen der Natur-wissenschaften und der sprachlichen Bedingungen der Prinzipienforschung bei Aristoteles.* Göttingen.

4. First Philosophy or Metaphysics

Albritton, R. 1957. "Forms of Particular Substances in Aristotle's Metaphysics." *Journal of Philosophy* 54: 699–708.

Arpe, C. 1938. *Das ti ên einai bei Aristoteles.* Hamburg.

Aubenque, P. 1972³. *Le problème de l'être chez Aristote.* Paris.

———. (ed.) 1979. *Études sur la Métaphysique d'Aristote.* Paris.

Burnyeat, M. (ed.) 1979. *Notes on Book Z of Aristotle's Metaphysics.* Oxford.

———. 1984. *Notes on Book Êta and Thêta of Aristotle's Metaphysics.* Oxford.

Elders, L. 1972. *Aristotle's Theology. A Commentary on Book Lambda of the Metaphysics.* Assen.

Fine, G. 1993. *On Ideas. Aristotle's Criticism of Plato's Theory of Forms.* Oxford.

Frede, D. 1970. *Aristoteles und die "Seeschlacht." Das Problem der Contigentia Futura in De Int. 9.* Göttingen.

Frede, M. 1978. "Individuen bei Aristoteles." *Antike und Abendland* 24: 16–39.

———. 1987a. "Substance in Aristotle's Metaphysics." In *Essays in Philosophy.* Oxford, 72–80.

———. 1987b. "The Unity of Special and General Metaphysics." In *Essays in Philosophy.* Oxford, 81–95.

Gill, M. L. 1989. *Aristotle on Substance. The Paradox of Unity.* Princeton.

Graeser, A. (ed.) 1987. *Mathematics and Metaphysics in Aristotle—Mathematik und Metaphysik bei Aristoteles. Akten des X. Symposium Aristotelicum.* Bern/Stuttgart.

Graham, D. W. 1987. *Aristotle's Two Systems.* Oxford.

Hafermann, B. 1998. *Aristoteles' transzendentaler Realismus. Inhalt und Umfang Erster Prinzipien in der "Metaphysik."* Berlin/New York.

Hager, F. P. (ed.) 1975. *Metaphysik und Theologie des Aristoteles.* Darmstadt.

Happ, H. 1971. *Hyle. Studien zum aristotelischen Materie-Begriff.* Berlin.

Hartmann, E. 1977. *Substance, Body, and Soul. Aristotelian Investigations.* Princeton.

Heidegger, M. 1958. "Vom Wesen und Begriff der PHYSIS." In *Wegmarken.* Frankfurt/M., 1967, 237–99.

Inciarte, F. 1994. "Die Einheit der Aristotelischen Metaphysik." *Philosophisches Jahrbuch* 101: 1–21.

Jaeger, W. 1912. *Studien zur Entstehungsgeschichte der Metaphysik des Aristoteles.* Berlin.

Krämer, H. J. 1967[2]. *Der Ursprung der Geistmetaphysik. Untersuchungen zur Geschichte des Platonismus zwischen Platon und Plotin.* Amsterdam.

———. 1973. "Aristoteles und die akademische Eidoslehre. Zur Geschichte des Universalienproblems im Platonismus." *Archiv für Geschichte der Philosophie* 55: 119–90.

Leszl, W. 1975. *Aristotle's Conception of Ontology.* Padua.

Lewis, F. A. 1991. *Substance and Predication in Aristotle.* Cambridge.

Liske, Th.-M. 1985. *Aristoteles und der aristotelische Essentialismus. Individuum, Art, Gattung.* Freiburg/Munich.

Loux, M. 1991. *Primary OUSIA. An Essay on Aristotle's Metaphysics Z and H.* Ithaca.

Manuwald, B. 1989. *Studien zum Unbewegten Beweger in der Naturphilosophie des Aristoteles.* Stuttgart.

Nortmann, U. 1997. *Allgemeinheit und Individualität. Die Verschiedenartigkeit der Formen in "Metaphysic Z."* Paderborn.

Oehler, K. 1973. "Der höchste Punkt der antiken Philosophie." In *Einheit und Vielheit*, ed. E. Scheibe/G. Süssmann. Göttingen, 45–59.

———. 1984. *Der Unbewegte Beweger bei Aristoteles.* Frankfurt.

Owen, G. E. L. 1960. "Logic and Metaphysics in Some Earlier Works of Aristotle." In Düring/Owen (see section 1), 13–32.

———. 1965. "The Platonism of Aristotle." *Proceedings of the British Academy* 51: 125–50.

Owens, J. 1978³. *The Doctrine of Being in the Aristotelian Metaphysics. A Study in the Greek Background of Medieval Thought.* Toronto, Pont. Inst. of Medieval Studies.

Preus, A./Anton, J. P. (ed.) 1992. *Aristotle's Ontology.* Albany.

Rapp, Ch. 1995a. "Allgemeines konkret. Ein Beitrag zum Verständnis der Aristotelischen Substanzlehre." *Philosophisches Jahrbuch* 102: 83–100.

———. 1995b. *Identität, Persistenz und Substantialität.* Freiburg/Munich.

———. (ed.) 1996. *Aristoteles. Die Substanzbücher der* Metaphysik *(Zêta, Êta, Thêta).* Berlin (Reihe Klassiker Auslegen).

Reale, G. 1994⁶. Il concetto di filosofia prima e l'unita della metafisica di Aristotele. Mailand.

Reiner, C. 1954. "Die Entstehung und ursprüngliche Bedeutung des Namens Metaphysik." *Zeitschrift für philosophische Forschung* 8: 210–37.

———. 1955. "Die Entstehung der Lehre vom bibliothekarischen Ursprung des Namens Metaphysik. Geschichte einer Wissenschaftslegende." *Zeitschrift für philosophische Forschung* 9: 77–99.

Scaltsas, T./Charles, D./Gill, M. L. (eds.) 1994. *Unity, Identity, and Explanation in Aristotle's Metaphysics.* Oxford.

Schmitz, H. 1985. *Die Ideenlehre des Aristoteles*, 3 vols. Bonn.

Spellmann, L. 1995. *Substance and Separation in Aristotle.* Cambridge.

Steinfath, H. 1991. *Selbständigkeit und Einfachheit. Zur Substanztheorie des Aristoteles.* Frankfurt.

Sykes, R. D. 1975. "Forms in Aristotle: Universal or Particular?" *Philosophy* 50: 311–31.

Tugendhat, E. 1988⁴. *TI KATA TINOS. Eine Untersuchung zu Struktur und Ursprung aristotelischer Grundbegriffe.* Freiburg i. Br.

———. 1983. "Über den Sinn der vierfachen Unterscheidung des Seins bei Aristoteles." In *Philosophische Aufsätze.* Frankfurt, 1992.

Wiggins, D. 1980. *Sameness and Substance.* Oxford.

Witt, Ch. 1989. *Substance and Essence in Aristotle.* Ithaca/London.

5. ETHICS AND POLITICS

Allan, D. J. 1963/64. "Aristotle's Criticism of Platonic Doctrine Concerning Goodness and the Good." *Proceedings of the Aristotelian Society* 64.

Anagnostopoulos, G. 1994. *Aristotle on the Goals and the Exactness of Ethics.* Berkeley. etc.

Annas, J. 1993. *The Morality of Happiness.* Oxford.

Aubenque, P. 1963. *La prudence chez Aristote.* Paris.

Barnes, J./Schofield, M./Sorabji, R. (eds.) 1978. *Articles on Aristotle*, vol. II. *Ethics and Politics.* New York.

Bien, G. 1973. *Die Grundlegung der politischen Philosophie bei Aristoteles.* Freiburg i. Br./Munich.

Broadie, S. W. 1991. *Ethics with Aristotle.* New York.

Charles, D. 1984. *Aristotle's Philosophy of Action.* London.

Cooper, J. M. 1975. *Reason and Human Good in Aristotle.* Cambridge.

Dahl, N. O. 1984. *Practical Reason, Aristotle, and Weakness of the Will.* Minneapolis.

Davidson, D. 1980. "How Is Weakness of the Will Possible?" In *Essays on Actions and Events.* Oxford.

Detel, W. 1995. "Griechen und Barbaren." *Deutsche Zeitschrift für Philosophie* 43: 1019–43.

Dihle, A. 1994. *Die Griechen und die Fremden.* Munich.

Dirlmeier, F. 1962. *Merkwürdige Zitate in der Eudemischen Ethik des Aristoteles.* Sitzungsber. d. Heidelb. Akad. d. Wiss., Phil.-Hist. Kl.

Engberg-Pedersen, T. 1983. *Aristotle's Theory of Moral Insight.* Oxford.

Gosling, J. C. B./Taylor, C. C. W. 1982. *The Greeks on Pleasure.* Oxford.

Hager, F.-P. (ed.) 1972. *Ethik und Politik des Aristoteles.* Darmstadt.

Hardie, W. F. 1968. *Aristotle's Ethical Theory.* Oxford.

Heinaman, R. 1988. "Eudaimonia and Self-sufficiency in the 'Nicomachean Ethics.'" *Phronesis* 33: 31–53.

Höffe, O. 1979. *Ethik und Politik.* Frankfurt.

———. 1987. *Politische Gerechtigkeit. Grundlegung einer kritischen Philosophie von Recht und Staat.* Frankfurt.

———. 1990. "Universalistische Ethik und Urteilskraft. ein aristotelischer Blick auf Kant." *Zeitschrift für philosophische Forschung* 44: 537–63.

———. 1996². *Praktische Philosophie—Das Modell des Aristoteles.* Berlin (1st edn. Munich/Salzburg, 1971).

Höffe, O. (ed.) 1995. *Aristoteles, Nikomachische Ethik.* Berlin (Reihe Klassiker Auslegen).

Hutchinson, D. S. 1986. *The Virtues of Aristotle.* London.

Irwin, T. 1992. "Who Discovered the Will?" In *Philosophical Perspectives* 6: 453–73.

Joachim, H. H. 1962². *Aristotle. The Nicomachean Ethics.* Oxford.

Kamp, A. 1985. *Die politische Philosophie des Aristoteles und ihre metaphysischen Grundlagen. Wesenstheorie und Polisordnung.* Freiburg/Munich.

Kenny, A. 1978. *The Aristotelian Ethics*. Oxford.

———. 1979. *Aristotle's Theory of the Will*. London.

———. 1992. *Aristotle on the Perfect Life*. Oxford.

Keyt, D./Miller, F. D. (eds.) 1991. *A Companion to Aristotle's Politics*. Cambridge, Mass.

Kraut, R. 1989. *Aristotle on the Human Good*. New Jersey.

von Leyden, W. 1985. *Aristotle on Equality and Justice*. London.

Loening, R. 1903. *Die Zurechnungslehre des Aristoteles*. Jena.

MacIntyre, A. 1981 (1984²). *After Virtue*. London.

Meikle, S. 1995. *Aristotle's Economic Thought*. Oxford.

Meyer, S. S. 1993. *Aristotle on Moral Responsibility*. Oxford/Cambridge, Mass.

Miller, F. D., Jr. 1995. *Nature, Justice, and Rights in Aristotle's* Politics. Oxford.

Milo, R. D. 1996. *Aristotle on Practical Knowledge and the Weakness of Will*. The Hague.

Moraux, P./Harlfinger, D. 1971. *Untersuchungen zur Eudemischen Ethik*. Berlin.

Mueller-Goldingen, Ch. (ed.) 1988. *Schriften zur aristotelischen Ethik*. Hildesheim/ Zurich/New York.

Mulgan, R. G. 1977. *Aristotle's Political Theory. An Introduction for Students of Political Theory*. Oxford.

Patzig, G. (ed.) 1990. *Aristoteles' "Politik." Akten des XI. Symposium Aristotelicum*. Göttingen.

Price, A. W. 1989. *Love and Friendship in Plato and Aristotle*. Oxford.

Reeve, C. D. C. 1992. *Practices of Reason. Aristotle's Nicomachean Ethics*. Oxford.

Reverdin, O. 1965. *La politique d'Aristote*. Geneva.

Rhodes, P. J. 1981. *A Commentary on the Aristotelian* Athenaion Politeia. Oxford.

Ricken, F. 1976. *Der Lustbegriff in der Nikomachischen Ethik des Aristoteles*. Göttingen.

Schleiermacher, F. 1817. "Ueber die ethischen Werke des Aristoteles." In *Sämmtliche Werke*, Dritte Abtheilung, Dritter Band. Berlin, 1835, 306–33.

Sherman, N. 1989. *The Fabric of Character. Aristotle's Theory of Virtue*. Oxford.

Sparshott, F. 1994. *Taking Life Seriously. A Study of the Argument of the* Nicomachean Ethics. Toronto.

Stein, S. M. 1968. *Aristotle and the World State*. London/Colchester.

Sternberger, D. 1980. "Der Staat des Aristoteles und der unsere." In *Staatsfreundschaft, Schriften IV*. Frankfurt, 35–52.

Stern-Gillett, S. 1995. *Aristotle's Philosophy of Friendship*. Albany.

Strauss, L. 1964. *The City and the Man*. Chicago.

Swanson, J. A. 1992. *The Public and the Private in Aristotle's Political Philosophy*. Ithaca/ London.

Teichmüller, G. 1879. *Neue Studien zur Geschichte der Begriffe III. Die praktische Vernunft bei Aristoteles.* Gotha.

Urmson, J. 1988. *Aristotle's Ethics.* Oxford.

Walsh, J. J./ Shapiro, H. L. (eds.) 1976. *Aristotle's Ethics. Issues and Interpretations.* Belmont.

Wolf, F. 1991. *Aristote et la politique.* Paris.

Yack, B. 1993. *The Problems of a Political Animal. Community, Justice, and Conflict in Aristotelian Political Thought.* Berkeley/Los Angeles/London.

6. Aristotelianism, Neo-Aristotelianism, Aristotle Studies

Arens, H. 1984. *Aristotle's Theory of Language and its Tradition.* Amsterdam.

Badawi, A. 1968. *La transmission de la philosophie grècque au monde arabe.* Paris.

Bianchi, L./Randi, E. 1990. *Le verità dissonanti. Aristotele alla fine del Medioevo.* Rome/Bari.

Blumenthal, H./Robinson, H. (eds.) 1991. *Aristotle and the Later Tradition.* Oxford (Oxford Studies in Ancient Philosophy, Supplementary Vol.).

Booth, E. 1983. *Aristotelian Aporetic Ontology in Islamic and Christian Thinkers.* Cambridge.

Brink, K. O. 1940. "Peripatos." In *Realencyclopädie der classischen Altertumswissenschaften,* Suppl. 7, col. 899–949.

Burnett, Ch. (ed.) 1993. *Glosses and Commentaries on Aristotelian Logical Texts: the Syriac, Arabic, and Medieval Traditions.* London.

Clagett, M. 1961. *The Science of Mechanics in the Middle Ages.* Madison.

Düring, I. 1954. "Von Aristoteles bis Leibniz. Einige Hauptlinien in der Geschichte des Aristotelismus." *Antike und Abendland* 4: 118–54 (repr. in P. Moraux (ed.). *Aristoteles in der neueren Forschung.* Darmstadt 1968, 250–313).

Flüeler, Ch. 1992. *Rezeption und Interpretation der Aristotelischen "Politica" im späten Mittelalter.* Amsterdam/Philadelphia.

Green-Pedersen, N. J. 1984. *The Tradition of the Topics in the Middle Ages. The Commentaries on Aristotle's and Boethius' "Topics."* Munich/Vienna.

Joest, W. 1967. *Ontologie der Person bei Luther.* Göttingen.

Kohls, E. W. 1975. "Luthers Verhältnis zu Aristoteles, Thomas und Erasmus." *Theologische Zeitschrift* 31: 289–301.

Kretzmann, N. (ed.) 1982. *The Cambridge History of Later Medieval Philosophy.* Cambridge.

Lohr, Ch. 1988. *Commentateurs d'Aristote au moyen-âge latin. Bibliographie de la littérature secondaire récente.* Freiburg i. Ü.

Lee, T.-S. 1984. *Die griechische Tradition der aristotelischen Syllogistik in der Spätantike.* Göttingen.

Lynch, J. P. 1972. *Aristotle's School. A Study of a Greek Educational Institution.* Berkeley.

Merlan, Ph. 1955. "Aristoteles, Averroes und die beiden Eckharts." In *Kleine philosophische Schriften*. Hildesheim/New York, 1976.

———. 1969. *Monopsychism, Mysticism, Metaconsciousness. Problems of the Soul in the Neoaristotelian and Neoplatonic Tradition*. The Hague.

Moraux, P. 1973. *Der Aristotelismus bei den Griechen. Von Andronikos bis Alexander von Aphrodisias*, vol. I. *Die Renaissance des Aristotelismus im I. Jahrhundert v. Chr.* Berlin/New York.

———. 1984. *Der Aristotelismus bei den Griechen. Von Andronikos bis Alexander von Aphrodisias*, vol. II. *Der Aristotelismus im I. und II. Jahrhundert n. Chr.* Berlin/New York.

Minio-Paluello, L. 1972. *Opuscula. The Latin Aristotle*. Amsterdam.

Oehler, K. 1968. "Aristoteles in Byzanz." In *Aristoteles in der neueren Forschung*, ed. P. Moraux. Darmstadt, 381–99.

———. 1969. *Antike Philosophie und Byzantinisches Mittelalter, Aufsätze zur Geschichte des griechischen Denkens*. Munich.

Peters, F. E. 1968a. *Aristoteles Arabus. The Oriental Translations and Commentaries on the Aristotelian "Corpus."* Leiden.

———. 1968b. *Aristotle and the Arabs. The Aristotelian Tradition in Islam*. New York.

Schmitt, C. B. 1983. *Aristotle and the Renaissance*. Cambridge, Mass./London.

Sorabji, R. (ed.) 1990. *Aristotle Transformed. The Ancient Commentators and Their Influence*. Ithaca/New York.

van Steenberghen, F. 1955². *Aristotle et l'occident. Les origines de l'Aristotélisme parisien*. Louvain, 1946.

Wehrli, F. (ed.) 1944–59. *Die Schule des Aristoteles. Texte und Kommentar*, 10 fascicles and 2 supplements. Basle.

———. 1983. "Der Peripatos bis zum Beginn der römischen Kaiserzeit." In *Die Philosophie der Antike* (Ueberweg), vol. 3, ed. H. Flashar. 459–599.

III. OTHER CITED WORKS

Arendt, H. 1960. *Vita activa oder Vom tätigen Leben*. Munich.

Bubner, R. 1990. *Dialektik als Topik. Bausteine zu einer lebensweltlichen Theorie der Rationalität*. Frankfurt.

Dihle, A. 1985. *Die Vorstellung vom Willen in der Antike*. Göttingen.

Ferber, R. 1981. *Zenons Paradoxien der Bewegung und die Struktur von Raum und Zeit*. Munich.

Höffe, O. 1993. *Moral als Preis der Moderne. Ein Versuch über Wissenschaft, Technik und Umwelt*. Frankfurt.

Höffe, O./Pieper, A. (eds.) 1995. *F. W. J. Schelling—Über das Wesen der menschlichen Freiheit*. Berlin (Reihe Klassiker Auslegen).

Horn, Ch. 1996. "Augustinus und die Entstehung des philosophischen Willensbegriffs." *Zeitschrift für philosophische Forschung* 50.

Lausberg, H. (ed.) 1973². *Handbuch der literarischen Rhetorik. Eine Grundlegung der Literaturwissenschaft.* Munich.

MacIntyre, A. 1990. *Three Rival Versions of Moral Enquiry. Encyclopedia. Genealogy. Tradition.* London.

Mayr, E. 1984. *Die Entwicklung der biologischen Gedankenwelt.* Berlin.

Quine, W. V. O. 1950. "Identity, ostension, and hypostasis." In *From a Logical Point of View.* Cambridge/London.

Raaflaub, K. 1985. *Die Entdeckung der Freiheit. Zur historischen Semantik und Gesellschaftsgeschichte eines politischen Grundbegriffs der Griechen.* Munich.

Salmon, W. C. (ed.) 1970. *Zeno's Paradoxes.* Indianapolis/New York.

Seidl, H. 1986². *Thomas von Aquin. Die Gottesbeweise.* Hamburg.

INDEX OF PERSONAL NAMES

d'Abano, P., 200
Abelard, P., 10
Abraham Ibn David, 193
Ackrill, J., 151, 202
Aelian, 8
Aeschylus, 43, 109, 137, 163, 177
Albert of Saxony, 197
Albertus Magnus, xv, 192–3, 195–7
Albritton, R., 118
Alcidamas, 175
Alexander of Aphrodisias, 190–1
Alexander the Great, 3, 6, 8, 9, 86, 173, 177
Althusius, J., 173
Ammonius Saccas, 191–2
Anaxagoras, 3, 63, 69, 89, 93, 96–7, 159
Anaximander, 70, 103
Anaximenes, 63, 103
Andronicus of Rhodes, 12, 24, 95, 190
Annas, J., 83, 171
Anscombe, G. E. M., 50, 203
Anselm of Canterbury, 151
Antigone, 45, 47, 148
Antipater, 9
Antiphon, 75, 177
Antisthenes, 49, 52
Apellicon, 190
Apollonius Dyscolus, 189
Aristarchus of Samos, 189
Aristophanes, 160
Arnim, H. v., 202
Aspasius, 144
Augustine, 10, 81, 143, 145, 197
Austin, J. L., 202–3
Averroes (Ibn Rushd), 190, 193, 196–7
Avicenna (Ibn Sina), 193, 196

Bacon, F., 25, 29–30, 69–70
Balme, D. M., 77, 86

Bar Hebraeus, 196
Barnes, J., 34, 50–1, 92
Bekker, I., 201–2
Bentham, J., 148
Bernays, J., 46
Bien, G., 155
Blau, U., 55
Bodin, J., 160
Boethius, 191, 194
Bolton, R., 36
Bonaventura, 197
Bonitz, H., 75, 201–2
Boole, G., 31
Brandis, Ch. A., 38, 201
Brecht, B., 43
Brentano, F., xv, 202
Bröcker, W., 203
Brody, W. A., 203
Bruno, G., 200
Bubner, R., 36
Buridan, J., 71, 197
Burnyeat, M. F., 42

Cajetan, 199
Callias, 33, 118–9
Callippus, 70, 105
Camus, A., 30
Cassirer, H., 92
Chambers, M., 183
Charlemagne, 192
Charondas, 185
Cicero, 10–2, 38, 40, 158, 189, 193
Clagett, M., 197
Cole, T., 40
Constant, B., 179
Cope, E. M., 40
Copernicus, N., 200
Corcoran, 32

Craemer-Ruegenberg, I., 71–2
Creon, 45–7
Critias, 91

Dante Alighieri, 141, 195
Darwin, Ch., xv, 86, 89–90
Davidson, D., 141
Democritus, 63, 69, 72, 74, 79–80, 86, 89, 93, 97
Descartes, R., xv, 25, 29–30, 50, 95, 97, 199
Detel, W., 34, 50, 53, 57, 83
Devereux, D., 36
Dicaearchus, 189
Diels, H., 43, 80, 93, 103, 177
Dihle, A., 143
Diogenes Laertius, 3, 9–10, 15, 189
Diogenes of Apollonia, 63, 90
Pseudo-Dionysius the Areopagite, 192
Dirlmeier, F., 130, 155
Driesch, H., 90
Düring, I., 3, 5, 86, 193
Duns Scotus, 193

Elders, L., 103
Empedocles, 63, 69, 91, 93, 97, 107, 142
Engberg-Pedersen, T., 139
Engels, F., 201
Epicurus, 80
Eriugena, John Scotus, 191
Eudemus, 8, 189
Eudoxus, 5, 70, 105, 135, 149
Euclid, 192, 195
Euripides, 44, 46–7, 163, 175, 177–8

al-Farabi, xv, 193
Ferber, R., 79,
Fichte, J. G., 121, 201
Fine, G., 122
Flashar, H., 13, 43, 46, 202
Foot, P., 203
Frede, D., 124
Frede, M., 118
Frege, G., 19, 31, 98, 125
Frederick II., 190
Fries, J. F., 50
Fromondus, 79
Fuhrmann, M., 43
Furley, D. J., 40, 42, 79
Furth, M., 92

Gadamer, H. G., 203
Galen, 189–90, 195
Galileo, xv, 10, 19, 69, 200
Gaskin, R., 124

Gauthier, R. A., 143
Geach, P. T., 50
Gerard of Cremona, 195
al-Ghazali, 193,
Gigon, O., 144
Gill, M. L., 71, 76
Glanvill, J., 200
Göckel, R. (Goclenius), 111
Goethe, J. W., 46, 120
Gorgias, 40, 43
Gosling, J. C. B., 149
Gotthelf, A., 86
Graeser, A., 83
Graham, D. W., 112
Gregory of Nyssa, 192
Grimaldi, W. M. A., 40
Grosseteste, R., 195
Grumach, E., 202

Haeckel, E., 90
Halliwell, S., 43, 46
Hamilton, W., 64
Happ, H., 74
Heath, T., 83
Hegel, G. W. F., xv, 16, 25–6, 28, 31, 35, 71, 108, 112, 121, 130, 137, 144, 176, 201–3
Heidegger, M., xv, 13, 71, 115, 202–3
Heinaman, R., 151
Hellwig, A., 41
Hennis, W., 38, 203
Heraclitus, 63, 97
Hermann, K. F., 13
Hermias of Atarnaeus, 6
Herodianus, 189
Herodotus, 64, 80, 163, 177–8
Hesiod, 63, 103, 108
Hilbert, D., 56
Hippocrates, 195
Hippo, 63, 91
Hobbes, T., xv, 19, 50, 165–6, 168, 170, 180, 199–200
Höffe, O., 43, 47, 130, 133, 135, 140, 142, 149, 151, 154–5
Hofmann, D., 199
Homer, 5–6, 43, 103, 108–9, 163, 178
Horace, 44–5
Horn, Ch., 143
Hugh of Siena, 200
Hume, D., 10, 144
Hunain (Johannitius), 192
Husserl, E., 26

Ibas, 192
Ictinus, 3
Inciarte, F., 99

Irwin, T. H., 36, 144
Isocrates, 40

Jackson, H., 5
Jacob of Venice, 195
Jaeger, W., 13, 100, 118, 160, 202
Jerome, 191
Job, 152
Joest, W., 199
John Italus, 192
John of Damascus, 196
Johnson, C., 76
Jolif, J. Y., 143
Jourdain, A., 202
Judson, I., 71
Justinian, 192
Kant, I., xv, 15–6, 19, 31, 33, 52–3, 55, 63, 66,
    81–3, 95–7, 109, 114–5, 121, 129, 133,
    135–6, 140, 144–7, 151, 153, 155–6, 159,
    199, 201–3
Kapp, E., 38, 112
Kelsen, H., 153
Kennedy, G. A., 40
Kenny, A., 130, 138, 144, 151, 203
Kierkegaard, S., 139, 144–5
al-Kindi, 193
Kohls, E. W., 199
Kosman, L. A., 73
Krämer, H. J., 103, 118, 190
Kretzmann, N., 124, 194
Kullmann, W., 86, 89

Lambert, J. H., 25
Lausberg, H., 40
Leibniz, G. W., xv, 10, 25, 79
Lennox, J. G., 71, 86
Leontius of Byzantium, 192
Lesky, A., 89
Lessing, G. E., 43, 46
Leszl, W., 112, 118
Leucippus, 63, 89
Levi Ben Gerson, 193
Liske, M. Th., 59, 112, 117
Lloyd, G. E. R., 92
Locke, J., 201
Loening, R., 137
Lucas, D. W., 43
Lukasiewicz, J., xv, 33, 55, 202
Luserke, M., 46
Luther, M., 199
Lycon, 189
Lycurgus, 185
Lysias, 40
Lysippus, 9

MacIntyre, A., 143
Maier, H., 202
Malebranche, N., 200
Mansion, A., 202
Mansion, S., 202
Marcus Aurelius, 190
Marquard, O., 203
Marsilius of Padua, 195
Marx, F., 40
Marx, K., 35, 157–8, 201
Mayr, E., 86
McKirahan, R. D., 50
Melanchthon, Ph., 196
Melissus, 61, 114
Meno, 8
Merlan, Ph., 190
Meyer, J. B., 86–7, 137
Mill, J. S., 53
Miller, F. D., 166, 171
Modrak, D. K. W., 57
Moore, G. E., 64, 131
Moraux, P., 10, 190, 202
de Morgan, A., 31
Moses Maimonides, 193, 196

Narcy, M., 55
Needham, J., 89
Nehamas, A., 40, 42
Neleus, 190
Nemesius, 192
Newton, I., 202
Nicholas of Kues, 197
Nicholas of Oresme, 195, 197
Nicomachus, 4, 6, 130
Nietzsche, F., 46, 95, 133
Nortmann, U., 34
Notger of St. Gall, 194
Nussbaum, M. C., 165, 182

Ockham, W. of, 10, 72, 197
Octavianus, 190
Oedipus, 45–6, 137
Oehler, K., 103, 106, 192
Origen, 192
Owen, G. E. L., 62, 92
Owens, J., 103, 112

Panaitius, 189
Parmenides, 61, 63, 69, 72–3, 97, 114, 116
Pascal, B., 108
Pasteur, L., 87
Patzig, G., 31, 33, 118, 130, 165, 175, 182
Perelmann, C., 38, 203
Petrarca, F., 200
Phidias, 3, 96

Philip II, 3, 6, 172
Philoponus, 9
Pindar, 180
Plato, 3–6, 8, 10, 12, 16, 26, 28–9, 35–6, 40–1,
    43–5, 49, 51, 57, 63–4, 70, 75–7, 79–80,
    82, 85, 91, 93, 97, 100, 104–5, 107, 111,
    114–5, 117–121, 124, 131–2, 148–50,
    155–7, 159–61, 163, 166–7, 171, 173,
    178, 180, 185, 190, 192, 197
Pliny, 86
Plotinus, 191–2
Pohlenz, M. von, 46
Polycleitus, 77, 96
Popper, K. R., 50, 52, 58
Porphyry, 13, 191, 193
Poseidonius, 71, 189
Prantl, K., 33
Priam, 152
Proclus, xv, 190–2
Protagoras, 3
Psellus, M., 192
Ptolemy, 189, 192, 195
Pufendorf, S., 155
Pythagoreans, 54, 63, 79–80, 91, 93, 97, 155
Pythias, 6, 9

Quine, W.V.O., 116–7, 203
Quintilian, 38

Raaflaub, K., 179
Raphael, 120
Rapp, Ch., 42, 55, 112, 116–8
Rawls, J., 64, 133, 157
Reale, G., 118
Reiner, H., 96
Ricken, F., 149
Ritter, J., 203
Robin, L., 202
Robinson, H. M., 76
Robinson, R., 142
Rorty, A. O., 40, 43, 130, 133, 155
Rose, V., 201
Ross, W. D., 33–4, 50, 202
Russell, B., 31, 98, 116
Ryle, G., 203

Saadja, 193
Salmon, W., 79
Sardanapal (Assurbanipal), 148
Schadewaldt, W., 46
Schelling, F. W. J., 121, 201
Schleiermacher, F. D. E., 130, 201
Schmitz, H., 118
Schofield, M., 92, 175

Schütrumpf, E., 92, 175
Schwegler, A., 202
Seidl, H., 196
Shakespeare, W., 132
Sidgwick, H., 64
Siger of Brabant, 197
Simplicius, 96, 191
Socrates, 5, 8, 32–3, 36, 40–1, 58, 61, 63,
    114–9, 141, 145, 164, 177
Solmsen, F. 40
Solon, 64, 152, 158
Sophocles, 3, 44–5, 47, 158, 163, 178, 181
Sorabji, R., 82, 92, 137, 190, 202
Spengel, L., 40
Speusippus, 5–6, 16, 63, 97
Spinoza, B., 50
Sprute, J., 37, 42
Stalley, R. F., 171
Stein, S. M., 6, 173
Stephanus, 192
Stoics, 24, 108, 125, 152, 154
Strato, 189
Strawson, P. F., 203
Strohm, H., 70, 190
de Strycker, E., 202
Sulla, 190
Sykes, R. D., 118
Syrianus, 191

Taurellus, 199
Taylor, C. C. W., 149
Teichmüller, G., 131
Tertullian, 191
Thales, 34, 63, 96–7, 103, 159
Theiler, W., 92, 94
Themistius, 191
Theophrastus, 6, 8, 9, 11, 40, 62, 71, 85,
    189–90
Thomas Aquinas, xv, 131, 144, 155, 157, 193,
    195–7
Thomasius, 199
Thrasymachus, 40, 148
Thucydides, 163, 185
Timpler, C., 199
Trendelenburg, A., 202
Tugendhat, E., 115, 203

Ulmer, K., 203

Verbeke, G., 202
Vico, G., 25
Viehweg, T., 38, 203
Voltaire, 148

Wagner, H., 71
Weber, M., 149
Wedin, M. V., 112
Weidemann, H., 117, 124
Welsch, W., 57
Whitaker, C. W. A., 124
Whitehead, A. N., 98, 202
Wieland, W. 34, 71, 78, 81
Wiggins, D., 116, 203
Wilamowitz, U. v., 189
William of Moerbeke, 195
Williams, B., 155
Williams, C. J. F., 76
Wittgenstein, L., 122
Wolf, U., 154

Wolff, Ch., 25, 155, 201
Wolff, C. F., 89

Xenocrates, 5, 7, 49, 52, 63, 97
Xenophanes, 61, 103
Xerxes, 177

Zabarella, G., 200
Zekl, H. G., 75
Zeller, E., 112, 118
Zeno of Elea, 79–80, 82

GENERAL INDEX

absence of governance (*anarchia*), 165, 168
Academy, 4, 6–8, 16, 31, 38, 62, 87, 111, 121, 160, 192
accident (*symbebêkos*), 19, 37, 116
speech act, 124
action (*praxis*), 45, 129, 131, 136
act, actuality (*energeia*), 19, 73, 94, 99, 106, 119, 142, 196
aesthetics of reception, 45
affect (*pathos*), cf. emotion, 91, 154, 171
agathon, *see* good
aisthêsis, *see* perception
aitia, *see* cause
akolasia, *see* intemperance
akrasia, *see* weakness of the will
akribeia, *see* precision
alienation (*xenikon*), 44
altruism, 171
amphiboly, 122
analytical philosophy, xv, 66, 112, 203
anankê, *see* necessity
anarchia, *see* absence of governance
andreia, *see* courage
anger (*thymos*), 137
anonymy, 123
anthropology, 3, 28, 30, 130, 152, 160, 165, 168, 177–78, 202
apeiron, *see* unlimited
apodeixis, *see* proof
aporia, aporetic
appetite (*epithymia*), 136–7
archê, *see* rule; *see* principle
aretê, *see* virtue
argument (logos), 42
Aristotelianism, 12, 24, 69, 93, 195, 198, 200
art(fulness) (*technê*), 24, 29, 74, 139
assembly (*ekklêsia*), 184
astonishment (*thaumazein*), 29
astronomy, 18, 27, 62, 105, 200

autarkeia, *see* self-sufficiency
autonomy, cf. Freedom, 135, 179–80
axiom, axiomatics, 50, 54–56, 57, 98–9

badness (*kakia*), 143
barbarians, 176–7
basic and human rights, 42, 165, 185
being (*on*), 111, 15–6, 151, 196
being *qua* being (*on hê on*), 98, 111
biology, 13, 27, 70, 85, 91, 166
bios, *see* life, form of
body (*sôma*), 91–2
boulêsis, *see* wishing
bouleusis, *see* deliberation
brutality (*thêriotês*), 141, 146

cardinal virtues, 155
categories, 11, 33, 52, 112–15, 150
cause (*aitia*): 49, 76–8; effective cause, 77; final cause, 77–8; formal cause, 77; material cause, 77
chance (*tychê*), 77–8
character (*êthos*), 39, 129, 153
chronology, 11
chronos, *see* time
circle, 52
cleverness (*deinotês*), 140
coherence, coherentist, 36, 56
comedy, 44,
common good, 180, 181ff., 185, 196
common sense, 64–5, 132
communication triangle, 123
communitarianism, 164–5, 171, 203
conclusion (*symperasma*), 32
constitution (*politeia*), 10, 180
contingentia futura, 34, 55, 124
continuum (*syneches*), 78–80, 82
convention (*synthêkê*), 124
conversion, 33

231

cosmology, 18, 70, 103–5, 190, 200, 202
courage (*andreia*), 154
critical theory, 49, 201, 203

decision (*prohairesis*), 137–9, 141, 143–5, 179
deduction, 28, 51
definition (*horismos*), 38, 53–4, 57
deinotês, see cleverness
deism, 108
deliberation (*bouleusis*), 138–9
democracy, 164, 178–80, 182, 183ff.
deon (the befitting), 147
desire (*orexis*), cf. striving, 93, 131, 135ff., 144, 147
diahairesis, see division
dialectics, 18, 23, 25, 35ff., 41, 87
dialogues, 10–1, 106, 189
didaskaliai (*Catalogues of the Dramas*), 10
dihoti, see why
dikaion, see just
dikaiosynê, see justice
division (*dihairesis*), 53
doctrine (*doxa*), 62–5
doxa, see doctrine
dynamics, 72, 200
dynamis, see possibility; *see* potentiality

economy, 18, 136
ecthesis, 33
eidos, see species; *see* form
ekklêsia, see assembly
eleutheria, see freedom
eleutheriotês, see liberality
emotion (*pathos*), cf. affect, 45, 46
empeiria, see experience
empiricism, 13, 27, 120, 199
endoxa, see (accepted) opinions
energeia, see actuality; *see* reality
Enlightenment, 135
entelechy, 73, 90, 92
enthymeme, 40, 42
epagôgê, see induction
epistêmê, see knowledge; *see* science
epithymia, see appetite
equity (*epieikeia*), 158–9, 180
ergon, s. function
essentialism, xv, 50, 56–7, 117, 131, 203
ethics, xv, 5, 18, 26–7, 39, 41, 47, 57, 88, 99, 109, 129–61, 171, 196, 202–3
ethics of science, 30, 63, 70
ethismos, see habituation
êthos, see character
eu zên, see good life
eudaimonia, see happiness

eupraxia, see good actions
evil, 145–6
evolution, 78, 90–1
example (*paradeigma*), 42, 58–9, 121
exoteric writings, 10, 189
experience (*empeiria*), 26–7, 76
experiment, 69, 90

figures (*schêmata*), 33
form (*eidos*), 19, 54, 73–4, 88, 196
freedom (*eleutheria*), 30, 178–9, 184, 190
friendship (*philia*), 165, 170ff., 176
function (*ergon*), 152
fundamental philosophy, 5, 16, 53, 97, 99–101, 122
fundamentalism, 50, 56–7

general/generality (*katholou*), 27, 31, 58, 118, 122
genos, see genus
genus (*genos*), 37, 88, 113–4
goal/purpose (*telos*), 64, 77–8, 99, 138, 140, 144, 150ff.; dominant goal, 151; inclusive goal, 151
god (*theos*), 100, 103–9, 151, 196
good (*agathon*), 99, 135, 144–6, 149–50, 152, 165
good actions (*eupraxia*), 18, 136, 172
good life (*eu zên*), 88, 136, 147, 167–8, 170, 172
grammar, 24, 44

habit (*hexis*), 153
habituation (*ethismos*), 57, 133
happiness (*eudaimonia*), 30, 38, 41, 130, 135–6, 139–40, 144–5, 147–53, 160–1, 169, 171, 196
hedonê, see pleasure
hekôn/hekousion, see voluntary
hereditary transmission, 89ff.
hexis, see habit
historiography, 7, 44
homonymy, 121
honour (*timê*), 132, 149, 154
horismos, see definition
hôs epi to poly, see mostly
hoti, see that
hylê, see matter
hypokeimenon, see substratum
hypothesis, 53

idea (*idea*), 100, 119–22, 131, 149–50
idealism, 13, 27, 95, 120–1, 201
idion, see unique property
imitation (*mimêsis*), 44, 47

immortality of the soul, 93, 191, 193
induction (*epagôgê*), 28, 42, 50–1, 57–9, 86
infinite regress, 52, 74, 81
intellect (*nous*), 94, 140, 190
intemperance (*akolasia*), 141–2

just (*dikaion*), 147, 155
justice (*diakaiosynê*), 155–9, 171, 178, 181,
    196–7; general justice, 157; specific justice,
    157; legal justice, 157; polis-legitimizing
    justice, 178; polis-normatizing justice, 178;
    justice of exchange, 157; distributive
    justice, 157

kakia, see badness
kalon (the good-in-itself), 147
katharsis, see purification
kinêsis, see motion
knavery (*panourgia*), 140
knowledge (*epistêmê*), 16, 18, 21, 24, 26, 28–9,
    49, 50; productive knowledge, 18, 29;
    practical knowledge, 18, 29; theoretical
    knowledge, 18; cf. science

language (*logos*), 122–5
law (*nomos*), 145, 155–6, 159, 180, 184
law of contradiction, 36, 55–6, 197
law of the excluded middle, 55
legality, 133
liberalism, 171, 179, 203
liberality (*eleutheriotês*), 154, 179
life (*zên*), 136, 166
life, form of (*bios*), 132, 139, 148–9; life
    devoted to enjoyment (*bios apolaustikos*),
    132, 139, 148–9; life devoted to gain (*bios
    chrêmatistês*), 149; moral/political life (*bios
    politikos*), 132, 149, 151, 159–61;
    theoretical life (*bios theôrêtikos*), 151,
    159–61
linguistic analysis, 66, 76
logic, 18, 21ff., 31ff., 38, 56, 192, 194, 199, 202
logica nova, 194–5
logica vetus, 193
logos, see argument; *see* language; *see* reason
Lyceum, 7–8

magnanimity (*megalopsychia*), 154
magnificence (*megaloprepeia*), 154
malakos, see soft
mathematics, 15, 18, 26, 50, 54, 56, 83, 98
matter (*hylê*), 19, 72, 74, 76, 88, 196
mean (*mesotês*), 153; mean for ourselves (*meson
    pros hêmas*), 153–4; objective mean
    (*pragmatos meson*), 153–4

medicine, 16, 46, 190
megaloprepeia, see magnificence
megalopsychia, see magnanimity
memory (*mnêmê*), 26–7
mesotês, see mean
metaphor, 40
metaphysica generalis, 99–100
metaphysica specialis, 99–100
metaphysics, 5, 12, 19, 97, 103–4, 130–1, 195,
    203
metaphysics, practical, 99
meteorology, 18, 71
method, 24, 28, 61–6, 200
metic (*metoikos*), 4–5, 179
mimêsis, see imitation
mind (*nous*), 57, 59, 90–1, 105
mixed constitution (cf. polity), 185
mnêmê, see memory
modal logic, 33–4
money, 157
morality, 133, 153
mostly (*hôs epi to poly*), 39, 134
motion (*kinêsis*), 11, 71–6, 105, 149
Münchhausen Trilemma, 50, 52
myth, 45

natural law, 158, 197
natural philosophy, 5, 18, 69–94, 105, 112,
    119, 197
nature (*physis*), 74–5, 77, 132, 165–6
necessity (*anankê*), 31, 34, 39
noêseôs noêsis, see thinking of thinking
nomos, see law
noûs, see spirit; *see* intellect; *see* mind,
number, 82

oligarchy, 183–4
on hê on, see being *qua* being
on, see being
onoma, see word
ontology, 18, 65, 98–9, 103, 105, 111, 114,
    122, 196, 203
opinions, accepted (*endoxa*), 35–6, 61
orexis, see desire, *see* striving
organism, 75, 89ff.
Organon, 5, 23ff., 191, 194
ousia, see substance
outline (*typos*), 93, 133–4

panourgia, see knavery
paradeigma, see example
paronymy, 123
passion (*pathos*), 39, 136
pathos, see affect; *see* emotion, *see* passion

peace, 196
perception (*aisthêsis*), 26–8, 51, 57–8, 93–4, 136
Peripatos, 7, 189–90
phenomena, 61–2
philia, see friendship
phronêsis, see prudence
physics, 5, 18, 69–83, 91, 99, 104, 200, 202
place (*topos*), 37–8, 81–2
pleasure (*hedonê*), 149
poetics, 31, 43–7
poiêsis, see production
poion, see quality
polis, see state
politeia, see constitution
politics, 5, 39, 41, 130, 163–85, 195–7
polity (cf. mixed constitution), 182, 185
positive law, 158
poson, see quantity
possibility (*dynamis*), 19, 73
potentiality (*dynamis*), 19, 57, 73, 80–1, 94, 98, 142, 196
practical philosophy, 63, 131–4, 203
practical syllogism, 141–2, 145
pragmateiai (treatises), 10–1
pragmatics, 39, 123–4
praxis, see action
precision (*akribeia*), 27, 99, 100, 133–4
predicables, 37
premiss (*protasis*), 32, 36–7
prepon (that which is seemly), 147
principle (*archê*), 28, 53, 59, 73, 96, 101
privation (*sterêsis*), 73
probability, 35, 42
procreation, 89
production (*poiêsis*), 19, 43, 129, 136
prohairesis, see decision
proof (*apodeixis*), 31, 51, 53–4
proof of the existence of God, 107, 191, 196
pros ti, see relation
pros-hen relationship, 116, 119, 123
protasis, see premiss
prudence (*phronêsis*), 24, 131, 139–40, 142, 153, 159
psychê, see soul
psychology, 18, 39, 41, 91–4, 131
purification (*katharsis*), 45–7

quality (*poion*), 11, 113, 119
quantity (*poson*), 11, 113

rationalism, 50
rationality, 31, 36, 39, 43, 168
reason (*logos*), 93, 136, 141, 152, 159, 161, 167, 172

reception, 18–9, 23, 31, 40, 43, 46, 153
reductio ad impossibile/absurdum, 33
relation (*pros ti*), 113
rhetoric, 5, 18, 35, 38–43, 201, 203
rule (*archê*), 178ff.

scala naturae, 88, 91, 93
schêmata, see figures
scholasticism, 18, 25, 32, 77, 98, 122, 136, 156, 199
science (*epistêmê*), cf. knowledge, 76, 139–40
self-sufficiency (*autarkeia*), 151, 159, 179–80
semantics, 123–4, 152
semiotics, 123–4
separation of powers, 180
sign (*symbolon*), 124
slavery, 164, 175–6, 180, 182, 196
soft (*malakos*), 141
sôma, see body
sophia, see wisdom
sôphrosynê, see temperance
soul (*psychê*), 82, 91–4, 191
species (*eidos*), 88, 99, 113, 117ff.
spirit (*noûs*), 9, 24, 93, 106, 140
state (*polis*), 5, 157, 160–1, 165ff., 171, 182–3, 196
sterêsis, see privation
striving (*orexis*), 72, 107
subsidiarity, 167, 169
substance (*ousia*), 19, 76, 99–100, 103–4, 111–9
substratum (*hypokeimenon*), 73
syllogism, syllogistics, 18, 25, 31ff., 35, 51, 59
symbebêkôs, see accident
symbolon, see sign
symperasma, see conclusion
syneches, see continuum
synesis, see understanding
synonymity, 123
synthêkê, see convention
system, 12, 16, 18, 23–4, 95, 158, 190

technê, see art(fulness)
teleology, xv, 13, 27, 61, 70, 77ff., 89, 107–8, 131
telos, see goal, purpose
temperance (*sôphrosynê*), 143, 145, 154
that (*hoti*), 26, 62
thaumazein, see astonishment
theology, 18, 95, 98, 100, 103–9, 119, 195–7; ethical theology, 108–9; theology of the cosmos, 105–8; ontotheology, 100, 103
theory (*theôria*), 19, 27, 95, 132, 159–60, 172, 201

theory of discourse, 15, 25, 37, 42–3
theory of science, 24–5, 49–59, 133, 200
thêriotês, *see* brutality
thinking of thinking (*noêseôs noêsis*), 104, 106–7
thymos, *see* anger
ti ên einai (what-it-was-to-be), 117
ti estin, *see* essence
time (*chronos*), 65, 79, 82–3, 115–6
timê, *see* honour
tode ti (a determinate this), 113, 117, 119
toionde (a such), 119
topics, 15, 24ff., 35–8, 203
tragedy, 43–7
tragic pleasure, 45–6
transcendental; transcendental philosophy, 55, 82, 112, 151, 199
transcendentalia, 196
truth (*alêtheia*), 5, 36–7, 39, 64, 134
tychê, *see* chance
typos, *see* outline
tyranny, 180–1

understanding (*synesis*), 140
unified science, 16, 41, 53
unique property (*idion*), 38

universals, 122, 197
unlimited (*apeiron*), 80–1
Unmoved Mover, 64, 71, 88, 104–5, 151, 191

virtue, 157, 169, 196; virtue of character (*aretê êthikê*), 153–5, 172; intellectual virtue (*aretê dianoêtikê*), 24, 139–40
voluntary (*hekôn/hekousion*), 47, 137, 145, 179; (involuntary: *akôn*, 138; non-voluntary: *ouch hekôn*,138)

weakness of the will (*akrasia*), 61, 141–3
welfarism, 181–2
why (*dihoti*), 26, 62
will, 135, 143–6
wisdom (*sophia*), 24, 27, 95, 140
wishing (*boulêsis*), 137, 144
woman, 164, 177–8, 182
word (*onoma*), 124–5
world state, 6, 173

xenikon, *see* alienation

zên, *see* life
zoology, 6, 16, 18, 57, 62, 70, 85–8, 114